BLACK FOLKLORE AND THE POLITICS OF RACIAL REPRESENTATION

JIM CROW.

Black Folklore and the Politics of Racial Representation

Shirley Moody-Turner

University Press of Mississippi   Jackson

Margaret Walker Alexander Series in African American Studies

www.upress.state.ms.us

The University Press of Mississippi is a member of the Association of American University Presses.

An earlier version of sections from chapters three and five appeared in "Anna Julia Cooper, Charles Chesnutt and the Hampton Folklore Society: Constructing a Black Folk Aesthetic Through Folklore and Memory." In *New Essays on the African American Novel from Hurston and Ellison to Morrison and Whitehead*, edited by Lovalerie King and Linda Selzer, 13–23. New York: Palgrave MacMillan, 2008.

An earlier and much abbreviated version of the argument in chapters four and five appeared in "Folklore and African American Literature in the Post-Reconstruction Era." In *A Companion to African American Literature*, edited by Gene Andrew Jarrett, 200–211. Oxford: Wiley-Blackwell, 2010.

Copyright © 2013 by University Press of Mississippi
All rights reserved
Manufactured in the United States of America

First printing 2013
∞
Library of Congress Cataloging-in-Publication Data

Moody-Turner, Shirley.
Black folklore and the politics of racial representation / Shirley Moody-Turner.
pages cm — (Margaret Walker Alexander series in African American studies)
Includes bibliographical references and index.
ISBN 978-1-61703-885-3 (cloth : alk. paper) — ISBN 978-1-61703-886-0 (ebook) 1. African Americans—Folklore. 2. African Americans—Race identity. 3. Race—Social aspects—United States. 4. Literature and folklore—United States. 5. Folklore in literature. 6. African Americans in literature. 7. African Americans—Intellectual life. 8. American literature—African American authors—History and criticism. I. Title.
GR111.A47M66 2013
398.2089'96073—dc33 2013018147

British Library Cataloging-in-Publication Data available

To my grandmothers
Ekaterini Frantzis and Elvenia Gaston Black

CONTENTS

ACKNOWLEDGMENTS

There have been many, many people who have given of their time, energy, and intellectual resources, helping me meet the challenges of this project with joy, rigor, and enthusiasm. Without them this book would not have been possible, and to all of them, I am eternally grateful. First among them I would like to thank Mary Helen Washington, whose enthusiastic support over the years gave me the confidence to stay the course. She asked the tough questions and would not settle for easy answers. Her engaged and uncompromising approach to scholarship provided a model I strove to emulate. I am likewise grateful to Barry Lee Pearson for fueling my early investigations into the intersections of folklore and race and for bringing to my attention how folklore operates in the customary politics of race relations. I owe a debt of gratitude to Gene Jarrett, who provided valuable feedback and guidance along the way and whose own work on the politics of racial representation has been so influential to my thinking about how nineteenth-century African American authors engaged various discourses of race and representation. I would also like to thank Robert Bernasconi, an unflappable mentor and advisor, whose keen insights and advice were indispensible in bringing this project to completion. There are a number of people who, in various ways, helped create the intellectual community in which different aspects of this project took shape, among them Carla Peterson, Beverly Guy-Sheftall, Vivian May, Elizabeth Alexander, Joycelyn Moody, Toi Derricotte, John Ernest, Sw. Anand Prahlad, Cheryl Wall, Evie Shockley, Phil Goff, Keith Wilson, and Robin Schulze. I would like to recognize the faculty and staff at Pennsylvania State University, especially the head of the department of English, Mark Morrisson; my colleagues Lovalerie King, James Stewart, Bernard Bell, Aldon Nielsen, Linda Selzer, Iyun Osagie, Keith Gilyard, and Kevin Bell; as well as my cohort at the African American Literature and Culture Society, James Peterson, Keith Byerman, Wilfred Samuels, Loretta Woodard, and again, Aldon Nielsen. I received first-rate research assistance from Sara Rudewalker,

Grégory Pierrot, and Alex Bohen; and the students in my graduate seminar in African American folklore and my proseminar in African American literature provided fresh insights and perspectives that helped me clarify and refine sections of the manuscript. I also would like to acknowledge the Africana Research Center's Post-Doctoral Fellows Program and the African American Literature and Language Emphasis reading group at Pennsylvania State University, as well as the African American and Diaspora Interest Group, led by Donavan Ramon at Rutgers University, for opportunities to work through different stages of the project.

The University Press of Mississippi has shown a commitment to African American literature and folklore, and their work in these areas has been crucial to growing and sustaining scholarship in these fields. I am especially grateful to Craig Gill for his confidence and unwavering support of this project; Katie Keene, for her editorial assistance with the preparation of the manuscript; and for the insightful feedback and comments provided during the review process.

I received institutional support for this book from the Ford Foundation; the Rutgers University African Diaspora Literature Post-doctoral Fellowship, created through the leadership of Cheryl Wall; and at Pennsylvania State University, the Department of English, the African Research Center, and the Institute for the Arts and Humanities.

I obtained much helpful research assistance from Donzella Maupin at Hampton University Museum's University Archives, the librarians at the Hawaiian Historical Society and the Mission Houses Museum Library's Manuscript Collections, the staff at the Moorland-Spingarn Research Center at Howard University, and Kylee Omo at the Punahoe School Library. Early on Donald Waters sent me a copy of *Strange Ways and Sweet Dreams: Afro-American Folklore from the Hampton Institute*, and it is my sincere hope that I have been able to realize his kind injunction to carry his foundational work forward and to advance the recovery project he began three decades ago when he called for the Hampton project to become the subject of expanded critical and scholarly investigation.

I also want to express my gratitude to my colleagues, friends, and family, who not only read multiple drafts of the manuscript but also frequently wrote alongside me. I truly would not have enjoyed this project had I not been able to work side by side with such brilliant and supportive women: while I was at the University of Maryland, Kaylen Tucker, Shaun Myers, Christie Williams, Robin Smiles, Kenyatta Albany, and Adrena Ifill; and at Pennsylvania State University, my cohort working on race and gender in the U.S. and throughout the African diaspora, Kathryn Gines, Solsiree del Moral, Gabeba

Baderoon, Alyssa Garcia, Kimberly Griffin, Jeanie Staples, Leticia Oseguera, Cheraine Stanford, Christine Buzinde, and Eden Renee-Pruitt.

Finally, I want to thank my mother, Celia Paulin, who was my very first "reader" and who has been unflagging in her support over the years, and my father, Keith Moody; our many conversations stoked my early and continued passion for social and racial justice. And to all my brothers, sisters, aunts, uncles, cousins, nieces, nephews, and grandparents, it was truly a family affair and everyone provided support and encouragement along the way. Thank you especially to my partner, TJ Turner, for walking beside me on this path, and for Amara Julia Turner, who has brought more joy into my life than I even imagined possible.

BLACK FOLKLORE AND THE POLITICS OF RACIAL REPRESENTATION

Introduction

> The children of Africa in America are in danger of paralysis before the splendor of Anglo Saxon achievements. . . . The American Negro cannot produce an original utterance until he realizes the sanctity of his homely inheritance. . . . The creative instinct must be aroused by a wholesome respect for the thoughts that lie nearest. And this to my mind is the vital importance for him of the study of his own folk-lore.
>
> —Anna Julia Cooper, Address to the Hampton Folklorists, 1894

While the origin of African American folklore studies often is traced back to an 1888 letter in the *Journal of American Folklore,* in which William Wells Newell announced an agenda for the 235 mostly, if not all, white members of the newly founded American Folklore Society that included the study of "Lore of Negroes in the Southern States of the Union,"[1] Anna Julia Cooper's 1894 statement on the significance of black folklore signals an alternative tradition of African American folklore studies. In the address from which this epigraph is taken, Cooper recognized that black folklore took shape within a larger context that often regarded African American cultural traditions in dismissive and/or derogatory terms. She recognized that white Western culture was held as the ideal against which black American culture was evaluated and, all too often, judged lacking. Within this context, Cooper advocated for the recovery of African American folklore through the complementary work of black authors and folklorists. Working in tandem, black folklorists and authors could document, recover, and indeed create a black folk tradition as an alternative to dominant cultural representations that often concealed and distorted African American culture and history; in their courageous hands, black folk tradition would be an emboldened David to confront the Goliath of white cultural imperialism and social and political domination. By locating black folklore within an activist cultural and political agenda, Cooper set forth an aesthetics of engagement that defied what would become the dominant approaches to the study and representation of black folklore in the late nineteenth and early twentieth centuries.

By beginning with Cooper's remarks rather than with the more recognized statements on the inauguration of black folklore studies, what I suggest is an alternative genealogy through which to approach both African American folklore studies and African American literary engagements with black folklore. This approach recognizes African Americans as active participants, rather than merely passive repositories, in the study and representation of black folklore. As such, this project takes as its subject a disparate group of African Americans—some formal folklorists, some informally enlisted in folklore collection projects, and some authors and scholars who engaged with black folklore in their creative, scholarly, and/or activist projects—whose works provide an essential, but too often neglected, perspective on the meaning and significance of early African American folklore studies.

Although I begin by considering the earliest folkloric investigations carried out at the Hampton Institute in 1878 and continue into the early years of the twentieth century, it is the work of the Hampton Folklore Society (1893–1900)—which, prior to the twentieth century, constituted the most sustained, active, and prolific folklore project undertaken by African Americans—that anchors this project.[2] At the end of the nineteenth century the Hampton Folklore Society functioned as a dynamic site for serious engagement with the politics, not just of black folklore, but also of black folklore studies. The society's project took place within the hostile context of the rapidly solidifying system of racial segregation and during the emergent institutionalization of folklore studies. Working out from the Hampton Folklore Society and the context in which the organization took shape, I contend that the Hampton folklorists, as a society and through their publication arm in the *Southern Workman*, engaged the racial politics of the time by representing black folklore in ways that informed and were informed by the literary and scholarly conversations about black folklore taking place among writers and scholars such as Anna Julia Cooper, Charles Chesnutt, and Paul Laurence Dunbar. Taken together, the literary texts and folkloric works of these diverse cultural figures establish the vitality, diversity, and complexity of African American theorizing about the significance of black folklore in the post-Reconstruction era. Their work, however, cannot be understood apart from dominant cultural and political discourses about folklore and race taking place at the turn of the twentieth century, and as such, this book also tells the story of how folklore became a linchpin in debates over Jim Crow segregation.

By examining the racial politics surrounding the cultural, ethnographic, and literary representations of black folklore in the second half of the nineteenth and the early part of the twentieth centuries, *Black Folklore and the Politics of Racial Representation* participates in the monumental and ongoing process of making visible the ways race has been simultaneously constructed and obscured. While the complicated story of how race became a global worldview stretches back well into the sixteenth century, as Audrey Smedley contends, it was not until the late nineteenth century that the social construction of race reached its full development, when "the legal apparatus of the United States and various state governments conspired with science to legitimize this structural inequality by sanctioning it in law."[3] Folklore—as field of scientific inquiry, as discursive practice, and as representational strategy—came to play an important role in justifying racial constructions and legitimating Jim Crow as the new status quo.

Within the plantation and minstrel traditions, for instance, folklore referred to the cultural materials that could be re-presented on the stage and in literature as a way to evoke an entire set of cultural practices and behaviors rife with implications for the constructions of race taking shape throughout the nineteenth century. Legal and political discourse often drew on meanings of folklore associated with tradition, customary behaviors, and popular usages in articulating justifications for upholding segregation based not only on racial difference, but also based on the notion that Jim Crow laws merely adhered to the popular norms and customs of the day. Within scientific and philosophic discourses, folklore could justify the racialized models of social and cultural evolution, providing evidence of a group's location on the evolutionary ladder. Conversely, folklore, particularly in a Boasian framework, could serve as evidence of the permeable boundaries of culture, detaching culture from race by showing how folklore could be transferred, adopted, and adapted between cultures, demonstrating what Brad Evans refers to as the ability of culture to "circulate."[4]

The relationship between conceptualizations of folklore and the construction of racialized structures of power and difference has received important attention over the years. George Frederickson's seminal study, *The Black Image in the White Mind,* argues that white notions of black identity, including popular depictions of black folklore, were driven by the ideological, social, and political desire to maintain (an illusory) white racial homogeneity and to protect the existing white power structure. George Stocking's works, particularly *Race, Culture, and Evolution,* track the relationships between race, evolution, and scientism in anthropology, with implications for related disciplines, such as folklore, while folklore historian and scholar Simon Bronner considers the formation of folklore studies in relation to U.S. national identity formations more generally. Sw. Anand Prahlad and John Roberts most directly interrogate the relationship between folklore studies and constructions of race, considering how the folkloric study of a racialized, removed, and pre-modern other enabled the construction of a modern, civilized white identity.[5] Each of these works focuses on how blacks were constructed as folk—primitive, uncivilized, and/or quaint and simple "others"—in an effort to buttress constructions of whites as inherently civilized, modern, rational, and ultimately superior beings endowed with the right and responsibility to rule over and/or be separated from inferior nonwhite others.

The master narrative of white cultural domination is well established in this literature, but in re-examining these dominant discourses, I further argue that we need to make central the range of theorizing about folklore and race generated by African American folklorists and cultural workers. In other words, we need to examine the intricate workings and deep structures of the relationship between folklore as a formalized institution of study, as documentable cultural material, and as lived social practice and the concomitant constructions of racial difference and hierarchy considering how this emerging concept of folklore was experienced and understood by those who were so frequently the objects of those discourses.[6] Our readings will enable us to refocus attention on the aspects of nineteenth-century discourses of folklore and race that African American writers and cultural workers variously engaged, negotiated, and critiqued when they took folklore as the subject of and/or basis for their creative, folkloric, and/or ethnographic work, compelling us to ask, for example: How did folklore and the folklore project register differently for African American writers and folklorists? How did folklore serve as an aspect of racial and/or cultural pride or, conversely, personal shame and humiliation? How did they interrogate the strictures as well as the slippages that characterized this multivariate concept? How did they engage folklore to expose its politicized and racialized role in constructing discourses of civilization? How did they interpret the relationship between folklore and modernity, race, gender, education, citizenship, and national belonging? In other words, how did they plumb the contours, nuances, and contradictions animating the relationship between folklore and race?

Recovering these voices requires expanding our definition of what "counts" as folklore studies and as theorizing.[7] Indeed, the African American folklorists at Hampton did not partake in folklore studies in the ways Newell prescribed and outlined for the members of American Folklore Society. They did not pursue careers or hobbies as full-time folklorists, and did not maintain objective distance in their work. Often they gathered "fieldwork" from their memories and lived experiences rather than from observations in the "field," and they experimented with various modes of representation. Their projects were admittedly both deeply personal and political. They tied folklore to cultural history and individual and collective identity, and they variously used folklore and folklore studies as a means to engage in contemporary debates and to document a viable African American tradition and culture. Their counterparts working in the literary realm similarly refused to allow the dominant conventions informing the collection and representation of black folklore to determine their ethnographic and artistic engagements with black folklore. The folklorists' literary peers called attention to the racialized politics dictating the representation of black folklore, remaining painfully aware of the social and political stakes inherent in depictions of black folklore, and using folklore as a vehicle to advocate for civic reform and to protest continued racial and gendered inequalities.

As Barbara Christian explains in "The Race for Theory": "people of color have always theorized—but in forms quite different from the Western form of abstract logic." She continues, "I am inclined to say that our theorizing (and I intentionally use the verb rather than the noun) is often in narrative forms, in the stories we create, in riddles and proverbs, in the play with language, since dynamic rather than fixed ideas seem more to our liking."[8] Taking Christian's cue, I draw on a range of texts, showing how African Americans theorized about the significance of folklore in an array of unlikely places—in prefatory remarks and obligatory disclaimers, couched within folktales and ethnographic reports, and veiled within letters, short stories, poems, and novels. Even Cooper, who engaged the most directly in constructing a literary theory of black folk aesthetics, utilized personal narratives, anecdotes, and recollections as vehicles for exploring the oppositional and liberatory possibilities of creating reciprocal relationships between African American literature and folklore.

Aside from the Hampton folklorists, however, many of the individuals in this study would not be recognized as folklorists in the traditional sense and their works would not be considered when recovering the history of African American folklore scholarship. And while it is not my intention to categorize or recover these figures as folklorists, I do argue that they contributed theories, perspectives, and analyses that should be included in our investigations of early African American folklore studies. Certainly, Charles Chesnutt's contributions to early African American folklore studies are as significant as the works of Joel Chandler Harris or William Wells Newell. It is my contention, then, that we need to consider the work of the Hampton folklorists not only in relation to the dominant white institutions, but in relation to the black intellectual community as well. The various figures in this study maintained connections, either directly or indirectly, with the Hampton Folklore Society. Cooper, for instance, maintained the most sustained relationship with the Hampton folklorists and offered an important perspective on both the politics of folklore studies and the need to cultivate a relationship between black folklore and African American literature. Dunbar and Chesnutt were both one remove from the society, sharing the same publication outlets, becoming involved in a variety of ways with the Hampton Institute, and through that involvement garnering various levels of contact with members of the society and their work. Beyond these material connections, Dunbar and Chesnutt are important figures because their decisions to engage folklore within the given cultural and political climate earned them dubious praise as impromptu folklorists whose works were often lauded for what were taken as authentic portrayals of black folk life. Like the Hampton folklorists, then, they had to find innovative strategies to negotiate and challenge their assigned role as "native informants," and thus their works are in conversation with the works of the Hampton folklorists in important and illuminating ways.

Recovering this expanded intellectual and historical context has important implications for, and joins conversations taking place in, both folklore studies and African American literary studies. Within folklore studies, attention to the cultural representation of folklore has prompted a general reevaluation of disciplinary origins—forcing contemporary folklorists to consider, for example, the role folklore scholarship has played in romanticizing African American communities or in creating the very notions of authenticity folklorists now often seek to challenge. In moving toward this end, a number of revisionist histories of folklore studies have considered how "particular groups got excluded and others essentialized" in the study of folklore.[9] While works such as Simon Bronner's *American Folklore Studies*, Rosemary Levy Zumwalt's *American Folklore Scholarship*, and Regina Bendix's *In Search of Authenticity* make vital contributions to the revisionist historiography of folklore studies, these works do not take into account the contributions of early African American folklorists in their surveys, and thus conversations about the politics of cultural representation continue to take place without fully considering how African American folklorists might have contributed to and been affected by those developments.[10] By presenting African Americans "as always the folk, but never the folklorists," both traditional and revisionist histories of folklore studies continue to perpetuate the idea, as Melvin

Wade states, that blacks appear as "peripheral participants in the evolution of their own intellectual history, fully involved in the performing of folklore, but rarely reflective about their involvement."[11]

Folklorist Elaine Lawless suggests we need to move away from self-reflexive attention to the politics of cultural representation that have characterized many revisionist projects in folklore studies to what she refers to as "reciprocal ethnography," asserting the need to shift from a myopic focus on the role of the ethnographer to an ethnographic practice where the "exchange of ideas and meanings is reciprocal." Lawless explains that in utilizing this reciprocal approach, we invite multiple voices to the table, recover the perspective of the "subjects" in the process of conducting fieldwork and writing ethnography, "learn from each other," and resist privileging one voice over the other.[12] Extending Lawless's framework to disciplinary historiography, I would argue, similarly, that it is not enough to be self-reflexive about the disciplinary origins of folklore studies—to recognize the ways in which folklore studies participated in creating a romanticized view of blacks as folk—but also that we must now invite previously silenced voices to the table as participants.

Heeding Wade's and Lawless's critiques, and responding to efforts by folklore scholars such as Adrienne Lanier Seward and John Roberts, there has been a turn in contemporary African American folklore studies both to recognize the politics of white folklorists' interpretations of African American folklore and to recover the role of African American folklorists in the development of the field. Seward's "The Legacy of Early Afro-American Folklore Scholarship" and Prahlad's "Africana Folklore" survey the history of African American folklore scholarship *and* African American folklorists' contributions to folklore scholarship, while Cassandra Stancil's study of Carter G. Woodson and Gerald L. Davis's work on Thomas Washington Talley recover understudied or unacknowledged African American forerunners of African American folklore studies.[13] This small but critical body of scholarship focuses much-needed attention on the recovery of African American voices in the larger revisionist and recovery projects taking place in folklore studies more generally. But while they document a tradition of African American folklore scholarship, all of their works recognize African American folklorists from the twentieth century forward. Hence, the work begun by these scholars beckons us to delve deeper, asking: Who were the nineteenth-century progenitors of twentieth-century African American folklore studies? How did they contribute to and intervene in the inaugural conversations about folklore studies that were taking place in national organizations like the American Folklore Society? How do their works provide us with insights into the tradition of African American theorizing about African American folklore?

In an effort to address these questions, my attention to the Hampton folklorists joins the handful of studies offering sustained attention to the work of nineteenth-century African American folklorists. Lee Baker's *Anthropology and the Racial Politics of Culture* and Daphne Lamothe's *Inventing the New Negro* include significant readings of the Hampton Folklore Society in relation to the civilizing mission of the Hampton Institute, and within the framework of William Wells Newell's scientific agenda, respectively. A recent dissertation by Ray Sapirstein explores how folklore studies at the Hampton Institute provided an orientation toward black folklore that informed related cultural projects, especially those conducted by the prominent white photographer Leigh Miner and the Hampton Institute Camera Club. Donald Waters's foundational history, *Strange Ways and Sweet Dreams*, interprets the work of the Hampton folklorists in relation to the civilizing project of the larger white institutions with which they were associated and offers an analysis of the Hampton folklore collection in terms of what those materials reveal about the values, beliefs, and worldview of slaves and former slaves living in the rural South.[14]

Like Baker, Lamothe, Sapirstein, and Waters, I too am interested in the relationship between the Hampton folklorists and the larger dominant institutions, and indeed, I argue that their work cannot be understood apart from this context. I am particularly interested, however, in recovering how the Hampton folklorists conceived of their project; how they negotiated their relationship to folklore within this context; how they interacted with other African American scholars and cultural workers who were also interested in the issues and challenges inherent in the collection, study, and representation of black folklore; and how, taken together, their work suggests a larger African American intellectual community approaching similar questions in sometimes complementary, sometimes contradictory, but always mutually informative ways.

Recovering this nexus of intersecting interests and concerns suggests not just an alternative genealogy for African American folklore studies, but also offers an alternative lens through which to view post-Reconstruction African American literary engagements with black folklore. Too often, post-Reconstruction African American writers' literary, aesthetic, and political engagements with black folklore have been situated merely as foils to later, more sophisticated treatments of black folklore that took shape during the Harlem Renaissance and were improved and perfected with each subsequent generation.[15] This assumption not only discounts the creative, aesthetic, and political accomplishments of post-Reconstruction African American writers, it also reproduces a teleology that views the African American literary tradition as moving toward a more perfect and sophisticated enunciation of a black literary aesthetic. While our contemporary period has seen a flurry of attention to the construction of the black "folk" in relation to questions of authenticity and racial identity, these works tend to locate sophisticated treatments of the politics of cultural representation and critiques of the relationship between folklore, identity, and authenticity as commencing in the 1920s with the Harlem Renaissance and associated movements.[16] However, as Henry Louis Gates notes, during the post-Reconstruction period, which he characterizes as a "new form of enslavement for blacks," the nation's political and economic backsliding and expansion of racist iconography was met by a dramatic resurgence of African American literary publishing through which African Americans "regained a public voice."[17] Gates's observation indicates that—despite the mounting social and political repression and the increasingly derogatory and circumscribed images of African Americans in popular culture and literature—African Americans in the post-Reconstruction era grew ever more determined to wrest back some control over the cultural representations that had become part and parcel of the solidifying edifice of racial segregation. Echoing Gates's assessment of the increase in African American literary production during the post-Reconstruction period, Barbara McCaskill and Caroline Gebhard, in their 2006 collection *Post-Bellum, Pre-Harlem, African American Literature and Culture 1877–1919*, argue against viewing the post-Reconstruction period as characterized by artistic stasis and black political subservience. Instead, they call for "new paradigms for understanding the unfolding of black art and politics" in the critical decades surrounding the turn of the twentieth century, insisting on a reappraisal of the era to establish it as a crucial stage in African American cultural and literary history, a period of high aesthetic experimentation and political dynamism.[18]

In creating these new models of interpretation, one not only has to move beyond the assumptions about the aesthetic stagnation of post-Reconstruction period literature, one must also incorporate and expand upon what have been the most far-reaching and influential approaches to interpreting the intersections of folklore and African American literature. Starting in the 1980s, vernacular theorists in the line of Gates and Houston Baker advanced a critical paradigm, exemplified by Gates's foundational study *The Signifying Monkey*, which turned to the tropes and figures of folk or vernacular expression as interpretative tools for analyzing African American literary texts.[19] In this seminal work, Gates argues that vernacular tradition "informs and becomes the foundation for formal black literature"; and in turn he proposes a literary criticism that is likewise informed by the strategies of language construction and interpretation arising out of African American vernacular practices.[20] Gates identifies "signifying"—which he defines as a "double-voiced trope," "a metaphor for formal revision," or the practice of engaging or rewriting with a difference—as the key practice adapted from African American (and by extension African) vernacular traditions and written into African American literary texts.[21] Thus, he asserts, an "indigenous black literary criticism" will take its cue from black vernacular culture and develop models for reading and interpreting the "signifying black difference" in African American literary texts.[22]

Significantly, Gates's work has served the important function of focusing attention on the stylistic features of folk forms and their textual transformations. He also extends this hermeneutic to provide a basis for analyzing the ways in which African American literary texts engage, while simultaneously critiquing and challenging, Western literary traditions. Gates has run into trouble with a bevy of contemporary critics, however, with his suggestions that "the black vernacular has assumed the singular role as the black person's ultimate sign of difference" and that those writers who incorporate black vernacular traditions do so "to ground [their] literary practice outside the Western tradition."[23] Both of these gestures seem to posit the individual or literary work that draws on vernacular traditions as more "authentically" black than those that do not rely on or reproduce cultural forms arising out of black vernacular. J. Martin Favor extends this critique, asserting that Gates's privileging of the black vernacular assigns a greater value or a "larger measure of authenticity" to literary representations emerging from constructions of the folk as lower class.[24] Favor maintains that this privileging of a lower class folk identity as what is authentic about blackness creates and enforces a literary canon restricted to black subjectivities that fit into the vernacular theory model.

Gates's identification of the form of signifying as the most significant of vernacular practices has drawn criticism as well. In her recent study *Renegade Poetics*, Evie Shockley argues that vernacular theorists such as Gates and Baker proposed a theory of African American literature that sought to "privilege the evidence of the text over the political ideology of the moment."[25] Shockley asserts that instead of locating blackness in adherence to a particular political ideology, which they associated with the art and politics of their Black Arts Movement predecessors, they instead sought to locate blackness within the cultural context and literary form and structure of a text. As a result, however, they were still attempting to "identify that which is black about these textual structures and, therefore, the texts that employ them."[26] The implication, then, is that African American literary texts that incorporate, in either structure or content, specific oral vernacular forms, typically forms associated with lower-class or rural communities, are regarded as more authentically black than texts that do not.

While I do not wish to jettison Gates's approach altogether, particularly his insights on how folk forms are often transformed in literary texts to posit an oppositional or "signifying" relationship with Western literary and dominant popular cultural discourses, I do wish to complicate his notion of the vernacular tradition as a measure of racial authenticity not only by emphasizing how writers incorporated folklore, but also by considering how they did so within a specific historical context and in relation to larger social, political, and cultural agendas. What I suggest is a way of reading driven not by identifying the "black difference" of a particular text, nor restricted to locating the origins for the formal features of folklore as it is transformed in a literary text (though both of these areas emerge at various points as sites of concern and negotiation), but instead by recognizing the contingent and constructed nature of categories such as "folk," "folklore," "authenticity," "blackness," and "race." As Robin Kelley has noted, categories such as "folk" and "modern" are "socially constructed and contingent . . . subject to the dynamics of class, gender and race."[27] In other words, these terms have a history that has everything to do with constructions of racial and national identity, and negotiating, exposing, and grappling with this history is one of the key features in the black folk "aesthetics"/strategies enacted by the writers I consider.

In the post-Reconstruction era, for example, black writers' engagement with folklore had to negotiate the emerging formation of folklore studies and the dominant cultural and scientific identification of Southern, rural African Americans as folk. They had to navigate the tension between their representations of folklore and the awareness that representations of certain forms of folklore and certain folk groups were one measure used by white society in determining the authenticity of black writers' texts and reifying notions of blackness that circulated in the national imaginary. Indeed, the writers I consider were as much engaged in the project of problematizing dominant society's notions of an authentic blackness, located in the folk practices of Southern, rural blacks, as they were interested in providing more accurate portrayals of black life.

What I propose, then, is not to expand Gates's hermeneutic to include one or two additional types of folk forms, but instead, to read engagements with folklore through a lens attentive to the cultural and political work carried out through these various representations. This approach allows us to see, for example, how *The Colonel's Dream,* which is not overtly rooted in black vernacular forms, is as much about folklore and the politics of cultural representation as *The Conjure Woman,* which *is* rooted in the folk practices of storytelling and conjure. It also allows us to recognize how, already in the 1890s, Dunbar's *The Sport of the Gods* exposed the role that representations of folklore could play in constructing racial difference, while simultaneously mounting a critique of idealized notions of black folklore as rooted in the rural South. More generally, this approach expands our context for understanding the deployment of black folklore in literary texts and public discourses, allows us to diversify what counts as folklore, and recognizes how constructions of folklore were tied to a racial and cultural politics that were inseparable from questions of national identity and belonging.

Chapter one begins by establishing the methodological, theoretical, and hermeneutical parameters advanced by William Wells Newell for the study of folklore, and specifically African American folklore. Then, locating the emergence of folklore studies in relation to the larger social, cultural, and political interests in folklore that converged during the second half of the nineteenth century, I historicize constructions of racial identity as carried out through representations of black folklore. I consider how constructions of the black folk in ante- and postbellum popular culture, as specifically located in the ironic figure of Jim Crow and the subsequent minstrel tradition, as well as Plantation Tradition literature, fed the national interest in black folklore and fueled white fascination with "authentic" black folks and/or black folk material. Reading at the intersections of "scientific" and popular representations of black folklore, and against the backdrop of the mounting debates over racial identity and segregation, chapter one suggests the complex protocols that influenced approaches to and representations of black folklore in the mid- to late nineteenth century.

Chapter two reviews the origins of black folklore studies at the Hampton Institute, with the first folklore collections conducted in 1878 under the auspices of Samuel Armstrong, the Institute's founder, and later reinvigorated by Alice Bacon and carried out by the Hampton Folklore Society. This chapter posits the influential role Armstrong played in establishing a reformist/assimilationist agenda for black folklore studies. I expand this context, however, to locate the roots of Armstrong's orientation toward folklore, education, and civilization in his early missionary work in Hawai'i. Investigations into Armstrong's youth allow us to align his conflicted approach to black folklore with assimilationist projects at home and U.S. imperialist expansion in the Pacific. As I illustrate in this chapter, Armstrong's disparagement of the African American practice of conjure is presaged in the missionary efforts to outlaw the hula, an effort Armstrong observed first-hand while living and working in Hawai'i. Armstrong's mission to excise folk practices from his African American students ironically led to the first extensive collection of black folklore materials at Hampton, as he enlisted his students in "spying out" and documenting, rather than concealing, what he saw as outdated and dangerous folk practices.

The second part of the chapter turns to the resurgence of folklore studies at the Hampton Institute when Bacon, a white teacher from Connecticut, established the Hampton Folklore Society in 1893. Unlike her predecessor, Bacon enlisted African American students and graduates of the Institute in what she identified as the serious and scientific study of black folklore. She established professional connections with the American Folklore Society, through which she endorsed and promoted a scientific approach to black folklore studies. She also, however, brought her own reformist background to the project, and thus her agenda for the society often embodied a tension between pursuing the scientific mission espoused by Newell and validating the perspectives and interpretations of the Hampton folklorists on the context-specific meaning of their own folk traditions. Despite her own orientation toward black folklore collection and study, Bacon created the Hampton Folklore Society as an open forum, thereby enabling ongoing and active participation from the wider black intellectual community. Thus it was under Bacon's leadership that the Hampton Folklore Society became a crucial site where the larger community, both black and white, engaged in dialogue and debate about the meaning and significance of black folklore.

Chapter three recovers the vested interest members of the black intellectual community—particularly, Anna Julia Cooper—had in the work of the Hampton Folklore Society, which came to be a site of lively discourse concerning black folklore's relationship to social change and justice. I argue that the work of the Hampton Folklore Society must be understood within, but also beyond, the bounds of both the Hampton Institute and the "scientific" frame offered by Bacon and the American Folklore Society. Recovering and re-reading several key moments in the society's history, I show how the folklorists resisted having their work confined to the ideology of the Hampton Institute as they questioned the politics of assuming a "scientific," and often objectifying, approach to the study of their own traditions. The second half of this chapter focuses on recovering Cooper's contributions to folklore studies and detailing the tension between her attempting to validate black folklore as a source for a distinctive African American literary tradition while still positing an anti-essentialist, non-objectifying approach to folklore study. I reveal how her emphasis on memory and personal experience was reflected in the methodology that some of the Hampton folklorists came to employ and how she saw black folklore as the basis for achieving an innovative, socially and politically engaged African American literary aesthetic.

Chapters four and five examine how the national conversation about black folklore intersected with the literary production and social change agendas of African American authors. I focus on the work of Paul Laurence Dunbar and Charles Chesnutt—the two African American authors who achieved mainstream notice, who maintained formal and/or informal relations with the Hampton Institute and Hampton Folklore Society, and in whom members of the society and the institute were most invested as representatives of and potential spokesmen for "the race." In these chapters I argue that Dunbar and Chesnutt resituated folklore in ways that extended beyond simply transposing historically identifiable items of folklore into their literary works. Both authors understood that through their literary engagements with folklore, they were entering deeply contested terrain. Writing at a moment when questions of racial identity and civil and political rights were increasingly played out through representations of black folk and folklore in popular culture, then naturalized through scientific discourses and practices, and finally institutionalized through legal decisions and legislation, Dunbar and Chesnutt introduced new literary strategies for contesting these various discourses as they struggled to find innovative ways to engage African American folklore, to critique the limits of popular representations of African Americans, and to enact New Negro social justice and uplift agendas.

More specifically, Dunbar, like the Hampton folklorists, had to negotiate the politics of being objectified as an embodiment of African American folklore and/or the folk communities he chose to represent. In his literary works, masking and dissimulation became his vehicles for exposing the many intertwined literary and cultural conventions that determined the range of black representation. In his 1902 novel *The Sport of the Gods*, he critiques idealized notions of folklore through the text's depiction of tensions within the Southern folk community. He further challenges the construction of folklore as a Southern, rural phenomenon by introducing a new geographic terrain—the urban North—in which to imagine black folklore, thereby introducing into African American literature alternative geographies for African American folklore, and thus providing one of the greatest affronts to the solidifying Jim Crow system: black folks who refused to remain in the segregated South.

Chapter five details how Chesnutt, from early in his career, experimented with African American folklore as a way to critique the existing epistemological approaches to understanding black culture and black history, and later turned his attention to exposing the white-supremacist forms of folklore that worked to reinforce existing structures of race relations. In his 1901 essay "Superstitions and Folk-lore of the South," Chesnutt assumes the positions of collector and translator as well as insider and outsider, with respect to black folk traditions. In this essay, he evokes "voice" as a trope for negotiating the shifting, yet circumscribed subject positions while simultaneously advancing his critique of dominant cultural representations of black folklore. In *The Conjure Woman*, his 1899 collection of short stories, Chesnutt incorporated the principles of conjure and ritual as formal strategies that allowed him to move beyond simply critiquing the conventions of the Plantation Tradition or even inverting the racial hierarchies steeped in the contemporary discourses of civilization, but instead to positing black folklore as an alternative way of constructing, perceiving, and responding to his current and historical realities. I close the chapter with an examination of Chesnutt's *The Colonel's Dream* (1905), a novel that painstakingly unravels the conflicting fictions of folklore and race by exposing the customary politics of race relations and the folklore that defines his white characters' attitudes about race, African Americans, and themselves. In this remarkable shift, Chesnutt turns the ethnographic gaze on the white characters, exposing the constructions of white racial perceptions and revealing the epistemological frames that were often employed to construct so-called knowledge about African Americans.

In concluding this project, I make an implicit call for a more nuanced genealogy of representations of black folklore from the post-Reconstruction era to what are typically considered the more "sophisticated" treatments of folklore in later African American literary and ethnographic works. In making this gesture, I do not want to insinuate that post-Reconstruction works merely anticipate later, more nuanced treatments of black folklore, but instead to recommend a more dynamic genealogy in which recognizing the complexity of post-Reconstruction engagements can render a richer understanding of subsequent treatments as well. This approach beckons us to recover another layer in the sophisticated and nuanced ways folklore and African American literature have intersected, not just in the post-Reconstruction period, or even in the Harlem Renaissance period and beyond, but indeed from the very foundations of the African American literary tradition.

1 "By Custom and By Law"

Folklore and the Birth of Jim Crow

Those who supported the myth of "separate but equal" were quick to adopt the rhetoric of folklore for support and protection. The notion that the social differences that were supposedly "created" by race could not be nullified by laws can be summed up in the famous adage often attributed to William Graham Sumner: "Stateways cannot change folkways."[1] This statement represents the proverbial soap that the country, particularly the Northern politicians and press, used to wash their hands of the segregation issue in the South. That American folklore studies grew up amid the fury over racial separation and difference is less a coincidence than a testament to the inextricability of folklore studies from the larger social, cultural, and political currents that defined the second half of the nineteenth century. At its founding, folklore studies was already invested in identifying and studying regional and ethnic groups—Negroes, Indians, bordering groups in Canada and Mexico—that existed within American borders and yet apart from mainstream American society. That these newly discovered "folk" possessed strange and peculiar habits observed and documented in this emerging field of study provided evidence that legislation could do little to change the habits and customs that defined race relations.

Whether wittingly or not, when William Wells Newell co-founded the American Folklore Society (AFS) in the late 1880s, he entered into a national public discourse on the meaning and significance of folklore that was rife with implications for African American cultural representation and social, political, and civic life. By examining several of Newell's statements on the emerging discipline of folklore, I argue that even though he sought to formalize a scientific and objective approach to folklore studies, there remained tensions and slippage between (and within) his scientific orientation toward folklore studies, competing theories of culture and race, and the place folklore occupied in the larger social, cultural, and political discourse. Despite Newell's attempts to rein in this most unwieldy of concepts, "folklore" maintained its multiplicity. In considering the confluence of discourses that drew on folkloric rhetoric, specifically in the popular cultural discourses that coalesced around representations of folklore in the minstrel and Plantation Traditions and the political and legal rhetoric that drew a curious line of support from the folkloric rhetoric of "customs and traditions," I seek to show how these intersecting discourses of folklore were variously deployed in constructing notions of race and nation in the late nineteenth century.

In an 1890 article in the *Nation,* T. F. Crane announced, "The interest in folklore seems to be steadily increasing in this country." He took as evidence of this growing interest "the large number of works on the subject . . . and the substantial support rendered to the American Folklore Society." He went on to note, however, that the bulk of interest in folklore had adhered around "popular tales," citing as a reason for their popularity their wide range of appeal to both "learned" and "unlearned" audiences and their adaptability in bolstering various theoretical interpretations.[2] His contemporary, and the founder of the rival Chicago Folklore Society, Fletcher Bassett concurred, remarking that folklore had indeed become "the subject of the day."[3] As the nineteenth century drew to a close, folklore became increasingly present in U.S. social and cultural consciousness. Leading members of AFS held positions at top universities and came from a range of occupations and disciplines. Founding members included Francis James Child and George Lyman Kittredge from Harvard, American psychologist Stanley Hall, a host of early anthropologists such as Franz Boas and Frank Cushing, philanthropists including Isabel Hapgood and Mary Hemenway, as well as Thomas Wentworth Higginson and Oliver Wendell Holmes. Joel Chandler Harris, Mark Twain, and Lafcadio Hearn, all members of AFS, rooted their literary writings in folkloric materials, and Harris's *Uncle Remus: His Songs and His Sayings* (1880) was a major catalyst in promoting the study of African American folklore.[4]

Despite its growing presence in American public discourse, however, the meaning of folklore in the mid- to late nineteenth century, as suggested by Crane's remarks on the reasons for folklore's wide appeal, was still very much in flux (as it remains today). Even as folklore studies became institutionalized in the United States through the work of AFS, Newell's repeated and urgent attempts to define and delimit the society's subject and its practice attest to the popularity, and mutability, of the concept of folklore. Indeed, Newell believed the AFS mission was under constant assault by the hordes of amateur collectors who were unable to achieve the requisite objectivity, due either to their fervor for documenting and celebrating their local folklore or ideological biases that colored how they presented the materials they had collected. To counter these tendencies, Newell sought to dissuade his fellow folklorists from engaging in what he saw as theoretical debates that would bias the objective collection and study of folkloric materials. More specifically, he did not wish to see folklore studies enlisted in support of what he considered discredited theories tying folklore and culture to racial or biological determinism. Instead, he repeatedly promoted theories of diffusion, arguing that folklore was not traceable to racial or national origins, but was transmitted through the diffusion of materials via the interaction of different cultures. Finally, for Newell, the underlying principle and major contribution of folklore studies was as a historical science, a project carried out in the interest of reconstructing history. As for the folkloric materials collected, their significance was as remnants of the past surviving in the present and used to interpret and illuminate the past. In other words, folklore comprised the historical record that could show how materials (songs, tales, customs) were diffused, circulated and adapted among cultures. In the discussion that follows, I show how Newell's methodological, theoretical, and historically-based orientations toward folklore exerted and reflected a powerful, though not uncontested, force in influencing late-nineteenth-century approaches to the study of folklore and culture.

In defining the parameters of American folklore studies, William Wells Newell was an especially significant figure. As co-founder and secretary of AFS and editor of the *Journal of American Folklore* (*JAF*), he exerted important influence over shaping the society's project and determining how folklore would come to be institutionalized in the United States. In articulating his agenda for the 235 members of his organization, Newell stressed the scientific nature of the AFS endeavor, and prioritized the need for the "objective" and extensive collection of folkloric materials. In an 1890 report on the first annual meeting of AFS, Newell used the term "collection" a dozen times in sixteen pages, noting that folklore gave a scientific basis to the "study of popular traditions" and provided for the "additional collection" of materials which the editor of *JAF* felt was "necessary to elucidate many problems of anthropology."[5] In his opening statement for AFS, Newell identified the "principal objective" of the society as establishing a "Journal, of a scientific character, designed (i) For the collection of the fast-vanishing remains of Folk-Lore in America."[6] Newell's almost obsessive emphasis on the scientific nature of folklore studies allowed him to validate his undertaking in relation to the professionalization of intellectual pursuits taking place at the end of the nineteenth century. As Simon Bronner points out, "the formation of folklore societies was part of a larger trend" in which over 200 learned societies were formed throughout the 1870s and 1880s.[7] These societies, Bronner notes, sought to distinguish themselves by establishing their scientific and intellectual authority in illuminating and building a systematic body of knowledge. To establish folklore studies within this milieu, Newell had to set his work apart from the "popular" collections that were not documented rigorously and whose resulting representations of folklore, he believed, were colored by the perspective of the collector and creative or political influences. To counteract this popular plundering of folklore material, Newell emphasized dutiful collection and faithful transcription of folkloric materials. If folklore was going to contribute anything to current debates on the nature and flow of cultural traditions, Newell insisted, "they cannot possibly be published in popular forms."[8] According to Newell, these popular forms did not preserve the integrity of the materials collected and so made them useless in charting the distinct history of traditions as they existed in popular oral culture.

According to Jon Cruz, in the post–Civil War years there was a shift in the interpretation of folklore—particular black spirituals—from the popular, romantic, "meaning-oriented" or "cultural" interpretations of the abolitionist period to the objectivist-oriented, taxonomical or "scientific" interpretations of the 1880s and 1890s. Whereas the abolitionists came to interpret folklore, and specifically the spiritual, through an avowedly cultural and political lens, as "cultural weaponry in the symbolic arsenal against slavery," this approach, Cruz argues, was eclipsed, displaced, and superseded by folklorists and social scientists: ". . . the interpretive tone changed from a concern with what was ostensibly moral and political to a preoccupation with what could best be grasped descriptively, taxonomically, and analytically within the larger intellectual schemas of objectification and classification."[9] Working within this context, Newell sought to move away from the previous popular, romantic interpretations of folklore and instead stressed an "objectivist-oriented" rather than "meaning-oriented" approach to folklore collection that was more interested in amassing and studying folkloric material and how these texts circulated, than in understanding what the materials might have meant to the people and groups who shared and passed on these traditions.

Hence, in the interest of scientific objectivity, Newell urged his fellow folklorists to avoid theoretical discussions of the materials that recapitulated the romantic nationalism, and hence the biological and racial determinism, he identified with popular approaches to folklore. In an 1890 essay, "Additional Collection Essential to Correct Theory in Folk-lore and Mythology," Newell went to work discrediting each of the prevailing models of interpreting folklore. In countering theories that supported folklore as a product of racial or national inheritance, Newell noted, "this theory . . . received a rude shock by the recent demonstrations that differences of race and language are not necessarily an indication of differences in tradition." As an example he cited the Basque people of Spain, who he maintained "do not seem to have retained any characteristic tales or songs which may be supposed derived from their ancient stock, but rather to have assimilated the lore of modern Europe."[10] Elsewhere, in a number of articles and books, he built a case against the Aryan origins theory, a version of the inheritance model, by arguing that Arthurian legends were products of French romanticism and not of Celtic folk origins. For Newell, the romantic nationalist approach to folklore was exemplified in the early-nineteenth-century folklore projects of Wilhelm and Jacob Grimm. In Newell's estimation, the Grimms, who did not maintain a strict adherence to accurate transcription of oral tradition and who adapted folklore to popular forms, believed folklore was "a racial heritage, transmitted from remote prehistoric epochs. . . . The traditions of any folk were regarded as truly expressive of its own distinct national genius, its peculiar way of assimilating nature and life." But this view, Newell asserted, was the result of "warm patriotism" and the desire to construct a unified Germany with a tradition every bit as poetic as the mythologies of ancient Greece.[11]

In each case, Newell sought to show that the search for national or racial origins was driven by political and ideological motives rather than by a scientific adherence to close and careful collection and analysis. Instead, he emphasized that the creation and transmission of folklore was the result of a complex process of diffusion that took place through the interaction between and among different cultural groups. This approach, at least in theory, allowed Newell to counter the evolutionary origins model, which suggested groups moved linearly through stages of evolution based on their mental and biological inheritances, and that their advancement was evidenced in their cultural or technological productions.

Newell's attention to the diffusion, rather than the evolution, of cultural material has been celebrated as his, as well as Boas's, great contribution to the study of culture. In *Before Cultures*, for example, Brad Evans argues that this early attention—especially as articulated by Franz Boas—to the ability of culture to circulate was meant to undermine the notion of racial inheritance and make cross-cultural affiliation, rather than race, the basis of identification.[12] While Newell's promotion of diffusion over evolution certainly posed a challenge to the prevalent biological determinism and racial essentialism of the late nineteenth century, the implication of this theoretical orientation supported an assimilationist approach to culture, suggesting the ease with which blacks and other non-European or marginal groups could assimilate to the more civilized white Western culture. Furthermore, despite his attempts to discount evolution as an inadequate model for studying the circulation and transmission of folklore, Newell's understanding of cultural groups was still rendered through an evolutionary schema that located groups at various stages of savagery, barbarism, semi-civilization, and civilization; in each case, white, Western culture being synonymous with civilization.

In addressing reports of Voodoo worship in Haiti, for instance, Newell took pains to show that the reports likely were overblown products of popular imagination and stereotype. He sought to trace the origins of Voodoo, not to African practices and customs, but to medieval European practices brought to Louisiana and Haiti by the French. As Newell stated, "I shall be able to make it appear: first, that the name Vaudoux, or Voodoo, is derived from a European source; secondly, that the beliefs which the word denotes are equally imported from Europe; thirdly, that the alleged sect and its supposed rites have, in all probability, no real existence, but are a product of popular imagination." In working toward these ends, Newell linked the practices associated with Voodoo more closely to medieval European witchcraft than to what he identified as the present-day savage customs of African cannibalism. Newell supported his contention through etymology and the collection and comparative analysis of reports regarding vaudoux and witchcraft, and concluded that the "Voodoos of Hayti are identical with the devout Waldenses of Piedmont."[13]

While Newell was unsparing in his critiques of folklorists who allowed their interpretations to be colored by their personal, political, or ideological biases, Newell's arguments in favor of European origins for African American folklore were not unaffected by such biases. Newell believed that blacks were assimilating so rapidly to white American practices that African American customs and tales actually bore the mark of the European remnants that persisted in white American culture rather than in African traditions and practices. This contention was supported by his belief that "in almost all cases folk-thought and folk-practice are imposed by the cultured races on the more barbarous, and that very little passes from the savage to the civilized." He continued, "I doubt whether a single instance can be cited of the adoption and assimilation, by a highly cultivated race, of any considerable body of barbarous ideas. Where two races are mixed together, as in America negroes and whites, the case is more complicated; yet here, also, the influence of the civilized part of the community is immeasurably in excess."[14] Within the context of the larger U.S. racial discourse, theories of diffusion, along with the geographic and environmental explanation for cultural similarities and differences, meant that African Americans could assimilate (and indeed had done so) to the more civilized practices and traditions of white Americans. As Cruz points out, this belief in assimilation grew out of the humanitarian reformists' views of the previous generation, but the new social scientists interpreted this cultural metamorphosis not through the moral and political lens of the abolitionists, but through a scientistic hermeneutic emphasizing classification and categorization.[15] In other words, the argument for circulation of cultural materials and the assimilation of racial groups was posed in an earlier guise, as the abolitionists and then reformists argued first for blacks' inherent humanity and second for blacks' ability to be educated and elevated to civilized standards. These ideas formed the intellectual tradition that Newell drew on to counter the biological determinism rooted in notions of essential, inheritable, and biologically determined racial differences. While the scientific impulse characterized in Newell's interpretative frame was legitimized within a rubric of objectivism, as Cruz contends, these orientations—the abolitionist/reformist and the scientific—"were never mutually exclusive" and indeed, "the benevolent attitude could blend with the managerial attitude to limit the value of cultural expressivity within larger structures of subjugation."[16] Furthermore, as John Roberts has argued extensively, the "discourse of folkness" that characterized nineteenth-century conceptions of folklore and interpretations of difference viewed Europeans as "the original folk and all other folk [as] mere imitators." This orientation greatly truncated interpretations of African American vernacular creativity. Furthermore, as Roberts maintains, from its very inception "American folkloristics obscured the most important source of difference claimed by African Americans—an African cultural heritage . . . [and] in a general sense, the history of African American folklore study can be characterized as an extended and extensive discourse designed to deny African American difference as a viable and vital sign of African cultural presence in the United States."[17]

In conjunction with his scientific orientation toward folklore studies and his commitment to theories of diffusion, Newell's historically based hermeneutic focused on folklore as a remnant or survival of the past. Working within a past-oriented paradigm, Newell often fell back on a "stages of culture" framework rendered in terms of savagery, barbarism, semi-civilization, and civilization. For instance, in his 1888 founding statement for AFS, Newell identified ethnic and regional groups warranting immediate study by the society's members. Although Newell conceded that in "the habits and ideas of primitive races much seems cruel and immoral to us," he emphasized the necessity of dutifully recording these habits and ideas, for in them, he argued, modern civilization was furnished with "a complete representation of the savage mind."[18] Since Native Americans were being exterminated at the hands of American progress, Newell included the "Lore of the Indian Tribes of North America" on his list, and urged his fellow AFS members to "preserve memorials" of their way of life.[19] Still set within the framework of rendering the savage mind accessible to the civilized, Newell identified the "Lore of the Negroes of the Southern States of the Union" as another pressing scholarly endeavor. Negro lore, he explained, represented "interesting and important psychological problems" for study by the learned society.[20] Ostensibly, Newell rejected the idea of using folklore as evidence of cultural evolution on the basis that folklore was not just a survival from a savage stage. Instead, he maintained, "folklore is found to exist among the most intelligent as well as among the rudest part of the population."[21] As such, he included on his list, alongside the Native American and African American lore, "the relics of Old English Folk-Lore . . . [and] Lore of French Canada, Mexico, etc."[22] As Roberts points out, however, Newell's shift from discussing the "lore" of Native Americans and African Americans to collecting the "relics" of the earlier stages of English folklore "made clear [Newell's] view that British descendants represented a contemporary and enlightened element in American society. . . . Their possession of relics made them not folk, but passive bearers of tradition."[23]

Indeed, the evolutionary schema hinted at in Newell's subtle shift in terminology, along with larger social interest and intent, made impossible the separation of folklore studies from theories of social Darwinism. Scholarly and public interest in folkloric materials hinged, in part, on what these materials revealed about the evolutionary stages of human development. In the report on the third annual meeting of AFS, for instance, Newell explained that systems of knowledge could be partitioned into three categories, noting that even among the "lowest" or "most savage people" there had been "attempts at such understanding," asserting that in general, a peoples' "system of explanation" could be correlated with these stages of development, consisting of "savagery," "barbarism," and "civilization." The folklore that existed among the "lowest people" provided a window into the "savage" or primitive mind, while the folklore that existed among the civilized provided a record of how the civilized had evolved to their current state.[24] For many, folklore studies offered a way to mark, categorize, and order the allegedly uncivilized elements that persisted in a civilized society. Lee J. Vance, for instance, stated that "folklore is only concerned with the legends, customs, beliefs of the Folk, of the classes of people which have least been altered by education, which have shared least in progress . . . this folklore represents, in the midst of a civilized race, the savage ideas out of which civilization has been evolved."[25] In his report on the third annual meeting of AFS, Newell noted that Otis Mason (who became president of the society in 1891) "remarked [that] . . . when all the world was looking forward, it was a relief . . . glancing backward, and considering the past as it appeared by its survivals in the present. The record of the past formed an essential element in the interpretation of the future."[26] Daniel Brinton, the second president of the American Folklore Society, similarly reasserted the association between folklore and the study of "survivals" or relics. And while Brinton, like Newell, claimed not to subscribe to the theories of social Darwinism or cultural evolution, he classified cultures in terms of stages of development, from savagery, to barbarism, semi-civilization, civilization, and finally to enlightenment, with folklore representing the remnants of the earlier stages of development that persisted, however fleetingly, in the face of progress and advancement.[27]

Like its American counterpart, European folklore studies, which had seen the formation of the British Folk-Lore Society in 1878, was just as firmly rooted in the concept of folklore as "survivals." Several of the British society's early presidents insisted that folklore comprised "survivals" from an earlier stage of development and identified groups in which folklore persisted.[28] In organizing the American Folklore Society, Newell borrowed organizational principles and theoretical approaches from European folklore studies, maintaining the European emphasis on collecting "survivals" or "relics." Nevertheless, Newell sought to distinguish American folklore studies from its European predecessors by finding uniquely American materials to collect. While theoretically consistent with European models, particularly in relation to the emphasis on "survivals," Newell's contribution, Rosemary Zumwalt insists, was to create a more inclusive and pluralist approach to American folklore studies. As Zumwalt explains, within a European framework the folk were seen as the peasant ancestors to the civilized members of modern society; thus, prior to the formation of AFS, "the American Indian as 'savage'" would not have been recognized as "folk" and as such "would be studied by the ethnologist and not by the folklorist."[29] Similarly, Roger Abrahams argues that Newell, in his more inclusive approach to "American cultures worthy of study," advocated a "radical vision" of American pluralism.[30]

While Newell may have found innovative ways to adapt European folklore studies to the American context, his identification of certain groups as "folk," which he variously equates with savage and primitive, marked these groups as a less evolved other to the mainstream, "civilized," white, Western norm. In an 1894 speech to the Hampton folklorists, for instance, Newell defines "folk" as synonymous with race, and "lore" as signifying the "learning or knowledge peculiar" to the race.[31] He maintains that folklore belongs to the primitive stage and as races move through the stages of culture en route to civilization, folklore provides a record of their evolution. As the "Negro" accepts more "advanced ideas, habits, morals and theology," Newell explains, he will take his place among the civilized human race and his folklore will provide a record of the stages through which he has passed.[32]

In considering his own racial identity, Newell notes that although he is of English ancestry, he truly can claim no racial affiliation other than that of the "human race."[33] Newell's comments suggest that concepts such as the "human race" were defined by his naturalized worldview and an assumption that white Western middle-class values equaled a universal, unquestioned norm. His notion that African Americans would eventually shed their distinctive folklore and move toward becoming merely part of the "human race" indicates that folklore was something that could mark racial difference and inferiority, but with proper training and education, one could shed these vestiges of savagery and enter the civilized domain. In linking folk to non-Anglo-American "races," and in identifying African Americans and Native Americans as folk—but himself as non-folk—Newell renders folklore within a racialized evolutionary power structure in which he and his cohort occupy the position of universal evolved/civilized authority, while the racialized others maintain lower positions on the evolutionary scale until they are able to shed their racially distinct (read: non-white) folklore and become "universal" (read: white).

Finally, despite his admonitions against "romantic nationalism" and his promotion of a rigid scientism, Newell's orientation toward folklore nevertheless was influenced by the anti-modern romanticism of the period. On one hand, as Bronner suggests, the swell of attention to the study of folklore was part of the trend of meeting the problems facing late-nineteenth-century America "in the safety of a distant past or removed place, rather than in the anxiety-ridden present."[34] As Bronner argues, industrial advances and improvements in transportation and communication had quickened the tempo of daily life and increased the quantity of goods and services. These advances also created the middle-class perception that "there was an abundance of new goods ready for consumption and an abundance of culture ready for collecting."[35] On the other hand, what Bronner identifies as an American tendency to confront the modern problems of the rapidly changing present in the safety of a timeless past can be read more specifically as the tendency to meet the problems of the post-Reconstruction racial crisis in the safety of the antebellum past. Through his past-oriented, survivals approach to folklore, Newell romanticized the folklore of others—particularly Native and African Americans—as more vital elements in the face of progress and modernity. He warned his fellow folklorists that their "encomiums on national prosperity" would not make amends for their lack of attention to what he referred to as their "obligation" to study the primitive culture of Native and African Americans.[36] In terms of African Americans specifically, Newell identified folklore as the survivals or remnants of slave culture, and his location of folklore in the slave past was reflected in Plantation Tradition ideology that located black folklore within a mythic Southern past.

Plantation Tradition literature emerged first in the 1830s but gained increased popularity in the 1880s and 1890s with the writings of Harris and Thomas Nelson Page. Works in the Plantation Tradition tended to romanticize the antebellum South as a simpler time and place, creating an idealized past valorizing white Southern patriarchy and supporting the notions that blacks had been happy and faithful under the master/slave system and that authority for addressing the "Negro problem" should once again be entrusted to Southern whites. This elaborate fiction allowed Northern whites to avoid the contemporary crisis precipitated by the social and political presence of free blacks by returning responsibility for the "Negro problem" back to the supposedly benevolent rulers of the former slaveocracy. Newell's attention to collecting the survivals of slave life as it had existed on the Southern plantation intersected with the era's preoccupation with African Americans who could be removed temporally and geographically from the current moment and located instead in the timeless imaginary of the antebellum South. To be sure, Newell's inclusion of the folklore of "Negroes of the Southern States of the Union" can be read as part of a pluralist agenda, and his attention to plantation folklore as a means of documenting the progress of educated African Americans can be seen as a progressive attempt to show that blacks were able to "evolve" by adopting the cultural practices and norms of dominant white society. Nevertheless, his identification of plantation folklore as that which was authentic about African American identity reified the prevailing Plantation Tradition ethos.

Alongside the growing popularity of Plantation Tradition literature, throughout the greater part of the nineteenth century, minstrelsy similarly spurred attention to black folklore, stoking debates about whether African Americans were capable of inventiveness and originality in their cultural productions or whether they merely imitated and "aped" white cultural forms. Simply stated, blackface minstrelsy refers to the pervasive popular cultural phenomenon in which white actors from about the 1830s onward darkened their faces and took to the stage performing parodies of black folklore and traditions. In the history of folklore studies, and of constructions of blackness in the United States generally, the significance of the minstrel tradition cannot be overstated. By the time the American Folklore Society was founded, the minstrel tradition had already constructed representations of African Americans as a distinct and peculiar folk group, replete with laughable habits, strange customs, and raucous songs and dance. With its conspicuous treatment and haphazard manipulation of black folk culture, coupled with the eventual use of black performers as the conduits of the material, minstrelsy marked black behavior as a subject for folkloric collection. As a prerequisite to understanding the conflation between the formation of folklore studies, the discourse of folklore, and the legalization of racial segregation at the end of the century, it is necessary first to consider briefly the ways in which minstrelsy shaped the national consciousness about race, particularly as this discourse centered on representations of black folklore as an indication of racial difference.

As a folk character made famous by the white minstrel performer Thomas Rice, Jim Crow ushered in a period of blackface performance that thrust the black image into the national and local entertainment spotlight. Rice's depiction of blackness quickened a cultural fascination with the black image that culminated in the immense popularity of minstrelsy. This juggling of racial identity eventually elicited enough attention to become a site of appropriation for the forming system of Jim Crow segregation. Tracing the career of Jim Crow reveals how popular culture, folklore studies, constructions of the black folk, and social and political agendas all converged around turn-of-the-century questions of racial identity and social order.

The birth of Jim Crow, the stage character, has typically been traced to an 1828 blackface performance by Thomas Dartmouth "Daddy" Rice. Rice, a white actor from New York's Seventh Ward on the Lower East Side of Manhattan, supposedly began "jumping Jim Crow" after a legendary encounter with Jim, the black stable hand. In *On the Real Side*, a study of humor in black entertainment, Mel Watkins recounts the event:

> Rice . . . reportedly saw a crippled and deformed black hostler or stable groom singing and performing a striking but peculiar dance as he went about his work. The actor, recognizing the potential appeal of the song—

> "Weel about and turn about, and do jis so. / Eb'ry time I weel about I jump Jim Crow"—and the black man's twisted, antic movements, memorized the lyrics and copied the dance.[37]

As the widely accepted story goes, Rice added several verses to the song, which he started performing between acts of *The Rifle*, and according to the legend, even bought the old man's clothes to "assure" the authenticity of his performance.[38] While the veracity of the encounter remains questionable, the legend has been continually reproduced because it provides a convenient explanation for the threatening appearance of ostensibly black folk material on the local and national stage. However, recent scholarship, as championed by W. T. Lhamon, asserts that this encounter was a fabrication of contemporary white journalists and middle-class monthly magazines contemptuous of the popularity of blackface performance and anxious about poor whites adopting black cultural material as an expression of dissatisfaction with their own stations in life. Instead, Lhamon's study shows Rice moved in culturally amalgamated circles and traveled extensively from New York's Five Points to Cincinnati, Mobile, Pensacola, Washington, Philadelphia, and New Orleans, arguing that it was during these travels and over the course of several years that Rice figured out how to adapt Jim Crow for the stage.[39] According to Lhamon, Jim Crow was "hardly a sudden or whimsical event" but instead was rooted in working-class affiliations across color lines and a lower-class desire to harness the subversive energy surging in black folk culture.[40]

Bringing his impersonations of black folk life to the stage, Rice became one of America's best-known comedians, riding the wave of American popular culture's fascination with blackness. But what of this popular culture fetish for ostensibly black folk material? Representing one end of the spectrum, Lhamon argues that this white fascination with black folk culture boiled up from poor whites' identification with the "charisma" that blacks exhibited in the face of oppression and servitude. Lhamon contends that it was the "liberating potential" of Rice's Jim Crow character that made it so wildly popular with poor white audiences on one hand and a ready target for racist appropriation by middle-class and elite authorities on the other.[41] Robert Tolls asserts, to the contrary, that as slavery grew into a national controversy and free blacks became increasingly present in the public sphere, minstrelsy served to satisfy Northern whites' curiosities about blacks, while it also organized the growing black presence into convenient stereotypes. Whether Jim Crow was first adopted by white actors for its cross-racial energy and liberating effects and later warped into a tool for segregationists' agendas, as Lhamon asserts, or blackface performance was always operating on the

Figure 1.1: "Thomas Rice as Jim Crow" (ca. 1830). Harvard Theater Collection, Harvard University.

basis of demeaning stereotypes, as Tolls contends, one thing is certain: early blackface performances played an integral role in forming the popular perceptions of the black folk. Rice's white contemporaries, for example, did not see him as an originator at all but lauded him as one skilled at impersonating the gestures and language of the black folk.

A London reviewer explained, "We will not say that we like Mr. Rice's performance, but there cannot be a doubt of its extraordinary reality. The shuffling gait, the strange whistle, and the more strange laugh."[42] Rice's manager Noah Ludlow claimed that his client's talent lay in "imitating the broad and prominent peculiarities of other persons, as was evident in his close delineations of the corn-field Negro, drawn from real life."[43] Rice's contemporaries regarded him not only as a performer of black folk material, but also as an ethnographer, translator, and representative of authentic Negro life. Early blackface actors were seen as purveyors, or in their own terminology, "delineators," of black folk culture, and thus these white actors took control of presenting American popular culture with its images of black folk life. Tolls, however, contends that these "blackface minstrels were not authentic, even in intention. They were not ethnographers, but professional entertainers, whose major concern was to create stage acts that would please their audiences."[44]

Thus, until the late 1860s and early 1870s, the major "black presence" in American popular culture was not black at all, but instead reflected white impersonations of black life. While elite sensibilities may have been offended by Jim Crow's disregard for social decorum and racial categorization, ultimately this stage character's strange behaviors and bizarre habits helped solidify a sense of social and civil superiority that justified the white elites' claims to a position farther along on the evolutionary scale. By 1840, any liberating and subversive potential that the early Jim Crow performances may have suggested had given way to the form of blackface minstrelsy, producing the damaging stereotypes that openly caricatured and ridiculed black life. Even Lhamon concedes that by the early 1840s, the form of blackface minstrelsy that followed Rice's Jim Crow performances inverted Rice's connections to blackness and made them "abhorrent."[45]

By the mid-1800s, minstrel performances used this "humor" to penetrate a national consciousness and shape an ideology of racial difference and degradation. What white audiences found most comical in the white minstrel performances of black life were the grotesque physical features attributed to blacks and the primitive, childish behaviors parodied for comic value, as the following description of the Virginia Minstrels' performance makes clear:

> They burst on stage in makeup which gave the impression of huge eyes and gaping mouths. They dressed in ill-fitting, patchwork clothes and spoke in heavy nigger dialects. Once on stage, they could not stay still for an instant.

Figure 1.2: "The Celebrated Negro Melodies as Sung by the Virginia Minstrels" (1843). Robert Cushman Butler Collection of Theatrical Illustrations, MASC, Washington State University Libraries.

> Even while sitting, they contorted their bodies, cocked their heads, rolled their eyes, and twisted their outstretched legs . . . their wild hollering and their bobbing, seemingly compulsive movements charged the entire performance with excitement.[46]

Coupled with this visual spectacle of black behavior, minstrel shows also satirized the popular social and political issues of the day. Minstrels in blackface would turn the topics of Emancipation, suffrage, and education into comic routines, at once undermining the seriousness of the issue being satirized while also insinuating blacks' inability to participate in serious political discussion. Minstrel shows were interspersed with pithy exchanges between actors, dialect-infused speeches, and boisterous song and dance. Many shows ended in "plantation extravaganzas," in which the plantation was presented as idyllic and blacks as contented and servile. These representations promoted pro-slavery and later pro-segregation interests and instilled the stereotypes of blacks as childlike, carefree, and in need of protection. These shows also portrayed blacks as vastly different from whites, more different perhaps, than even Northern whites had imagined.

Blackface minstrelsy remained wildly popular with white audiences up to and through the Civil War. Its representation of black folk life reflected and solidified public opinion. At best, it showed blacks as natural, primitive, and carefree juxtaposed to evolved, modern, and civilized society. At worst, it branded blacks as immoral, stupid, lazy, and inferior. Watkins aptly states, "by focusing on and exaggerating the supposed earthy peculiarities of blacks, black-faced mimics provided the simple, folksy entertainment that white audiences demanded and assured them that, indeed, they were superior to their enslaved brethren."[47]

After the Civil War, in the Reconstruction and post-Reconstruction eras, minstrel caricatures and stereotypes passed from white performers in blackface to black performers. By and large, whites controlled the management and profit of black minstrel troupes, and blackface minstrelsy had set the parameters of minstrel performance decades earlier.[48] When black performers inherited the stage from white people in blackface, they found themselves trapped within the confines of caricature and rewarded for their ability to personify the stereotypes conjured up by white minstrel performances. In the post-Reconstruction era, seeing whites act like blacks was no longer quite as funny as it was to see blacks act like whites expected them to act. When black minstrels went before their white audiences, they provided the corporeal evidence that blacks were, at best, different and peculiar and, at worst, grotesque and degenerate. Here was physical proof that blacks were an anomaly to be exploited in popular entertainment and a curiosity to be investigated in the emerging social sciences. Promoters and reviewers emphasized that these were not shows involving entertainers or performers, but displays of natural, uninhibited black life. Black minstrel troupes were promoted as "the real thing," "real nigs," and "genuine plantation darkies."[49] Black performers were able to modify these stereotypes by adding detail, nuance, and more significantly, by creating in-group meanings among themselves and their black audiences. The stereotypes and caricatures forged by the white minstrels were too deeply ingrained and culturally useful, however, for the white audiences to discard. Therefore the black minstrels found that, far from creating satirical critiques, their performances reinforced the racial stereotypes, adding physical evidence that verified the white audience's expectations.

Figure 1.3: Oliver Scott's "Refined Negro Minstrels" (1898). Minstrel Poster Collection, Library of Congress, Prints and Photographs Division.

The print for Oliver Scott's "Refined Negro Minstrels" (see Fig. 1.3) depicts the medley of stereotypes that had come to dominate the minstrel shows and capture the public imagination. Jim Crow, Zip Coon, and the enduring and infamous Grinning Darkie of the old plantation South ousted the Yankee and the backwoodsman from national prominence. In the Scott print, the dandy poses in a flashy yellow coat, sporting pencil-thin legs and holding a cane. A Topsy-like character dances around a figure whose spectacles mark him as a caricature of the black intellectual. In the background, standing erect, are five "gentlemen" who could be a spoof on the Hampton Student Singers or Fisk Jubilee Singers, groups known for their dignified manner and impeccable dress. In front of the student singers is the ever-popular parody of the cake-walk couple: an ornately dressed Southern belle towering over her stocky, diminutive companion. In the foreground, a mammy figure and a variation of the Jim Crow character dominate. The Scott print illustrates aptly how representations of black folklore—the "songs and dancing" promised in the print caption—and the different possibilities for black identity and representation, were mocked and curtailed through the evocation of easy and convenient stereotypes. The black intellectual, the Northern gentleman, the Southern rural folks, as well as the sophisticates, were all turned into comic relief on the minstrel stage.

It was also protocol for black minstrels to legitimize themselves by playing on the audience's desire to see real, authentic blacks. To stress that they were genuine Negroes, most black minstrels ceased darkening their faces with burnt cork. The variety of hues among the actual black faces was another authenticating feature that allowed the black minstrels to claim that they were not "uniformly painted imitations" like their white minstrel predecessors, and critics even began to denounce white minstrels as "base imitators" of the real thing.[50]

The cultural obsession with the "natural" and "spontaneous" behavior of these black figures continued to grow, climaxing in 1895 with the arrival of a "Negro Village" in Brooklyn's Ambrose Park. As Tolls explains, the plantation literally came to New York. The minstrel show "Black America" created a plantation fantasy in the midst of the city, complete with Negro cabins, hen yards, chickens, mules, and peopled with 500 blacks identified as "genuinely southern Negroes . . . brought direct from the fields." The show was billed as an "ethnological exhibit of unique interest," and blacks were referred to not as entertainers, but as participants. The show promised "no imitation, nothing but what is real." The Negro Village, as one viewer commented, "might have been hundreds of miles from civilization."[51]

Just two years before the Negro Village captivated audiences with images of "genuine plantation Negroes," the World's Columbian Exposition in Chicago had enthralled fairgoers with its architectural masterpiece, the White City. The White City, ostensibly named for the white paint that covered every building within the exhibit, showcased the accoutrements of modern civilization. The Court of Honor stood at the center of the city, surrounded by the marvels of modern civilization. Enormous white buildings ran along the canals surrounding the Court of Honor and housed exhibits of modern industry, art, agriculture, and electricity. Women, after protesting their exclusion, received one building located on the edge of the White City. Blacks, however, were excluded from the White City altogether. In fact, non-white, non-Western participants were relegated to the Midway Plaisance. German and Irish exhibits were located near the entrance of the Midway, followed by Turkish, Arabic, and Chinese "villages." Finally, the American Indians and Dahomans were situated at the end of the Midway.[52] As the *Chicago Tribune* reported, "What an opportunity was here afforded to the scientific mind to descend the spiral of evolution tracing humanity in its highest phase down to its animalistic origins."[53]

As Gail Bederman notes, just as whites "insisted tenaciously that civilization was built on white racial dominance, African Americans were equally tenacious in insisting that civilization was not necessarily white."[54] Frederick Douglass and Ida B. Wells vehemently objected to the exclusion of blacks from the exposition. In their protest pamphlet, *The Reason Why the Colored American is Not in the World's Columbian Exposition*, they argued that the African American best demonstrated the advances of civilization, having overcome the hardships of slavery to survive and excel, while the white Americans' exclusion of black Americans from the exposition only further illustrated that white America lacked the decency and civilization it professed.[55] Anna Julia Cooper, too, denounced the exclusion of African Americans from the Fair, noting, ". . . foreigners from all parts of the globe, who shall attend our Columbian Exposition," would come away with images of African American subjugation or exclusion. The barring of African Americans from any kind of substantive participation in the White City, she continued, said more about the lauded, but in her view illusory, "impartiality and generosity of our white countrymen" than it did about African Americans' state of or contributions to civilization.[56]

Juxtaposing the White City to the Negro Village and the Midway Plaisance reveals by stark contrast the racialization of the discourses of folklore and civilization. These grand spectacles combined popular entertainment, representations of "authentic" folk, and scientific discourse to reinforce for the American public that white was synonymous with civilization and black with primitivity. It was the folklore of the Negro that provided a foil against which the modern, evolved, rational society could be measured. The Negro occupied a different place on the evolutionary ladder and was not figured as an ancestor to the civilized middle-class American, but instead was seen as a living example of the primitive stage. As the superimposition of the rhetoric of evolution onto the discourse of black folklore makes clear, the black folk were not just within, but apart from, American society; they were behind and below modern civilization. The ideology of social, cultural, and biological evolution coursed through the entire conversation, providing "scientific" justification that this was indeed the natural order of things.

Throughout the nineteenth century, minstrelsy had an indelible impact on emerging social, cultural, and intellectual institutions. Minstrelsy furnished "the jokes that were told and retold, the songs that were on everyone's lips, and the vivid, literally living . . . minstrels in effect evolved a kind of '*national folklore*'—a constellation of images, definitions, symbols and meaning that most white Americans could and did share."[57] By yoking the stage stereotypes to claims of a folk authentic, minstrelsy created a potent black folk image that intrigued the social scientist and provided ready support for the rapidly solidifying system of Jim Crow segregation. While minstrelsy provides an ideal trope for examining constructions of racial identity around representations of black folklore, the ostensibly racially based differences caricatured in Jim Crow minstrel performances also received literary treatment in works from the so-called Plantation and Lost Cause traditions. The Plantation Tradition, epitomized in the works of Joel Chandler Harris and Thomas Nelson Page, gained efficacy through the manipulation of black folklore so that it became an emblem of childish behaviors and "the good ole days before the war."[58] The images of happy, industrious, and loyal "darkies" and of kind and just plantation owners helped absolve Northern whites of a race issue that by century's end had come to stand in the way of the profitable reconciliation many Northern and Southern whites now desired. Where the Plantation Tradition left off, literature of the Lost Cause picked up. Works in this tradition, exemplified by Thomas Dixon's *The Leopard's Spots*, provided a storehouse of the more damning stereotypes of blacks as lazy, thieving, and sexually voracious, while idealizing the pre–Civil War South and its lost culture.[59]

Alongside these popular-culture representations, early submissions of black folklore to *JAF* added an air of scientific authority and objectivity to the public's beliefs about the black folk. Newell, editor of *JAF* from 1888–99, noted that since blacks, "for good or ill, [were] henceforth an indissoluble part of the body politic," their lore warranted rigorous investigation.[60] Accordingly, *JAF* published over 100 articles and notes on black folklore in its first twenty-five issues, and Newell assured the readers that, "in conformity with the spirit of modern scholarship," the folklore materials presented were of "sufficient scientific status to make them worth recording."[61]

From its founding days, however, *JAF* betrayed the tension that existed between Newell's continual injunctions that the journal submissions focus solely on documenting folklore materials and the propensity of the contributors to theorize about the materials they presented. Thus, some of the contributions on black folklore are relatively straightforward and strive for a degree of objectivity. Stewart Culin in his "Reports Concerning Voodooism," for example, notes, "it is popularly asserted in Hayti and San Domingo that the negroes perpetuate Voodoo orgies, and that cannibalism is still practiced." Culin, to the contrary, states, "I believe that meetings are held, but do not think they are accompanied with human sacrifices."[62] He then provides a secondhand account of how Voodoo rites and rituals were used to secure a marriage, to bring harm to an enemy, and to cause a mysterious death. He imparts these accounts not as a way to pass judgment on the participants or practitioners, but instead to suggest the importance of belief and performance in the Voodoo ritual.[63]

Alcee Fortier's "Customs and Superstitions of Louisiana," in contrast, provided just the type of scholarly report that proved useful in depicting the black folk customs that sustained the plantation ideology and, by extension, Jim Crow segregation. Fortier begins his contribution to *JAF*'s second issue by stating:

> In order to understand fully the customs of a past age and of plantation life before the war, we must bear in mind that the planters lived in the greatest opulence and possessed many slaves. These were, as a rule, well treated by their masters, and in spite of slavery, they were contented and happy. Not having any of the responsibilities of life, they were less serious than the present freemen and more inclined to take advantage of all opportunities to amuse themselves.

Fortier goes on to explain that New Year's Day on the plantations was an occasion of great merriment and pleasure for the slaves, when they would gather around the big house and receive "a piece of ox killed expressly for them, several pounds of flour, and a new tin pan and spoon." Fortier further observes: "The scene was most striking, interesting and weird. Two or three hundred men and women were there in front of the house, wild with joy and most boisterous, although always respectful." Recounting the celebration, Fortier notes that the slaves' "strange and savage music . . . [and] grotesque and extraordinary faces" provided "great amusement" to the children, and although the tradition was "less entertaining" to the parents, "they never interfered, as they considered that, by well-established custom, New Year's Day was one of mirth and pleasure for the childlike slaves." Fortier concludes that the scene he has documented is "very different . . . from those described in 'Uncle Tom's Cabin,' for the slaves were certainly not unhappy on the plantations."[64]

Perhaps not incidentally, Fortier's description of slave life sounds remarkably similar to what was a well-known 1878 Plantation Tradition poem by Irwin Russell, "Christmas-Night in the Quarters," in which Russell describes the festivities of an antebellum Christmas celebration on a large plantation: "When merry Christmas-day is done, / And Christmas-night is just begun; /. . . The darkies hold high carnival. / From all the country-side they throng, / With laughter, shouts, and scraps of song." Russell's poem continues, explaining the source of the slaves' unbridled enthusiasm: "Original in act and thought, / Because unlearned and untaught. / Observe them at their Christmas party: / How unrestrained their mirth—how hearty! / How many things they say and do / That never would occur to you!" Russell explains that the slaves are justified in their celebration because the next day they will return to the fields and resume their diligent service and hard work. In his poem, the slaves continually appeal to "Mahsr" to forgive and "bless" them, since they cannot restrain the inevitable call to dance.[65]

The similarities between Fortier's folklore document and Russell's Plantation Tradition poem suggest the close, at times intertwined, relationship between early folklore studies and mainstream popular culture, particularly black folklore and popular cultural materials associated with the minstrel and Plantation Traditions. In a journal purportedly devoted to the objective and scientific study of folklore, Newell saw fit to publish Fortier's submission containing so many assumptions sustaining the post-Reconstruction segregationist platform. Was this an oversight, or were the ideas that Fortier advanced, linking representations of folklore to the politics of the Plantation Tradition, so pervasive that they were published, evidently uncontested, in a journal devoted to the *scientific* study of Negro folklore?

In a society fraught with racial tensions, it would be difficult to overestimate the impact of the popular representations of the black folk, coupled with the intellectual and "scientific" assessments of black folklore, on turn-of-the-century racial politics. The rhetoric of folklore achieved currency in the political and legal discourse of segregation because it was easily translated into support for the separation of the races and the inferior position of blacks. The combination of the minstrel and plantation images of black folklore, along with the scientific framework provided by the newly emerging field of folklore studies, supplied segregationists with a convenient apparatus for legitimizing a system of racial separation predicated on two premises: 1) racial distinctions could be demarcated, if not through one's blood or physical appearance, then at least through the observation of what were ostensibly racially differentiated behaviors, practices, and characteristics, and 2) the separation of blacks and whites followed the existing customs, traditions, and habits of the people and therefore could not be regulated by law. Many cultural commentators, past and present, have observed that, given the reality of a racially "mixed" population, discerning racial identity came with a host of attendant difficulties. The judges and legislatures who constructed and supported the "one drop rule" recognized the difficulty of visually distinguishing race, realizing that racial identification had to move beyond physical markers.

But if discerning race based on physical appearance was difficult, identifying the color of a person's blood presented an obvious paradox.[66] This dilemma required new indicators of racial identity, and those indicators were found, in part, through attention to what were ostensibly racially differentiated behaviors, i.e., folk customs. There was an insistence, for example, that blacks could not imitate whites, that the behavioral differences, if not inherent, were so ingrained that they had become "spontaneous" and "natural." Dominant interpretations of black minstrelsy as inherent and authentic worked to legitimize segregationist agendas by supplying examples of the kinds of uncivilized behaviors that blacks supposedly exhibited as vastly different from those of civilized white society. At the same time, there was a growing consensus that legislation could do little to change the folkways, habits, social practices, and/or folk customs that inherently separated the races. In establishing a precedent for the *Plessy* decision, Justice Henry Billings Brown turned to *Roberts v. City of Boston* (1849), citing State Supreme Court Chief Justice Lemuel Shaw, who casually noted in his majority opinion upholding segregation in Massachusetts public schools that racial "prejudice, if it exists, is not created by law and probably cannot be changed by law."[67] As Rayford Logan has documented, this sentiment was echoed in the Northern press. The New Haven *Evening Register*, for example, voiced "grave doubt if the question of social principles can be settled satisfactorily by legislation," and as Logan notes, like opinions were expressed in similar language in a number of major city newspapers.[68]

Indeed, the very phrase "by custom and by law," which was popularly used to describe how Jim Crow segregation was enacted, borrows from folklore studies the term used to denote both the traditional way of doing things (i.e., customary) and the things done in the traditional way (i.e., customs). In other words, the notion that racial separation and difference are accomplished "by custom" implies they are a result of the force of tradition, or in everyday parlance, just the way things are. It also implies, however, that racial distinction is evidenced in the "customs," or characteristics and behaviors, distinguishing the two races. Justice Henry Billing Brown's majority opinion in the *Plessy* case illustrates how the dual meaning operated. When Brown declared that it was legally permissible for the state of Louisiana to act in accordance with the "the established customs, traditions and usages of the people," he was drawing on the first meaning of the term, allowing that the "reasonableness" of the statute was confirmed by its adherence to existing customs. When he later stated that "if one race be inferior to the other socially, the Constitution of the United States cannot be expected to put them on the same plane," he was basing his constitutional interpretation on the second meaning of custom, implying that in the absence of the ability to rely on "admixture of blood" or even appearance, it was blacks' inferior social behaviors that distinguished them from whites and relegated them to a separate sphere in the public and private life of the nation.[69]

This concept was articulated most overtly in the Mississippi Supreme Court *Ratliff v. Beale* (1896) case, in which the court deferred to the 1890 Mississippi State Constitution in supporting its decision upholding poll taxes. The court stated:

> By reason of its previous condition of servitude and dependence, this race had acquired or accentuated certain peculiarities of habit, of temperament, and character, which clearly distinguished it as a race from that of the whites—a patient, docile people, but careless, landless, and migratory within narrow limits, without forethought, and its criminal members given rather to furtive offense than to the robust crimes of white. Restrained by the Federal Constitution from discriminating against the Negro race, the [Mississippi State] Convention discriminated against its characteristics.[70]

In this decision, the justices found that the Mississippi State Constitution did not discriminate against blacks because of their race, but instead held that it was due to blacks' inferior characteristics that they found themselves disenfranchised. In other words, the voting qualification of two years of consistent payment of the poll taxes was not meant to discriminate against blacks as a race but against the characteristics of carelessness, transiency, and criminality, to which blacks just happened to be prone.

This mode of reasoning is characteristic of the form of "historicist racial rule" that, as David Theo Goldberg asserts, rose to dominance in the second half of the nineteenth century. Distinguishing between the "historicist" and "naturalist" forms of racial rule, Goldberg explains that in the "naturalist" paradigm, which dominated from the seventeenth century until well into the nineteenth century, black inferiority was rooted in or determined by African Americans' biological makeup. In its ideology and operation the "naturalist's" program tended to be "viscerally vicious," "cruel," and "direct concerning racist presumptions and commitments."[71] "Historicist rule," on the other hand, employed a version of cultural evolutionism, arguing, according to Goldberg, that black inferiority was a product of culture and environment (i.e., "their previous condition of servitude") and that "those not white are . . . developmentally immature, historically not yet capable of self-governance."[72] While there was certainly plenty of cross-fertilization between the historicist and naturalist modes of reasoning, and as Goldberg notes, the rise of historicist racial rule hardly displaced the naturalist forms of rule, the historicist mode allowed the state legislatures and the local, state, and federal courts to pass and uphold laws that could appear non-discriminatory on the surface and yet, in fact, be deeply discriminatory.

Thus the Supreme Court, and state courts and legislatures, followed the scientific and social scientific discourse, popular culture, and vocal public opinion in favor of racial segregation in accepting as fact that racial distinctions existed as a matter of custom, while black inferiority was a consequence of blacks' culture, environment, or biology, but certainly not of law. Conciliatory rhetoric notwithstanding, the *Plessy* decision, in effect, gave the federal stamp of approval to a state-by-state travesty already under way when the justices decided they could not sway social ideas or customs, thus authorizing the disenfranchisement of African Americans and condemning them to second-class citizenship for the next five-plus decades. It would be fifty-eight years before the Supreme Court would recognize the racism, prejudice, and discrimination buried in the ostensibly non-discriminatory rhetoric and reasoning of the *Plessy* decision.

While the Supreme Court was slow to admit the discriminatory nature of its decision, there were those, like Charles Chesnutt, who understood clearly what pulsated beneath the Court's ruling. In "The Negro and the Courts," Chesnutt opined:

> The most important and far reaching decision of the Supreme Court upon the question of civil rights is that in the case of *Plessy vs. Ferguson*. . . . The opinion is a clear and definite approval of the recognition by State laws, of color distinction. . . . It establishes racial caste in the United States as firmly as though it were established by an act of Congress. . . . a more humiliating, insulting, and degrading system is hardly conceivable under even a nominally free government.[73]

Similarly, in an important but unheeded dissenting opinion, Justice John Harlan recognized that the federal institutions were authorizing a travesty, predicting, "It is, therefore, to be regretted that this high tribunal . . . has reached the conclusion that it is competent for a state to regulate the enjoyment by citizens of their civil rights solely upon the basis of race. . . . the thin disguise of 'equal' accommodations . . . will not mislead anyone, nor atone for the wrong this day done."[74]

The confluence of forces that congealed around the formation of folklore studies in the late nineteenth century did not go unremarked upon by African American intellectuals and cultural workers. While Newell's scientific hermeneutic and emphasis on diffusion allowed for an expansion in thinking about cultural formations that pushed beyond a strict adherence to biological or racial determinism, the political and cultural implications of his orientation toward folklore became areas of concern for several African American cultural commentators. African American folklorists and cultural workers, ranging from Anna Julia Cooper and Alexander Crumell, to W. E. B. Du Bois, Paul Laurence Dunbar, and Pauline Hopkins—all deeply aware of the racial politics of representing and studying black folklore—imagined alternative possibilities for African American folklore and folklore studies. Cooper, for instance, challenged the vaunted objectivity embraced by Newell. Instead, she advocated for a more intimate and reciprocal relationship between folklore and African American literature, embracing folklore's role in creating an African American literary tradition, not so much as part of a racially essentialist project, but as conscious cultivation of an oppositional perspective and history embodied in black folklore. Hampton folklorist Robert Moton, on the other hand, participated in categorizing and classifying black folk songs but resisted examining folklore as detached remnants of the past, and instead advocated for an understanding of folklore in context.

Indeed, as national constructions of black folklore and the black folk image were increasingly implicated in white supremacist ideologies and segregationist agendas, the Hampton Folklore Society emerged as one of the first societies comprised mainly of African Americans dedicated to the collection, preservation, and study of black folklore and cultural traditions. Like the American Folklore Society, the Hampton Folklore Society cannot be understood outside of the social, cultural, and political debates surrounding constructions of racial identity and segregation. The history of the Hampton Folklore Society, however, is predicated on the emergence of folklore studies at the Hampton Institute, which began as early as 1878 with a decidedly reformist orientation. Recovering the history of the folklore studies at the institute introduces a more specific context in which to locate the emergence of the Hampton Folklore Society, thereby allowing us to gain a deeper understanding of the range of theorizing about black folklore in relation to the racial politics of folklore studies at both the local, national, and transnational levels.

2 From Hawai'i to Hampton

Samuel Armstrong and the Unlikely Origins of Folklore Studies at the Hampton Institute

The story of folklore studies at the Hampton Institute is framed by racialized discourses of civilization within and beyond the permeable national borders of the United States. It is a story about modes of resistance and agency within the dynamics of asymmetrical power relations, and it is a story about redefining the meaning of black folklore within a literary, cultural, social, and political context. I begin my recounting of this story in a rather unexpected place, tracing the journey of Hampton Institute founder Samuel Armstrong from Hawai'i to Hampton to reveal how Armstrong's missionary background played an influential role in determining the educational principles that would serve as the cornerstone of the institute while also shaping his attitudes toward black folklore. As part of his mission to educate and civilize his black students, for instance, Armstrong sought to expose and eradicate black folklore as a relic of an uncivilized past. Ironically, in an effort to realize this objective, Armstrong came to oversee the initial collection and publication of black folk materials at Hampton.

Armstrong's aggressive policy toward extricating residual folk elements en route to civilizing his black students, however, was an area of ongoing contention. For the members of the Hampton Folklore Society the legacy of the Armstrong position posed a fundamental challenge. In the second half of the chapter I examine the formation of the Hampton Folklore Society in the last decade of the nineteenth century, arguing that under the leadership of Alice Bacon, the society continued to operate in relation to the founding ideology of the institute but also introduced important innovations to the study of black folklore, questioning the established dynamics of folklore collection and incorporating a range of perspectives and approaches into their work. Locating the Hampton folklorists within this larger institutional, national, and transnational context suggests both the limitations and parameters placed on their early collection efforts as well as the reach of their cultural contributions and folkloric innovations.

While the Hampton Folklore Society was not founded until 1893, the idea for both the institute and the collection of black folklore was planted in Maui and Oahu, Hawai'i, where Samuel Armstrong lived from his birth in 1839 until his departure for Williams College in 1860. When Armstrong's parents, Richard Armstrong and Clarissa Chapman Armstrong, arrived in Honolulu in 1832 along with seventeen others from the Fifth Company of missionaries, the American Board of Commissioners for Foreign Missions had already spent eleven years building schools and churches, printing newspapers and books, translating the Hawaiian language into writing, establishing businesses, and performing advisory roles for the Hawaiian ruling class.[1]

By the late 1840s, the missionaries believed that they were entering the next stage of their project. In this phase, they were to secure a permanent stronghold in Hawai'i, extending their missionary influence throughout the Pacific islands. To accomplish this they first would have to establish and maintain secondary and advanced schools for their children. As Edward Beckwith, Richard Armstrong's son-in-law, fundraising partner, and future president of Oahu College, explained, the "married missionaries" would not then feel "constrained to return to [the United States] . . . to make provisions for [the education of] their children."[2] The alumni of these schools would then serve as missionaries for other ventures throughout the Pacific. Both of Armstrong's Hawaiian alma maters—Punahou, founded in 1841 by Hiram Bingham for the primary and secondary education of the missionary children, and Oahu College—were manifestations of missionaries' desires to establish, maintain, and expand control in the Pacific.

In tandem with this first objective, the missionaries commenced securing for themselves and their children key positions in government and industry. Richard Armstrong inherited from William Richards the position of Minister of Public Instruction, while Armstrong's brother, William Nevins Armstrong, would go on to become Attorney General of Hawai'i in 1880.[3] This pattern was replicated numerous times in the garnering of powerful appointments for missionary progeny as they extended their influence from ministry and education to Island administration and commerce. Daniel Dole, for example, who arrived as a missionary and served as the first principal of Punahou, was the father of Sanford Dole, who became President of the Republic of Hawai'i when Queen Lili'uokalani was deposed in 1893. Once in office, Sanford Dole immediately requested that the United States annex

Hawai'i, though this would not occur until 1898.[4] In the year after annexation, Sanford's cousin, James Drummond Dole, who would become known as the "Pineapple King," arrived. He would become owner of the Hawaiian Pineapple Company, which would later become half of the Dole Company.[5] Samuel Northrup Castle and Amos Starr Cooke, who also arrived as missionaries, established the Royal School for the education of the missionary children and the children of Hawaiian royalty. They served as advisors to the king and were soon running the fourth largest company in Hawai'i; their venture would become the other half of Dole.[6]

This influential network of Protestant missionaries and their children, referred to as the Cousins (later formalized as the Hawaiian Mission Children's Society), either remained on the Islands to assume powerful and lucrative positions or returned to the United States to undertake other endeavors. Writing about "[w]hat a grand old institution the 'Cousins Society' is," Armstrong exhorted, ". . . seeing our Fathers have done more for poor Hawai'i than all others besides, and that we are natives of the soil, the Islands are our *lawful inheritance*."[7] In this fervent declaration, Armstrong claimed for the Protestant missionaries, as opposed to the "foreign" missionaries (i.e., the Catholics and Mormons), a "lawful inheritance" to the lands of Hawai'i. The Kanaka Maoli (native Hawaiians) were displaced as rightful occupants of the land, and Armstrong claimed for the missionaries familial and legal rights to assume ownership of Hawai'i, assigning the Kanaka Maoli the place of fortunate beneficiaries of the missionaries' goodwill.[8] Armstrong's comments were representative of the larger discourse regarding the future of the Hawaiian Islands. In late-nineteenth-century deliberations over who would control, inherit, and direct the future of the islands, neither the Hawaiian people nor their rulers were even considered legitimate players in the negotiations. Their rulers were viewed as childlike at best, or racialized, denigrated, and dismissed, as was the case with Queen Lili'uokalani, at worst.[9] The Kanaka Maoli people were seen as hopelessly benighted and desperate for the kind of rule that could come only from the U.S. missionaries and in need of the kind of reform that came only through hard work. It was in this milieu that Armstrong formulated his ideas about civilization, folklore, race, work, and education. And while Armstrong did not remain in the Islands, as many of the other "Cousins" did, he was greatly influenced by his experiences in Hawai'i and remained convinced throughout his life that the missionary project in Hawai'i served as a precursor to and a lesson for the Hampton Institute.

On January 1, 1848, Armstrong's father Richard transitioned from missionary pastor to Minister of Public Instruction. In the journal entry marking the day, Richard Armstrong opined, "The subject of this office has cost me a long and severe mental conflict. To accept of it I could not and to reject it I dared not; to be brought into so close contact with the government, has seemed extremely objectionable and repugnant to my feeling, and yet to let the school system go down . . . I could not do." He would, of course, accept the position, conceding, "But the conflict is over. . . . I must now go forward."[10] In a formal letter of acceptance sent to King Kamehameha III, Armstrong reveals his more overt motives for accepting the position, namely that education could be as potent a tool for "re-making" the people as religious ministering: "Education, intellectual, moral and physical, is the great lever by which philanthropists of every land, are seeking to redeem and elevate the mass of people." He then goes further to suggest that the very existence of the Hawaiian people is dependent on their learning and practicing Christian moral values, prophesying, "[I]f depopulation here is to be arrested; if vices which are consuming the natives are to be eradicated; if an indolent and thriftless people are to become industrious and thrifty; if Christian institutions are to be perpetuated, the work must be accomplished mainly where it has been so prosperously begun, *in the education of the young*."[11] As Lee Baker has argued, Richard Armstrong sought to implement his plan by connecting manual labor to education in the schools he oversaw—approximately 500 in total.[12] In the elder Armstrong's formulation, education, industry, and Christian morality formed the holy triumvirate that would save the Hawaiian people from their own supposed vices and their corrupt and inept leaders.

Throughout his father's tenure as Minister of Public Instruction from 1848 until 1860, Samuel Armstrong observed and absorbed the process of using industrial education as a means of instilling Protestant values in non-Western populations. Accompanying his father on visits to the schools, the young Armstrong internalized his father's emphasis on manual labor as a tool for indoctrinating the Protestant work ethic and for transforming the supposedly heathen native population into civilized Christians.[13] In *Lessons from the Hawaiian Islands*, Armstrong reflected, "These schools, over which my father as Minister of Education had for fifteen years a general oversight, suggested the plan of the Hampton School." He noted the "many striking similarities" between "the negro and the Polynesian," explaining, "[O]f both it is true that not mere ignorance, but deficiency of character is the chief difficulty, and that to build up character is the true objective point in education. . . . Especially in the weak tropical races, idleness, like ignorance, breeds vice." He concluded, ". . . [I]f man is to work out his own salvation, he must learn how to work."[14] Based on his experiences in Hawai'i, Armstrong came to believe that in facing the challenges of transforming a "native" population, accumulating the accoutrements of civilization was just one aspect. The more dire challenge had to do with altering the deeply imbedded, but not wholly immutable, racial character of the group. The character deficiencies of the "weak tropical races" might just be remedied, he believed, through a rigorous program of "proper training," which revolved around labor. The missionaries easily translated this ideology into justification for using labor as a tool for civilizing the so-called native or heathen peoples.

Redeeming the character of the native populations through labor and hard work, however, was beset by dangers, one of the most prominent being the traditional customs and practices of the Kanaka Maoli. In 1851, while accompanying his father on an inspection of all the schools in the Islands, Armstrong noted that the people had Bibles and offered family prayers, but their old customs and traditions persisted, leading the missionaries to wonder if the Hawaiians could ever truly become "English Christians" or enlightened, civilized citizens. In a departure from his father's view on the efficacy of using the Hawaiian language to enact the missionaries' educational agenda, the younger Armstrong believed the Hawaiian vernacular language, seen as the connective thread between the people and their customs, had to be replaced by English. He exhorted, "[S]avage dialects are a part of a low, sensuous life, that must be forsaken together with its other belongings. English is a tonic for both mind and soul."[15] The destruction of the Hawaiian language was an intricate part of what Ngugi wa Thiong'o refers to as the "cultural bomb" or the annihilation of "a people's belief in their names, in their languages, in their environment, in their heritage of struggle, in their unity, in their capacities and ultimately in themselves."[16] This kind of "linguistic genocide" not only attempted to prevent people from preserving and passing on their own stories, songs, traditions, beliefs, and histories, but also, as Noenoe Silva points out, it was more convenient for the missionaries turned businessmen and plantation owners to have laborers who understood English.[17]

While serving as chief clerk to his father, who was then editing the government-sponsored Hawaiian-language newspaper, *Ka Hae Hawaii*, Armstrong further witnessed the disparagement of cultural practices that fell outside the Protestant missionary moral economy. In particular, the hula became the object of missionary censure. In 1857 his father's newspaper ran an editorial arguing that the Hawaiian royalty had "no power in the law to agree to the hula," and that "the pono [or "morality" in a Christian context] of the hula encourages idleness."[18] Silva, Noel Kent, and Amy Stillman have variously argued that while objections to the hula were sometimes expressed as outrage against what the missionaries interpreted as savage and immoral displays of sexuality, those objections were secondary to the real opposition, which revolved around issues of work, labor, productivity, and economics. According to Kent, in an effort to maintain a productive labor force, the missionaries sought to "expunge those Hawaiian customs that seemed to undermine the grand objective of material accumulation."[19] In 1858 the missionaries circulated a petition listing reasons that hula should be legally banned. As Silva explains, reasons one and two asserted that people became absorbed in hula and would not attend to their work, thus the lands became unproductive; the third was because it encouraged licentiousness. Only at the end of the petition was the "spiritual welfare" of the people mentioned. Silva further notes that in a separate editorial, the writer of the petition issued a muted warning, stating that an additional threat of the hula was that "the natives are reverting to an old amusement which is essentially national."[20] The editorial suggests that the hula embodied a form of "national" identity based on distinct cultural practices and traditions that stood in opposition to the missionaries' attempts to remake Hawaiian identity in their own image.

As the debates over the hula reveal, the missionary effort to reform the people involved not just exacting adherence to white, Western religious and cultural norms, but more importantly, ensuring the creation of productive and efficient laborers. Cultural traditions and folklore were impediments to the process and in need of being expunged, not merely on the basis that they represented the customs of a less civilized people, but more importantly, because they thwarted productivity, maintained cultural identity and autonomy, and formed a basis for cultural resistance and subversion.[21]

In reflecting on the significance of the missionary work in Hawai'i, Armstrong wrote to the Cousins:

> Its [Hawaii's] influence is both strong and constructive. . . . To me the work of our fathers has been of unspeakable interest and value. I have tried to analyze and criticize to see mistakes—mistakes teach more than anything else—and while looking in a cold daylight as possible, at their methods and work, not to find fault, but to discover ideas and principles to apply when there was rise for them. . . . it is our duty and privilege to learn the lessons of Hawaiian life.[22]

When Armstrong founded the Hampton Normal and Agricultural Institute in 1868, he adapted from the Hawaiian missionary project an emphasis on work as pedagogy and a pronounced suspicion of folk culture and traditions.

He saw African Americans, like the Hawaiians, as a people in need of being civilized at the foot of the missionary contingent, but he was more aggressive than his father in enlisting the people to exorcise the cultural traditions and practices that persisted in their own homes and communities, and he devised more direct strategies for utilizing students as agents in the civilizing process.[23]

Before founding the Hampton Institute, however, Armstrong would leave Hawai'i, studying at Williams College for two years before eventually serving as brevet brigadier general of black troops in the Union Army.[24] Armstrong's wartime letters illustrate the transformation of conscience he underwent as his military service brought him into close and regular contact with African American troops. Prior to the war, in a letter to Archibald Hopkins, Armstrong explained that he supported the war out of a sense of Christian obligation but felt no personal commitment to black Americans: "I am a sort of abolitionist, but I have not learned to love the Negro. I believe in universal freedom; I believe the whole world cannot buy a single soul. . . . So I go in for freeing them, more on account of their souls than their bodies."[25] By the time the Emancipation Proclamation was signed, Armstrong's position had grown more sympathetic toward the slaves; writing again to Hopkins in 1863, Armstrong exclaimed, "I hope that until every slave can call himself his own, and his wife and children his own, the sword will not cease from among us, and I care not how many evils that attend it; it will all be just."[26] In October 1863 Armstrong applied for a position as an officer of Negro troops, and it was in his experience as a major, then a colonel, and later a general of the Eighth Colored Regiment that Armstrong's belief in the potential for black moral improvement was fostered. In a letter to his mother he lauds his troop's deportment: "[M]y men fell fast, but never flinched—they fired coolly and won great praise."[27]

Armstrong's missionary and military experiences, along with his formal associations with the Freedmen's Bureau and the American Missionary Association (AMA), convinced Armstrong that it was through industrial education that he could best attend to the work of civilizing and training former slaves, who in turn would carry out the work of educating and civilizing other rural blacks.[28] Through his employment with the Freedmen's Bureau, it became obvious to Armstrong that the bureau offered only a temporary solution to a long-term problem. In fact, the growing sentiment in the post–Civil War era was that freed blacks now represented a political threat and a national problem. Francis Peabody, the Harvard professor who authored the apocryphal account of the Hampton Institute, *Education for Life*, stated that the freed slaves "had to be incorporated in the life of the nation, or remain a permanent menace both to its welfare and its self-respect." He maintained that the only way to ensure "national security was through a comprehensive scheme of education."[29]

While Armstrong did not deny that blacks were morally and intellectually deficient, lacking in the development of character associated with civilized society, he did believe that blacks possessed the potential for mental and moral advancement if properly trained and educated. Armstrong forcefully articulated his position in direct response to a series of well-known articles on "the African problem" published from 1884 through 1890 in *Atlantic Monthly* by noted Harvard geologist Nathan Shaler. In *Strange Ways and Sweet Dreams*, Donald Waters perceptively argues that Armstrong and Shaler both agreed that black Americans suffered from intellectual and moral deficiencies. Shaler, however, wed those deficiencies to the genetic makeup of black Americans. Armstrong, on the other hand, opposed Shaler's assertions that black Americans' intellectual and moral deficiencies were genetic and instead tied the supposed deficiencies to blacks' experiences in slavery. As Waters explains, Armstrong held that the conditions of slavery had created great moral deficiencies in the slaves by absolving African Americans of responsibility for their actions and behaviors. According to the Armstrong hypothesis, the slaves' lack of responsibility under slavery resulted in the loss of the faculties of moral reasoning and common sense. Therefore, Armstrong concluded that the Institute's primary function was to provide "proper training" to improve African Americans' moral condition.[30]

Armstrong formulated a definitive philosophy and program detailing the values he considered indispensable for improving African Americans' moral condition and the process through which these values were to be imparted. Armstrong's mission, as embodied in the Hampton idea, was threefold. Students were to acquire vocational training and an education, primarily industrial, which would provide them with the skills to earn a living in the predominantly agricultural and trade-based Southern economy. In Armstrong's model of education, industry was stressed, in terms not only of production but of productivity. The second part of the Hampton idea maintained that, through industrial training, students would learn the proper values of industriousness, honesty, and diligence; as such, Armstrong's program also functioned as a moralizing and civilizing force, teaching values and building character. Finally, the students, after receiving a Hampton education, were to return to their home communities and become teachers to those who remained behind. What happened in practice, however, is that the Hampton

Figure 2.1: "The Old Folks at Home." The Hampton Album. Photograph by Frances B. Johnston. Courtesy of the Hampton University Museum.

Figure 2.2: "A Hampton Graduate at Home." The Hampton Album. Photograph by Frances B. Johnston. Courtesy of the Hampton University Museum.

idea came to define the moral, educated, and civilized black student against the immoral, uneducated, and uncivilized black folk.[31]

Indeed, nothing more aptly illustrates the civilizing effect of a Hampton education than the images in *The Hampton Album*, a series of photographs created between 1899 and 1900 by the photographer Frances Johnston, a white woman born in Grafton, West Virginia.[32] This photo exhibit, commissioned by Hollis Frissell for display at the 1900 Paris Exposition, consisted of forty-four photographs representing the transformation from a folk to civilized people that Hampton students underwent as a result of their education and training. The photographic exhibit as whole suggests that, in little over a generation, Armstrong's Hampton idea had been successful at incorporating African Americans into the national fold, thus saving them from remaining, as Francis Peabody had put it, "a permanent menace."[33]

In the opening photograph, "The Old Folks at Home," an elderly black couple is shown in their rude surroundings with only functional kettles and earthenware lining the mantle and resting upon the cabinet. A shawl hangs from iron hooks in the corner and the walls are lined with peeling and frayed paper. The woman wears a checkered handkerchief on her head and dons a gingham apron. The couple eats at a bare table, their eyes averted from the gaze of the camera.

"A Hampton Graduate at Home" appears on the adjacent page. The placement of the two photographs is clearly intended to illustrate the dramatic difference between "The Old Folks" and "A Hampton Graduate." In contrast to the cheerless and rudimentary setting in "The Old Folks," "A Hampton Graduate" shows a middle-aged man and his wife with their three children sitting in a well-lit dining room around a covered table. The wall is decorated with a landscape painting and a few well-placed decorations sit on top of the piano—the quintessential symbol of Western high culture. Aside from the decorative, as opposed to functional, objects adorning the house, the two-story Hampton graduate's home also implies economic prosperity and class status.

The next two sets of photographs in the collection reiterate the distinction conveyed in the first pairing. One set shows "The Old-Time Cabin," which is, again, a crude structure—unpainted and unadorned—juxtaposed with "A Hampton Graduate's Home," which is a well-manicured, two-story white house with contrasting black shutters, intricate woodwork, and a covered porch. The next set shows "The Old Well," a rudimentary contraption created with trees, long branches, a rope, and buckets opposite "The Improved Well," a metal push-lever water pump sitting atop the covered waterhole. The photographs, along with their oppositional placement and respective captions, create a palpable dichotomy. The folk signify the old, outdated, primitive ways and are the antecedents to the educated students, who embody the modern, fashionable, civilized future.

The rest of the photographs in the series show Hampton students engaged in a variety of educational activities. Beginning with the youngest students, immaculately clad in petticoats, caps, and bonnets, the photographs show children saluting the flag, studying plant life, learning domestic skills, and receiving a "Thanksgiving Lesson," complete with model log cabin. In *American Archives*, Shawn Michelle Smith argues that these activities constitute rituals of American national identity, demonstrating the success of Hampton's social reforms by exhibiting "the American character of Hampton students."[34] In other words, the photographs depict the power of Hampton to both civilize its black students and bring them into the fold of modern American society as productive and industrious workers, their transformation evidenced by their distance from the unreformed rural black folk against whom their images are set.

Figure 2.3: "Stairway of Treasurer's Residence. Students at Work." The Hampton Album. Photograph by Frances B. Johnston. Courtesy of the Hampton University Museum.

Subsequent photographs represent older students situated in a variety of academic settings, affecting the most orderly, attentive, and studious postures. The photographic narrative leaves the viewer with an image of the students as contained, industrious, and well behaved. Having documented the students' transformation through white, Victorian middle-class norms, the successive images place the now-refined country folk in a variety of vocational settings. They have become dairy farmers, better masons and builders, and better domestics. Having received their Hampton education, they are now able to enter the Western economy as more refined, less vulgar workers. Armstrong's Hampton idea moved the former enslaved peoples from unskilled, rural country folk to well-mannered, well-disciplined, skilled laborers ready to take their place among the civilized in the new economic structure of the postwar South.

As this photographic narrative shows, the Hampton idea calcified the dichotomy between the folk and the educated, the immoral and the moral, the ignorant and the civilized. To move into the category of moral and civilized required not only education and training but also the relinquishing of old folkways for new civilized habits and customs. At both the ideological and practical levels, the embedded assumption was that the ways of the white Northern missionaries were synonymous with morality and civilization, and blacks were instructed to emulate the white Northern missionary models of behavior. The Hampton idea participated in solidifying the concept of the folk as ignorant, immoral, Southern, and rural while also reinforcing the Plantation Tradition image of the black folk as a relic of the past and an exclusively antebellum phenomenon.

For Armstrong nothing more clearly represented the intellectual and moral deficiencies created by the system of slavery than the foolish superstitions and old-fashioned beliefs preserved in black folklore. However, he maintained a hierarchical view of black folk traditions. The Negro spirituals and slave songs, for example, comprised the commendable form of black folklore, and the value of the Negro music caused Armstrong to pause in his usually aggressive scheme of educating and civilizing. In a letter to his wife, he pondered the melodic beauty, as well as the cultural and historical value, of Negro music: "Few people have any idea of the deep and essential music there is in these people . . . these songs are but the cry of their desolate hearts unto their God—once uttered in long agony of their oppression and now sung by their children as the songs of their home and nation."[35] The music, he explained to his wife, "makes the matter of civilization a puzzle. . . . Should we educate them out of all this that was needed to carry them through slavery?"[36] Armstrong's comments to his wife betray an often muted awareness that the process of "civilizing" the former slaves and free blacks was not without cost. In his letter, Armstrong acknowledges that educating blacks, according to his model, also meant distancing blacks from valuable aspects of a legacy that preserved the story of their struggles from slavery to freedom.

Perhaps as a way to continue his scheme of education while addressing the problem he wrote about to his wife, Armstrong created the Hampton Student Singers, a student group that performed refined versions of plantation songs at capacity concert halls around the country, and in the process, raised money for the construction of new buildings at the school.[37] As historical accounts of the Hampton Student Singers attest, to many white observers Negro spirituals or plantation songs represented a deep, even if uncultivated, religiosity. The songs testified to the slaves' capacity for moral uplift, and their melody, rhythm, and lyrics were often interpreted as evidence of the slaves' natural pathos and humility, expressing not coded cries of dissatisfaction or secret desires for escape—as later commentators would assert—but instead embodying deep acceptance of and sorrow over the harsh conditions of slavery.

For Armstrong, the Hampton Student Singers came to represent the best that could be achieved through the Hampton idea. As Hampton Institute teacher Helen Ludlow wrote in 1874, "[T]he peculiar strength of the Hampton Chorus is the faithful rendering of the original slave songs." Ludlow noted that the students became proficient in "cultivating their voices to a degree capable of executing difficult German songs with a precision of harmony." Ludlow further explained that choir director Thomas Fenner had "succeeded in preserving . . . that pathos and *wail* which those who have listened to the singing on the old plantations recognize as the 'real thing.'"[38] At least one consequence of the touring performance of the slave songs was that it taught, cultivated, and trained black Americans to perform the "real" traditions of African Americans, traditions which tied blacks to the antebellum South and traditions that many whites interpreted as evidence of blacks' sad but simple perspective on the hardship and suffering that characterized slavery and freedom. According to folklore scholar Regina Bendix, the assumed anonymity and authenticity of the spirituals allowed the white observers to sympathize in a general way with the suffering of the ex-slaves, while not attributing individuality or creativity to the black performers. Northern whites, Bendix asserts, "could confess to [black music's] emotional appeal and profess to their feelings of affinity" with the music of an anonymous collective that emerged out of an idealized past and expressed a transcendent spirituality.[39] Equally telling is Ludlow's response to what she identified as the often-asked question, "Has not a constant appearance for many months before the public injured their [the Hampton Student Singers] characters or changed their tastes?" To this question, Ludlow responded, "[T]hey have . . . behaved surprisingly well. School discipline has been kept up through all their wanderings; the greatest care has been taken of their manners and morals, and their health. . . . They all appear to be as loyal to right work as the students at Hampton."[40]

Thus, the rendering of the spirituals allowed Armstrong to preserve what he deemed to be the valuable legacy and authentic expression of black folk spirituality, while also allowing his school to profit from the performances. In turn, the performances highlighted the school's mission, illustrating that blacks possessed raw materials ripe for cultivating; within the strict parameters of the Hampton model, the Hampton Student Singers would not be derailed by lofty ideas or aspirations acquired during their travels but would remain humbly devoted to the school's mission of moral uplift. Ironically, many blacks in the post–Civil War era had begun to see the spirituals and slave songs as a "badge of slavery" and adamantly resisted performing them. According to Robert Engs, the Hampton students' dissatisfaction with performing the slave songs grew increasingly vocal after Armstrong's death in 1893 and culminated in a 1927 student strike in protest of having to perform the slave songs for white visitors.[41]

If plantation songs comprised the acceptable form of black folklore, Armstrong identified Negro religion, preachers, and, most of all, conjure practices as forms of wholly unacceptable black folklore, the brand of folklore that his teachers were to "spy out" and eliminate.[42] Armstrong explained that there was "plenty of religion" among both his students and their families, but that it was "too often a religion that regards more the emotional part of nature than the moral, and so aids little in the work of checking the evil tendencies of these growing lives."[43] He made it the work of the Hampton Institute to educate the folk ignorance out of the students. Armstrong exhorted:

> [I]f the height of ignorance and deadly superstition still rests upon the race . . . it should be the chief concern and effort of every more fortunate individual of the race not to hide the foul burden, but to lift it. . . . To them [the young teachers] we say again and again: You cannot be the friends your people need, unless you are brave enough to tell them their faults, and work, not for their thanks, but for their good.[44]

Once they had acquired the requisite traits, the black students were expected to venture forth in the missionary tradition, spreading the Hampton idea of civilization and proper behavior throughout the rural South. According to Engs, "Armstrong intended, quite literally, to educate the entire black race by creating those who would be its leaders and teachers."[45] Once the Hampton students received proper intellectual and moral training, they could then venture out into the rural communities to expose and eradicate the folk ignorance and superstitions that lingered among their uneducated students, friends, and family members.

Ironically, Armstrong's seek-and-destroy attitude toward most forms of black folklore laid the foundation for Hampton's earliest collections of black folklore. In 1878, as part of his project of exposing and eradicating folk ignorance, he began soliciting reports on black folklore from his students and recent graduates that he then published in *Southern Workman*. Two rather unexpected outcomes resulted from Armstrong's early folklore project. First, Armstrong's circulation of the "deadly folk superstitions" elicited protests from other educated black teachers, who resented what their Hampton education had taught them to see as their race's depravities being displayed to the general public. In a letter to the editor, Hampton teacher W. I. Lewis argues against publishing the folklore reports in *Southern Workman*, pleading: "I fail to see what is gained by your repeating this dark legend of a by-gone day. Experience teaches that unless we are reminded of excellencies, we will ourselves hardly become excellent. . . . you will find it best, in many instances, to omit the mentioning of such things."[46] Armstrong's editorial response negates Lewis's appeal that *Southern Workman* only focus on the achievements of the students and teachers—seemingly a very Hampton-esque position—stating that "no great wrong or folly of mankind has ever been got rid of without public exposure, yet none has ever been exposed without a pained outcry for concealment."[47]

Second, in attempting to "civilize" the young black students and teachers away from their folk traditions, Armstrong was continually baffled by the persistence of folk beliefs among his educated students. In a project intended to expose the absurdity of black folklore, many of his students expressed a continued belief in their folk practices. One student, in a submission on conjure doctors, concluded his paper by stating, "I believe in the conjure Drs. [*sic*] and all this that I have written I can vouch for myself." Armstrong replied, "[T]wo years more in the school will change his ideas."[48] Despite his confidence in the "civilizing" power of the school, Armstrong must have been especially miffed by the prevalence of conjure doctors among rural blacks and the persistence of the belief in conjuration among his students. Even Armstrong had to concede that many of the students maintained a belief in folk practices, such as conjuration, but were reluctant to share them with the public. In his commentary on the entrenched belief in folklore, Armstrong noted that "nothing is harder to eradicate from the mind than early-acquired superstition, and there is little doubt that many who are less frank in its acknowledgement are by no means free from it."[49] Armstrong's comments suggest that students suppressed their views toward black folklore out of fear of being deemed ignorant; therefore, even in letters where students provide first- and secondhand accounts of conjuration practices, many conclude with an obligatory disclaimer, formulaically identifying the folk practices as ignorant and then disavowing any personal belief in such practices. For example, one student shared a narrative account of a conjure woman providing a cure for another woman who had been sick "for a whole year" and unable to walk. After taking the cure, the woman got better and was soon able to walk again and "has been walking every day since." The student confirmed, "[T]his is the truth, what I saw with my own eyes." However, at the conclusion of the letter, the student adds, "You can judge from this how ignorant they are to believe in such things."[50]

This student letter illustrates the orientation toward black folklore that students had to display in order to participate in Armstrong's system of moral education. As Armstrong explained, "[A] natural hesitation—partly fear, and partly shame—was felt by many of our students, at the idea of thus revealing the superstitions of their people, until they were made to perceive the motive and importance" of such work.[51] In other words, the students were encouraged to reveal the folklore of their homes and communities so long as it was part of the necessary process of exposing and removing it from the black community. Membership in the civilized class demanded the renunciation of these cultural traditions, especially folk beliefs and practices associated with conjuration. In Armstrong's estimation, the conjure doctor, who, as Philip Bruce reported in 1899 was "invested with even more importance than a preacher," was the personification of all that was backward, immoral and uncivilized.[52] Armstrong attributed the belief in conjuration to what he identified as the Negro's "love of the supernatural and dense ignorance of the laws of living, a more excitable nature and nearly as loose a hold on life."[53]

More to the point, however, was that the conjure doctor stood as an affront to Armstrong's system of industrial education, which operated not for the sake of profit—at least not for the students' profit—but instead as a means of building moral character. In all but one of the student letters, the writers identified the conjure doctor as being one of the only people in the black community who was paid, quite handsomely and in cash, for his or her services. Additionally, each of the letters demonstrated the conjure doctor exercising a great deal of agency, offering the people either a cure for a physical ailment or a mixture to be used for influencing the behavior of another. For Armstrong, the power of the conjure doctor to secure private profits, to offer an alternative solution to the problems rural African Americans faced, and to defy the power of Christian religious beliefs, posed both a real and a symbolic challenge to the moral, industrial education he was trying to instill in his students and propagate among rural African Americans. Further, as Jeffrey Anderson argues, conjure practices in the second half of the nineteenth century were often used by whites as a way to mark African American difference.[54] Popularly identified as a relic of a savage African past that persisted among ignorant rural blacks, conjure practices became just one of the cultural markers that white Southerners could point to as evidence of their distance from and above their black neighbors. For Armstrong to demonstrate the efficacy of his particular brand of social reform, conjure practices needed to be expiring in the light of reason, Christian morality, and civilization. As Armstrong asserted, the belief in conjure threatened not only blacks' ability to cross over into civilization, but also the very existence of the Negro race. He explained that the student letters revealed "the work that must be done among them if they are to be raised to civilization or even saved from extinction."[55] The Hampton idea, as conceived and executed by Armstrong, was bound in the ideologies and rhetoric of civilization so pervasive in post-Reconstruction discourse. In tying the education of freedmen to a comprehensive program based on moral training and the attainment of civilization, Armstrong assumed the moral superiority of white, Western, Christian civilization while invalidating black culture and black values. Given the times and the circumstances, Armstrong's position was hardly unique. His aggressive mission to replace black culture with civilized mores and his proximity to the black community, however, made his position an especially influential one. By the time of his death in 1893, Armstrong had built his institute, consisting of over twenty buildings, employing 80 staff members and enrolling almost 700 students. By 1893, Hampton could boast that it had produced 797 teachers who had taught 129,475 children. With twenty-five years at the helm of the Hampton Institute and as the architect of the Hampton model of education, Armstrong left an indelible mark, not only on the institute and all those who attended its classes and taught at its schools, but also upon the construction of the folk as Southern, rural, black, uneducated, and immoral in opposition to the civilized who were, by contrast, Northern, white, educated, Christian, and moral. Additionally, Armstrong's view of black folklore supported a hierarchy that deemed Negro folk songs valuable, while damning conjuration as dangerous and immoral. In Armstrong's final estimation, black folklore was seen as an impediment to, and thus a necessary even if somewhat regrettable casualty in, the advancement of the race.

After Armstrong's passing, Hollis Frissell, Armstrong's successor, launched a national campaign to gain support for Hampton's plans for implementing regional systems of black industrial education throughout the South. According to James Anderson, in the years following Armstrong's death, and in spite of criticism that its model perpetuated a system of white dominance and black subordination, the Hampton Institute was determined to advance its industrial model of education by garnering the support of both Northern and Southern whites. As Hampton Board of Trustees member Robert Ogden stated, "The main hope is in Hampton and Hampton ideas. Our first problem is to support the School; our second to make the School ideas national."[56]

By the time of the changing of the guard from Armstrong to Frissell, antiblack racism—supported by social and cultural Darwinism and biological racialism, customary and legal segregation, and popular culture caricatures of blacks and black folklore—had reached a new low. Perhaps as a result of Armstrong's own eradication policy toward black folklore, by 1893 Hamptonians were beginning to bemoan what they perceived as the loss of black folk heritage through both the misrepresentations of black folk in popular culture and literature and willful forgetting on the part of educated blacks. Frissell, for example, lamented that the descendants of freed slaves tended to disavow the remnants and reminders of slavery and thus allowed "a priceless inheritance," borrowing the phrase Armstrong had coined, to slip away. Consistent with the position supported by his predecessor, Frissell felt that the loss of spirituals and plantation songs, which "reprised something of the best that was in them," was particularly regrettable.[57]

What prompted the resurgence of a folklore movement at Hampton in the years after Armstrong's death is uncertain. Perhaps Frissell felt that a folklore society would cultivate attention to what he may have presumed would be safe black culture, i.e., the socially acceptable plantation songs and spirituals. Based on the previous work on black folklore under Armstrong, Frissell had no reason to suspect that a group devoted to the collection of black folklore would be inconsistent with the Hampton idea. Additionally, scholarly attention to black folklore, from groups such as the American Folklore Society and the Chicago Folklore Society and notable figures such as Joel Chandler

Harris and George Washington Cable, may have validated folklore studies and created exigency for the formation of a Hampton folklore society. The only certainty, however, is that the Hampton Folklore Society was formed at the behest of one of its teachers, Alice Bacon. Thus, in 1893, folklore studies was reborn at the institute, this time in the form of the Hampton Folklore Society.

Alice Bacon's approach to black folklore departed in significant ways from that of her predecessor. While Armstrong sought to identify and exorcise the black folklore traditions that persisted among his students, Bacon envisioned the work of the new folklore society in terms of collection and preservation. She turned to the African American students and graduates of the Hampton Institute, not as foot soldiers in a war against pesky folk traditions but as partners in a project she believed was of deep cultural and historical import. Her ideas about the preeminence of white, Western civilization, too, were less fixed than those that had informed Armstrong's attention to folklore a decade and a half earlier. Thus, when she reconvened folklore studies at Hampton she sought support for the project from entities that extended beyond the walls of the institute. She looked most overtly to William Wells Newell and the American Folklore Society. Through Newell's emphasis on the "scientific" study of folklore materials, Bacon found an ally in her pursuit of what she identified as the "serious" study of black folk traditions.

To be sure, Bacon was not free of the ideology of reformist missionary uplift that informed the Hampton project, nor was she fully able to see black folk traditions beyond the hierarchies of developmental evolution that informed both Armstrong's and Newell's approach to folklore; however, she was able to construct an inclusive framework for the society, enabling the exchange of often competing methodologies and perspectives.[58] Indicative of this inclusive approach, in the December 1893 and January 1894 issues of *Southern Workman* Bacon reprinted letters of support she had received for the newly conceived folklore society. The letters came from "prominent men" in the fields of science and literature, including Newell and Shaler, as well as authors Thomas Wentworth Higginson and George Washington Cable. Sentiments ranged from general declarations of support ("Your plan is one which will receive all possible aid and support from our Society [AFS]"), to recommendations for specific lines of inquiry, to suggestions regarding what should be done with the collected materials.[59] Bacon acknowledged the "aid, approval and encouragement" offered in the letters, but noted, "[A]ll of these would have been of no use, if the plan had not already received the hearty approval of some of our own graduates. To them we went before laying the plan before any outsiders."[60] She further explained, "[W]e have besides consulting with resident and visiting graduates . . . written to some prominent colored people."[61] The African American supporters included Booker T. Washington, who gave his general endorsement of the project; Alexander Crummell, who suggested the folklorists look for African retentions in the "ancestral remembrances" and folk materials they were to collect; and Anna Julia Cooper, who saw the project as an opportunity to validate black folklore as a distinctive and generative aspect of African American literature and culture.[62]

Bacon's prefatory comments and the varied letters of support highlight the range of interests at play in the founding of the Hampton Folklore Society. They indicate the divergent, often competing ideas about the meanings of black folklore circulating in the late nineteenth century and locate the work of the Hampton folklorists within the concentric circles formed by nineteenth-century discourses on folklore, race, education, and civilization. Recovering the Hampton Folklore Society as an important site across which these discourses were negotiated allows us to recover multiple perspectives, including those of the often silenced and overlooked folklorists themselves, on the vexed relationship between folklore and race in the late nineteenth century.

Bacon's involvement with the Hampton Institute began at an early age. When she was twelve years old she was sent to Hampton to stay with her sister Rebecca Bacon, who was then serving as Armstrong's assistant principal. Her stay at Hampton was cut short, however, when Rebecca Bacon resigned in 1871 over a disagreement with Armstrong's fundraising strategy.[63] Alice Bacon returned to the Hampton Institute from 1883 to 1890, where she worked as a teacher, served as an editor for *Southern Woman*, and founded both the Hampton Folklore Society and the Dixie Colored Training School for Nurses. In 1888, she took a one-year hiatus from the institute to accept an invitation from her friend and former houseguest Countess Oyama to teach at the Peeresses' School in Japan.[64] Whereas Armstrong's ideas about the preeminence of Western civilization were fortified by his missionary work in Hawai'i, Bacon's notions about civilization were brought into question by her transnational experiences.

As Robert Rosenstone notes, Japan presented a paradox to nineteenth-century American visitors, emigrants, and explorers. Observing Japan's "complex, sophisticated urban life and a rich heritage," American interlopers, Rosenstone asserts, were often left questioning the measures by which one could judge civilization.[65] Bacon was no exception. After living in Japan, Bacon remarked, "[T]here is certainly a high type of civilization in Japan, though differing in many important particularities from our own."[66] While she could not escape the nineteenth-century U.S. obsession with measuring "foreign" cultures against white Western standards, her experiences in Japan led her to question ingrained ideas about the superiority of Western civilization. Informed by her observations of Japanese cultural and social traditions, Bacon reflected, ". . . [T]he word 'civilization' is so difficult to define and to understand, that I do not know what it means now as well as I did when I left home."[67] In writing about her time in Japan, Bacon recognized that her perceptions were inherently "much affected by [having passed] through the medium of an American mind,"[68] and she explained of her 1893 publication, *A Japanese Interior*, that even while she offered an extensive catalogue of Japanese customs and traditions, the book, comprised of letters she had written to her siblings while in Japan, was "more a picture of the life of one foreigner among the Japanese, and a record of her thoughts about their civilization and her own, than it is an authority on Japan in general, or on any particular phase of life there."[69] These comments, even if localized and left largely under-developed, indicate that Bacon was cognizant of her own subjective position in observing and interpreting Japanese culture. Recognizing that her viewpoint represented only one limited perspective, she attempted to expand the purview of her study through dialogue with her Japanese hosts, explaining that her description of Japanese life in *Japanese Girls and Women* was "largely the result of the interchange of thought through many and long conversations with Japanese ladies." She enlisted assistance from her friend and colleague at the Peeresses' School, Umé Tsuda, who, as Bacon notes, "carefully revised and criticized" the collection, offering "many valuable additions."[70] Bacon's notion of cultural understanding, facilitated through interaction and exchange, as well as her shifting ideas about civilization and her awareness of the ways in which one's observations were filtered through one's own cultural location, proved foundational in her construction of the Hampton Folklore Society.

Upon her return to the Hampton Institute, Bacon continued to question the imbedded assumptions latent in the prevailing ideas about civilization. Specifically, Bacon criticized Hampton's music department, lamenting what she referred to as the "process of civilizing into regular written forms" the traditional Negro songs:

> We hear again and again of someone who has recently come into the school with such beautiful new plantation songs, and then they are taken down by the music teacher, and the choir is drilled in the rendering of them, and

> the whole school in time follows the choir's interpretation of them, and in a short time that song, with time and tune and spirit altered, becomes a totally different thing.[71]

Bacon's critique of the "civilizing" of plantation songs into standard form contradicted Armstrong's Hampton idea by suggesting that the plantation songs, unaltered by the Hampton music directors, were valuable in their own right. Indeed, the civilizing of the unrefined folk songs was one of the most lucrative ventures in Armstrong's fundraising efforts, since the students' performances of plantation songs showed the still distinct, but now refined, African American students Hampton could produce. While founded at the Hampton Institute, the Hampton Folklore Society was not simply a reiteration of Armstrong's earlier attention to folklore.

Determining the story that Bacon sought to tell through the collection of black folklore in the years surrounding the *Plessy* decision, however, is not as straightforward a task as it might seem. While her experiences in Japan suggest that she began to question Western ideas about civilization, the prevalence of anti-black racism and the historical location of blacks in the United States made her application of those ideas to African Americans difficult. While she was able to recognize the beliefs of rural African Americans as a "reasoning philosophy," she still saw their epistemological system as "childlike" and underdeveloped.[72] She initiated the Hampton project to preserve and document the customs and traditions of rural blacks, customs, and traditions she felt were being "eradicated" in the face of common education, and yet she was deeply entrenched in the missionary industrial-education project she implicated in the destruction of black folk traditions.[73] She charged the Hampton folklorists with the task of "serious and reverent" collection of black folk traditions and insisted that the folklorists were to see in folk beliefs and customs "no occasion for scorn or contempt or laughter."[74] At the same time, she identified those who visited the conjure doctors as "dupes," and noted that the customs and beliefs of rural African Americans were "happily passing away."[75]

These multivalent objectives and orientations suggest that Bacon was propelled by contradictory motives. In adopting a "scientific" approach to folklore she was attempting to embrace a new methodology, but her work was still informed by the ideology of cultural evolution that defined early attitudes toward black folklore. Her commitment to the missionary model of industrial education espoused by the Hampton Institute meant that the closer her students came to embodying the ideals of white, middle-class, Victorian norms, the more successful was the work of the institute. The persistence of the folk customs and traditions of rural blacks was antithetical to such a project, and the tenets of cultural evolution allowed her to reconcile attention to folklore within the frame of the Hampton model.[76] But Bacon was also propelled by the desire to collect black folk traditions in a way that could illuminate their historical and current significance, and thus she supported studying those traditions in context and as one component in a complex cultural whole. She recognized the prejudices of her time as an impediment to the "serious" collection of black folklore, and was aware of the particular impact of those prejudices on the work of white folklorists like herself. She experimented with a rudimentary form of self-reflexive ethnography in her studies of Japanese culture, and while she could not extend those practices to her own research on black folklore, she enlisted the African American students at the institute to work as folklorists in an attempt to sidestep some of the challenges she saw as hindering cross-racial folklore studies. In conjunction with her efforts to find new methods for the collection of black folklore, she continued to invite and consider various approaches to black folklore studies throughout her tenure with the folklore society, welcoming varied, and at times opposing, input from the larger intellectual and academic community.

As Waters suggests, in a very general way Bacon found inspiration for the folklore society in the series of articles Shaler had published in *Atlantic Monthly* in which he called for the collection of additional data in assessing the condition of the "Negro." But Shaler was an adherent of racial determinism who held that blacks were biologically inferior to whites, who tied traits like intelligence to race, and who believed that racial mixing resulted in genetically inferior "half-breeds . . . more inclined to vice and much shorter-lived . . . than pure races."[77] And while Bacon credited Shaler for "originally suggesting the idea to us" in determining the focus and orientation of the folklore society, she was not wed to Shaler's ideology or to his suggestion that the group focus their investigations on tracing "pure" versus "mixed" bloodlines and identifying the concomitant racial traits.[78]

Instead, in finding validation for the academic pursuit of black folklore, the project at Hampton gained more sustained support from the American Folklore Society. In an 1893 letter, Newell assured Bacon that her plan would "receive all possible support from our Society"; the two societies did, in fact, enter into an ongoing relationship in which they attended each other's conferences and meetings, published in each other's journals, and openly exchanged collected materials. Both Bacon and Newell recognized that the complex racial politics that informed the fieldwork often hampered the efforts of white folklorists to collect materials from African American informants, and both saw the Hampton project as a way to address these shortcomings by enlisting African Americans in collecting materials from their own present or former communities. Because Newell conceived of black folklore as relics of the slave past, he saw it as slipping away with the older generations of formerly enslaved peoples and suggested that Hampton Folklore Society focus on collecting the "survivals" of this past before the materials associated with it were gone forever. Newell further suggested that the Hampton folklorists might then "desire to send the material collected up here [to the AFS] for examination and perhaps part of it could best appear in the *Journal of American Folk-lore*," and he hoped that the Hampton Folklore Society would eventually become the Virginia branch of the American Folklore Society.[79] While Waters asserts that this acquisition did in fact take place, letters and statements published by Bacon indicate that this arrangement may have never been formalized and that the Hampton Folklore Society maintained its operational autonomy from the American Folklore Society, as well as its own publication outlet. In the same issue of *Southern Workman* in which she published Newell's letter of endorsement, Bacon explained that the graduate residents at the Hampton Institute "have already formed a Folk-Lore Society among themselves," and she hoped that "other local societies will be formed in correspondence with the *Workman*." She allowed that "when the time comes, we hope to follow out Mr. Newell's suggestion and form them all into a Negro Branch of the American Folk-Lore Society," but left it to the reader to determine "[w]hether our plan works successfully or not . . . as they look in the Folk-Lore corner of *Workman* from month to month."[80]

In the months and years following the inauguration of the Hampton Folklore Society, readers would, in issue after issue of *Southern Workman*, encounter the Hampton Folklore Society's reports, findings and calls for submissions. Indeed, as late as 1898, Bacon published an overview of the works and methods of the Hampton Folklore Society in the *Journal of American Folklore*, in which she explained that the Hampton Folklore Society had its own constitution, president, vice-president, treasurer, and secretaries.[81] While the two societies were certainly interested and engaged in each other's work, the Hampton Folklore Society maintained its autonomy by generating its own organizational structure, by keeping its status as a society of the Hampton Institute, and by continuing to publish the vast majority of its materials in the monthly "Folk-lore and Ethnology" column of *Southern Workman*.

Further, while Bacon tended to emphasize the "customary" practices of black folklore as an area for study, Newell identified "oral" traditions as the defining feature of folklore studies. In an effort to distinguish folklore from literature, and the American Folklore Society from its early rival, the Chicago Folklore Society, Newell repeatedly defined folklore as unwritten oral tradition and oral lore. Oral tradition, Newell argued, characterized the various subcategories of folklore: "By folk-lore it is to be understood oral tradition," or information and belief transmitted from generation to generation "by word of mouth and without the intervention of writing."[82] According to folklore historian Rosemary Zumwalt, the American Folklore Society "developed a more restricted definition of folklore." Because folklore was considered a part of anthropology, and not literary studies, Newell and fellow AFS founding member Franz Boas reasoned that anthropology comprised the study of culture, broadly defined, and folklore represented the study of the *oral* aspects of culture. In contrast, the Chicago Folklore Society housed folklore studies within literary studies, considering literary studies to be concerned with written traditions, while folklore accounted for both verbal art *and* traditional life ways.[83]

Although directly associated with Newell and the American Folklore Society, Bacon's definition of folklore was more closely aligned with that of the Chicago Folklore Society as she repeatedly identified attention to customary folklore as well within the purview of the Hampton folklorists' work. According to Bacon, oral folklore could be most readily identified as the proverbs, rhymes, jokes, tales, and songs of a folk group; the text of these oral forms could easily be transcribed, indexed and compared (a prominent activity, in fact, of the AFS's first president, Francis James Child, who collected hundreds of variants of Scottish ballads through various written texts and submissions). Customary folklore, on the other hand, was more difficult to recognize and collect. According to Bacon, folk customs and habits had to be observed as they circulated among the folk and as they were passed from one group member to another. Bacon further suggested that all forms of folklore had to be observed and understood in their lived context, noting that folk songs, for example, had a "foreordained and appropriate setting in some part of the complicated negro religious ritual. . . . The music cannot be studied apart from the rest of the religious service with any hope of understanding either its origin or its present status."[84] Bacon further argued that given the racial climate in the late nineteenth century, even the most well-intentioned white fieldworkers would have trouble both gaining the trust of rural blacks and approaching black folk traditions in a way that was not predetermined by the racial stereotypes prevalent in contemporary popular culture.

While contemporary folklorists recognize the inseparable nature between oral and customary forms of folklore,[85] Bacon's attention to both customary folklore and the performance setting in which folklore was enacted served to refocus attention on the lived context of the folklore event and the ways in which a white folklorist might affect the performance and interpretation of African American folklore. Her assumption that the African American students at Hampton could seamlessly enter the fieldwork situation with Southern rural African Americans by virtue of their racial identification and perhaps familial affiliation overlooked the cultural and class differences that may have existed between the students and their former communities, differences created in part through their participation in the Hampton project. It also assumed that the African American folklorists at Hampton would be free from the influence of the degrading images of black folklore, an assumption that often proved false. Indeed, the Hampton folklorists had to negotiate often conflicting pressures resulting from their connection with the Hampton Institute, their participation in the Hampton Folklore Society, and their relationship to the larger African American community.

Despite Bacon's failings, her interest in creating Hampton as a center for the collection of black folklore produced a dynamic space where ideas about black folklore were generated, exchanged, and debated. Her emphasis on collecting customary folklore within a lived context constitutes an early attempt to move beyond a text-centered approach to folklore collection, and her recognition of the racial politics inherent in interracial fieldwork collection inspired her to privilege the position of African American collectors in the collection of African American folklore. In these ways, she moved folklore studies at Hampton beyond the restrictive and exacting approach of her predecessor, encouraging African Americans to assume a voice in a field traditionally dominated by white folklorists and collectors.

3 Recovering Folklore as a Site of Resistance

Anna Julia Cooper and the Hampton Folklore Society

In *The Hampton Project*, her provocative 2000 exhibition at Williams College, Carrie Mae Weems invited contemporary audiences to step into the spaces, intersections, and divides that characterized early African American and Native American educational projects, symbolized most prominently by the mid- to late-nineteenth-century work of the Hampton Institute. The installation-based exhibition consisted of "word photography," audio narratives and ceiling to floor panels of diaphanous cloth depicting digitally rendered images of Hampton students alongside various sites of contestation. Some of the photographs were "re-purposed" from Frances Johnston's *Hampton Album*; others were digital enlargements of salient images representing moments of contact between whites, Native Americans, and African Americans.

On one level, Weems's exhibit laments the cultural loss and psychological damage precipitated by the religious and educational projects that were driven by civilizing agendas. The exhibit's accompanying audio narrates this process: "Your progress now measured / by your successful distance / from your past . . . Educated away from yourself / you gave up Ogun, Ife, Yemoja, Obatala & Wankan alike."[1] At the same time, the exhibition suggests that one's cultural heritage and individual and collective identity can never be entirely made over into something else without echoes of that past continuing to survive, haunt, and challenge the present. Indeed, in *The Hampton Project* the folk past refuses to remain muted and invisible, but instead plays along the edges of the present, calling for remembrance and recognition. In Weems's recitation, "Hampton Alums" are still "survival's people," and—through enlarged and digitally reproduced images of the Hampton students and graduates flowing throughout the exhibit—the past continues to peer out from "behind history's veil." We are told that these students, "graduates of a stripped people," demanded more than "reserved land / peanuts & twenty acres." And yet, as they quested for more than they could get from their industrial education, our omniscient, first-person narrator explains that she still saw them lured by the promises of the institute as they smiled "at the sweet smell of success."[2]

Probing the interplay between past, present, and future, complicity and resistance, self-determination and self-effacement, Weems's *Hampton Project* resists reductive dichotomies and easy answers. Are the students' cultural traditions snatched away or relinquished? Did their participation in the Hampton project enable them to re-enter American society as productive and valuable members of the modern economy? Or did it sequester them to second-class citizenship and cultural dislocation, barring them from full participation in American political, social, and civic life and increasing the distance between them and their former communities by way of education and the adoption of Americanized manners and mores? By recovering the intricately multivalent histories that characterized early attempts to utilize industrial education as what some would consider one of the more humane responses to the "Negro problem," Weems invites us to examine this process anew, to see, and see through, the layers of the past that can both illuminate and obscure this history. I open this chapter with reference to Weems's powerful and controversial exhibition to suggest that, like Weems, we must reread the relationship between the Hampton folklorists, their home institution, and the wider black community. Such analysis leads to a better understanding of these early African American folklorists' contributions to the study of and artistic engagements with black folk traditions, both in the context of their own historical moment and in relation to subsequent ethnographic and creative engagements with black folklore.[3]

In this chapter, I examine several key moments in which the Hampton folklorists sought to define their project in terms that extended beyond the bounds of both the Hampton Folklore Society and the Hampton Institute. It is in recovering these moments that we see the Hampton folklorists attempting to imagine an epistemology of black folklore that was neither overdetermined by the representations in popular culture nor trapped within the notions of "progress" and assimilation espoused by their educational institution. The goal of this chapter is not to assert that the Hampton folklorists were entirely free from the ideologies espoused by their home institution; but it is to suggest that their approach to collecting and representing black folklore was not entirely defined by the Hampton idea, either. As Donald Waters has argued, the folklorists were able to generate alternative orientations toward black folklore through their associations with Bacon and Newell, who offered a "scientific" approach to the collection of folk materials. The folklorists, however, were also working in relation to the larger black intellectual community. Like Bacon and Newell, a number of African American scholars and activists, such as Anna Julia Cooper, Alexander Crummell, W. E. B. Du Bois, William Scarborough, Paul Laurence Dunbar, Charles Chesnutt, and Pauline Hopkins, all of whom were either directly or indirectly connected to the Hampton Folklore Society, were also experimenting with new understandings of folklore and culture while remaining deeply cognizant of the politics of racial representation in the years surrounding the *Plessy* decision. It is by locating the Hampton folklorists in relation to the larger interest in black folklore, expressed by both white and black academics and artists, that we are able to more fully appreciate their contributions to the study of folklore, race and culture at the end of the nineteenth century.

Founded at the Hampton Institute in 1893, the Hampton Folklore Society was comprised of approximately thirty members who attended the society's meetings and/or sent contributions to be included in the society's collection. Hampton graduates Fred Wheelock and Frank D. Banks, also institute treasurer, served as society president and vice president, respectively, and members included African American students and graduates, white teachers, and black and white institute staff members.[4] Some of the folklorists submitted materials collected from their students while teaching in rural schools throughout the South, while others shared information they remembered from their own experiences or had heard from family or community members. Many of the Hampton folklorists went on to take prominent positions within the African American community. Vascar Barnette, for example, accepted a position in 1902 as the circulation manager for the African American–run *Colored American Magazine*, edited at the time by Pauline Hopkins, while Robert Russa Moton succeeded Booker T. Washington as the second principal of the Tuskegee Institute.[5]

As Ronald Sharps has shown, the student and graduate members of the Hampton Folklore Society were generally a close-knit group. They worked together, went into business together, sent their children to Hampton, remained involved in the activities of the Hampton Institute, and "even tended to marry other Hampton graduates."[6] Because of their continued involvement with the institute, and because many of the students and former students spoke affectionately about the institute's founder, Sharps concludes, "[I]ndustrial education had fashioned the Hampton group *and* determined their approach to folklore."[7]

While it is true that the Hampton Institute exerted a powerful influence on those who attended the school and, as Waters asserts, most of the members of the Hampton community were in general agreement that African Americans possessed the capacity for educational advancement,[8] public documents and private letters suggest the students at Hampton were willing to expose and challenge some aspects of the racial politics latent in the institute's founding ideology. In 1885, for example, Barnette drafted a resolution objecting to the white faculty's appropriation of the black students' kitchen. In 1889 Barnette, joined by Wheelock and others, issued another protest against the Institute's segregated eating facilities.[9] Moton, who would appear to be an exemplary Hampton man—serving as institute disciplinarian and successor to Washington at Tuskegee—expressed his distance from the Hampton idea in his own retrospective writing, *What the Negro Thinks* (1930). In this text, he criticizes what he identifies as the white perspective that assumes to know both what African Americans think and how best to solve the "Negro" problem. A letter written by Du Bois further suggests that Moton, in his personal communications, had shared with Du Bois his critiques of his Hampton education. In one of his scathing reports on the shortcomings of the Hampton model, Du Bois condemns Hampton for the disservice it has done to men like Moton. In a letter responding to an inquiry from Paul Hanus of Harvard University about the work of the Hampton Institute, Du Bois writes: "Take, for instance Major Moton. He is an excellent man and a friend of mine. He has done and will do good work, but he is going to be forever handicapped by the fact that Hampton deliberately kept him from being a broadly educated man. He is handicapped by his training and he feels it."[10]

In addition to critiques put forth by Barnette, Wheelock, and Moton, Hampton folklorist Portia Smiley, who attended Hampton but earned her degree from Pratt Institute in Brooklyn, New York, and worked and taught in numerous schools and settlements before gaining notoriety in the 1920s in Boston as a culinary expert, similarly expressed her disenchantment with the institute in letters written over a number of years. In 1912 she rebuffs Hollis Frissell for his slow-coming recognition of her achievements, writing, "[F]or years you would not accept my loyalty." In 1918 she declined Hampton's accolades, writing to an acquaintance, "Miss Hyde's niece said that Hampton was proud of me, but it is Pratt Institute who is." Again in 1922, she hints at her lingering disregard for Hampton over the ambiguous terms of her dismissal, noting in a personal letter, "[T]hey think I am a Hampton graduate from what they show in their papers. Now what do you think about that matter? Nevertheless, I shall help them in their prospect."[11] In her letters Smiley exposes and resists the storied Hampton tradition of claiming, documenting, and publicizing the accomplishments of its graduates as evidence of Hampton's success. Instead, she critiques this process, even as she eventually relents and allows Hampton to lay claim to her success as part of their reformist agenda.

Although it is true that most of the students and graduates embraced the opportunities offered by the Hampton Institute, they were still aware of the sometimes overt, sometimes muted racial politics that pervaded the institute's policies and practices. While the student members of the Hampton Folklore Society generally remained involved in the activities of the Hampton Institute long after they graduated or moved on from Hampton, they did not accept wholesale the ideas or practices of the institute and were willing to challenge its founder and his successor when they felt the institute violated their rights.

Working within but also beyond the bounds of the institute, the members of the Hampton Folklore Society, over the course of the society's more than six-year existence, introduced the public to a range of theoretical and ideological orientations toward black folklore while also presenting an extensive and varied collection of black folk materials. The compilation of materials collected by Hampton folklorists and published most extensively in *Southern Workman*, represents a broad swath of folklore. It includes "acceptable" forms of folklore, such as spirituals, religious lore, and animal tales, but draws heavily on less reputable forms, including numerous submissions of superstitions, signs, and conjuration. There are several examples of various genres of oral folklore, such as rhymes, riddles, animal tales, folk tales, warning tales, and songs. Also included are descriptions of customary practices, such as courtship rituals, conjuration, rites of passage, religious ceremonies, games, foot-washing ceremonies, and ring-plays, as well as lists of material artifacts containing special spiritual or magical qualities. Some entries provide lists of folkloric items with no contextualizing comments, such as the lists of superstitions and riddles submitted by J. W. Bendenbaugh from Bradley, South Carolina.[12] Other items are framed with elaborate context ranging from personal narratives to commentary on performance situations and transmission to evaluative remarks.

In one of the most distinctive submissions in the collection, a woman named Mrs. Cabot shares letters she has secured from her mother, Chloe Cabot Thomas. In the letters, Mrs. Thomas, who states that her mother's first cousin was Phillis Wheatley, shares a detailed family history: her grandparents' capture in Madagascar, the cleaving apart of her family as they were forced onto slave ships, and their eventual reunion in Salem, Massachusetts.

Responding to "further questioning" from Bacon, Mrs. Cabot secures from her mother another letter elaborating on "physical peculiarities and customs" of the Madagascar peoples, and further explains the circumstances of Wheatley's separation from and reunion with her mother. Mrs. Thomas's letter then relates how her defiant mother greeted freedom when Massachusetts banned slavery in 1780: "The madam told Chloe that if she was going to be insolent that she would send her home back to Salem. Miss Chloe told her that she would not go because 'I am free, Daddy and Mammy Smith told me so' . . . [she] left them and went to live with another lady who paid her for her work until she got married. This my mother told me."[13] Mrs. Cabot goes on to share how she and her brother had to devise strategies to protect her husband, who had escaped from North Carolina to Vermont. The letters preserve and pass on what was shared orally by Mrs. Thomas's mother by merging oral and written accounts.

In these letters, Mrs. Cabot and her mother utilize personal narrative to relate their family history. They then situate the Cabot-Thomas family history within a transatlantic history marked by the capture of African peoples, the resultant ruptures to families and communities, and subsequent enslavement in the North. In the face of these horrific forces, however, tales of freedom, defiance and self-determination propel their family history. While this set of submissions is unique in both content—its attention to slavery in the North, for instance—and form—the use of personal narrative and family history, as well as the combination of oral and written narratives—it attests to the diversity represented by the collection.

While it is beyond the scope of this present study to provide more than a cursory overview of the society's extensive collection, works that do offer detailed analyses of the society's materials are Waters's *Strange Ways and Sweet Dreams* and Sharps's *Happy Days and Sorrow Songs*. Interestingly, Waters and Sharps read the same materials in markedly different ways. Waters argues that before Southern blacks could put their norms into practice, "they, like all people, had to discuss and evaluate them with respect to particular situations."[14] Referencing various parts of the collection, Waters illustrates how Southern blacks used folklore to present norms of behavior, to evaluate those norms in given situations, and then to persuade members of the community to follow those norms. After the establishing of community norms and values, Waters asserts, signs, superstitions, and conjuration enforced the behavioral norms. Waters's analysis of the Hampton folklore collection challenges the premise of Armstrong's Hampton idea—which linked the "folk" with immorality/amorality and the "educated" with morality—by showing that the folk communities in which these materials circulated had established their own ethical systems for evaluating, instilling, and perpetuating values, norms, and beliefs.

In contrast, Sharps argues that the materials in the collection can be read as direct support for the tenets embedded in the Hampton idea. In his analysis, the emphasis on work ethics and morality presented in the collection was an expression of the Hampton principles of entrepreneurship, labor, and economic development. He argues that work songs are included in the collection because they support the Hampton idea of industrial education, and that the courtship rituals documented by the society embody Victorian middle-class norms of decorum and chivalry. While some members' desires to present black folklore in a positive light may have led them to collect materials that could be read as support for the Hampton idea, I would argue that the materials in the collection as a whole exceed its bounds. For example, Sharps acknowledges that according to the Hampton idea, superstition was "the great stumbling block" to African American development, and therefore Sharps's analysis necessarily leaves unaccounted the pervasive presence of superstitions, signs, and folk beliefs.[15]

Sharps's and Waters's varied interpretations of the Hampton collection stem not only from the ideological ends to which scholars have employed the various materials, but also from the diversity represented in the range of materials presented. Different parts of the Hampton collection tell different stories. For example, conjure practices are variously represented as evil hoaxes perpetrated by practitioners who derived their powers from the devil and as beneficial acts carried out by doctors who had been divinely ordained. Taken as a whole, the Hampton folklore collection documents an elaborate system of values and folk knowledge representing a cross-section of rural black communities throughout the South. Some materials can be read as reinforcing the values latent in the Hampton idea, as Sharps contends, while other materials blatantly contradict those values.[16] At the most fundamental level, what the collection reveals is a collage of communities that did have an elaborate system of values, morals, ethics, traditions, and beliefs that were communicated and negotiated through their various forms of folklore.

In addition to providing a rich assemblage of cultural materials, the collection serves as a palimpsest, documenting the racialized politics of folklore collection and representation. In particular, the "moments of contestation," to borrow Weems's phrase, between the folklorists and members of the larger scientific and intellectual community suggest the complex negotiations the folklorists undertook to participate in a folklore project endorsed by the white scientific establishment while still working to advance their own divergent cultural and political agendas.

One especially laden account, described by Lee Baker in *Anthropology and the Racial Politics of Culture* and documented in the 1895 issue of *Southern Workman*, narrates the participation of four Hampton Folklore Society members at the annual American Folklore Society meeting in Washington, D.C. In the report, Bacon explains that Frank Banks, Robert Moton, William Daggs, and J. H. Wainwright "delivered a paper on Negro Folk-Songs made up of material contributed by the club, and compiled by one of its secretaries."[17] Moton read the paper while intermittently rejoining his fellow folklorists to perform the songs referenced in his discussion. In his presentation, Moton confronts two popular constructions of black folklore. First, he contests the popularly held belief that black folklore and related African American cultural and intellectual productions are essentially imitative; second, he confronts the notion that black folklore, as performed in the minstrel and plantation traditions, is representative of black difference and inferiority. Simultaneously, he legitimizes his authority to intervene in both the popular discourse around black folklore and the dialogue perpetuated by the white folklore studies establishment, with whom he and the other Hampton folklorists were not necessarily in agreement.

Moton begins his talk by identifying Negro folk songs as "our subject," noting that it has "widened out before us." He likens his discussion to a metaphorical journey to the land where folk songs reside, what he refers to as the "land we are bound for."[18] By using first-person plural pronouns, Moton not only becomes a synecdoche for the Hampton Folklore Society as a whole, but also positions himself rhetorically as speaking both to and with his AFS audience, creating a sense of shared identity as academic folklorists and establishing his authority as guide and purveyor on the subject. Moton's informed and technical discussion of folk songs shifts his position from that of folk performer to trained researcher and expert. He then sidesteps the question of "origins," while claiming for African Americans a distinct and original cultural contribution, noting that "whenever or wherever that music may have originated, it is to-day a part of the life and heart of colored people of the South, a true body of folk-songs, the outgrowth of the conditions that surrounded in the past, an oppressed and humble, but highly emotional race." Moton then makes a distinction between "'real' Negro music" and both the "imitation[s] created by white 'nigger' minstrels . . . composed with the view of making the religious experiences of the Negro a joke for white audiences" and the picturesque plantation songs, such as "Swanee River" and "Old Black Joe," created by white men.[19]

In an ironic reversal of the dominant construction of African Americans as "imitative," Moton suggests that blacks adapted, integrated, and created distinct cultural traditions in response to their lived conditions, while it was whites, in fact, who were crude imitators of black cultural traditions. While his reversal does not necessarily recognize the subtle dynamics of cultural exchange, Moton strategically deploys this kind of essentialism to challenge dominant ideologies that dismissed African American cultural contributions as unoriginal, imitative, and, hence, invalid or nonexistent. On the contrary, Moton explains that there are three distinct types of "Negro folk-songs": "Corn-Songs" or work songs, "Dance-Songs," and "shouts or Spirituals." In presenting "corn songs" to the attendees of the American Folklore Society meeting, Moton contextualizes the performance of the songs by explaining that "they were used largely to expedite the labor at the great annual corn shuckings. . . . the rhythm sets the time of the work on which all are engaged, and the beating of feet, the swaying of the body or the movement of the arms may be retarded or accelerated at will by the leader." In recognizing and documenting the customary behaviors that accompanied the music and lyrics, Moton is able to theorize that the songs functioned as part of the "plantation discipline and may be said to have had an economic value in carrying on the productive labor of the South."[20]

Moton would not, however, be confined to presenting materials that, as Sharps suggests, supported the Hampton idea by promoting productive labor and discipline. Directly following his presentation of the "Corn Shucking Song," the quartet renders "Run, Nigger, Run, de Patteroler'll Ketch Yer." Unlike the former song, the ethos of the latter is clearly one of protest and bearing witness to the hardships the slaves faced at the hands of duplicitous white slave owners and "patterolers." The song relates a slave's experiences with a "patteroler" who "hit yer thirty-nine and sware 'e didn't tech yer" and a "mistis" and "master" who promise they will set the slave free upon their deaths, but neglect to do so, instead leaving "dis nigger er shellin corn."[21] The slave decides to run away after bearing these abuses and the refrain of the song, "run, nigger, run," repeated at the end of each stanza, serves as an eerie threat propelling his flight.

Moton also presented the dance song "Juba," which, instead of functioning to maintain the efficiency of the plantation economy, facilitated African American entertainment and leisure. Although he found this particular dance song not as advanced as some others—stating that it had the effect of "heathen festival" in an "African forest," thereby reinforcing a racial-cultural hierarchy—he shared it, along with his assessment, as an example of the songs used to "set the time of the dances, plays, or marches in which plantation Negroes indulged when work hours were over." He concluded his discussion and the group's presentation with the rendering of several plantation spirituals and his final summation that "[n]o truer folk-music can be found in this or any other country, than the religious songs of the black peasantry of the South."[22]

Despite Bacon's claim that the Hampton Folklore Society did not include "a single scientific folk-lorist," Moton showed that he could go beyond simply providing materials for other "trained," white folklorists to interpret and analyze.[23] As Waters has argued, many of the Hampton folklorists saw the chance to participate in what Bacon defined as the "serious" and "scientific" study of black folklore as an opportunity to pursue another, ulterior motive: to save black folklore from the ridicule they saw it subjected to in various forms of popular entertainment. In his 1921 autobiography, *Finding a Way Out*, Moton writes that, upon arriving at Hampton, he was disturbed to hear students singing Negro spirituals. "They were negro songs," he explains, "and we had come to Hampton to learn something better . . . and then too, I objected to exhibiting the religious and emotional side of our people to white folks."[24]

Waters argues that Moton, aware of the ways in which minstrel caricatures could support demeaning stereotypes of black people by presenting black folk traditions to white audiences as humor and entertainment, became committed to preserving black folklore from public ridicule. Moton did this by conducting critical investigations of the social value of black folk music and presenting black folk traditions in relation to their historical and lived context. By distinguishing between "imitations" and "true" Negro folk music, and by focusing attention on the varied contexts in which the songs were performed, Moton was able to theorize about the significance of black folk songs while simultaneously enacting his larger cultural agenda, which was to collect and present black folklore as a way to critique black representations in popular entertainment.[25]

While Moton assumed the role of academic folklorist and studied expert on Negro folk songs as a way to move beyond folk performer at the AFS meeting, he established his authority by way of his training *and* his shared racial affiliation with his informants, positioning himself as a kind of cultural insider. Moton participated in a system predicated on locating the "authentic" folk material by adopting the objectifying gaze of the omniscient researcher, and by offering to pull back the veil to reveal "true" African American folklore to a group of cultural outsiders. In this interaction, he "plays tour guide," facilitating what Rosemary Hathaway refers to as a "touristic reading," or "the fallacious practice whereby a reader [or in this case, an audience] assumes, when presented with a text where the writer and the group represented in the text are ethnically different from herself, that the text is necessarily an accurate, authentic, and authorized representation of that 'Other' cultural group."[26] The touristic approach leaves intact preexisting notions of authenticity, creating the perception that the representation is, oxymoronically, even more authentic because it has been "authorized" by someone sharing a racial or cultural identification with the group being depicted. While Moton's donning of the folklorist's attire allows him to contest popular constructions of black folklore, his counterstrategy, in this instance, does not necessarily expose or challenge the deep structures linking "authenticity," race, and folklore.

Indeed, while Moton's performance was received enthusiastically by his AFS audience, which included Boas, Newell, and Frank Cushing, the academic legitimacy of the Hampton folklorists was continually in question. According to Lee Baker, following Moton's presentation Newell and Thomas Wilson requested "an encore performance" by the quartet so they could capture one of the negro folk songs on a phonographic cylinder. Bacon was so impressed by the "considerable exactness" of the phonographic reproduction that she began a persistent, though ultimately unfulfilled, quest to secure a graphophone to capture later performances by the folklorists.[27]

As Daphne Lamothe asserts, Bacon, Newell, and the other AFS members "believed they were witnessing a moment of cultural authenticity as opposed to a demonstration that might approximate the music in its indigenous setting."[28] Unable to secure the graphophone to record folkloric materials for the 1898 AFS meeting in New York City, Bacon offered up Daniel Webster Davis as the "real thing," noting in a letter to Newell that Webster is a "full-blooded Negro" whose renditions of the songs are "rather better than a phonographic reprint as he gives it."[29] Moton's and the other Hampton folklorists' negotiation of the roles of folk performer, native informant, and trained folklorist attest to the difficulty of escaping the conflicted position in which many African American folklorists and ethnographers found themselves. To assume the role of legitimate folklorists within the established power structure constituted a form of empowerment and resistance, but this counterstrategy left intact the subject/object binary that posits the ultimate knowability of the object of scientific inquiry. Although Moton may not have been able to go far enough in exposing the politics of cultural representation, he was able to unsettle the prevailing binary in which African Americans were considered as always the folk but rarely the folklorists.[30]

Additionally, outside of his prominent role at the American Folklore Society annual meeting, Moton collected and contributed materials highlighting the racialized power relations endemic in the politics of authenticity that defined "scientific" approaches to black folklore. In a Hampton Folklore Society public meeting attended by William Scarborough, Moton shared a Master and John tale to illustrate the adage "to talk at the big gate," which Moton translated as "to brag behind one's back." In Moton's version of this fairly popular tale, John receives a Christmas gift of five dollars from his "Master." When the other slaves inquire how John received this monetary gift, he explains that he "cursed the Master . . . 'cursed him all to pieces.'" Incredulous, but hopeful, three of John's compatriots head off to the big house and begin cursing the Master to his face. After receiving a "handsome flogging," they return to John to find out why his stratagem failed them, to which questioning he replies, "'Yes I did curse him, but I cursed him at the big gate.'"[31]

As Susan Meisenhelder explains, the John tales "depict the slave's strategies for dealing with apparent powerlessness. Many of them demonstrate graphically the impossibility of open defiance and the need for indirection in battling oppressive whites."[32] In this tale, John receives the five dollars from the Master, but still expresses his discontent, thus denoting the gift's inability to either assuage John's grievances or compensate for his labor. Given the unequal power relations, however, John is unable to "curse" the Master directly, although his telling of the tale acts as a form of wish fulfillment. Instead, John secures what he can in the given situation, while keeping his true feelings concealed from the Master. Beyond documenting dissimulation as a traditional African American survival strategy, the tale serves the pedagogical function of teaching other slaves the meaning of the concept "to talk at the big gate," while also emphasizing the importance of deciphering John's coded language. The failure to read and interpret John's tale within the existing power dynamics results in severe censure for the uninitiated. In contributing this tale, Moton demonstrates his willingness to document materials that fall outside the bounds of what would be considered "acceptable" folklore, recovering and recreating a tale of subversion and dissimulation that illuminates how African Americans might gain from a socio-economic system while still protesting its injustices. This tale is also significant because it utilizes oral storytelling to pass on the oppositional values and knowledge of this particular African American community.

In *What the Negro Thinks* (1930), Moton revisits this process of dissimulation and subversion, explaining that African Americans often created a smokescreen around their practices and beliefs as a way of defending against unwanted attention from whites. For this reason, Moton argued, the white American cannot know the Negro, although he often professes that he does. Moton further explained that this assumption, epitomized in the phrase "I know the Negro," "has been commonly employed to support the opinions and sustain . . . the existing customs and practices which give to the Negro a different status in social and civic life from that occupied by his white neighbors." Quite to the contrary, Moton asserted that "there are vast reaches of Negro life and thought of which white people know nothing whatever, even after long contact with them, and sometimes on the most intimate terms."[33]

In addition to contributing subversive John tales, Moton also served as the informant for at least eleven Irishmen tales recorded by Alice Bacon in 1899. Although the first installment of the Irishmen tales published in the May 1899 issue of *Southern Workman* is unsigned, and the Irishmen tales attributed directly to Moton were not published until 1922 in a *JAF* article by Elsie Clews Parson, it is possible that at least some of the tales published in *Southern Workman* in 1899 can be attributed to Moton, who was at the time actively engaged in sharing the tales for Bacon to record. The Irishmen tales collected by the Hampton folklorists play on stereotypical representations of the Irish and generally turn on Irishmen's supposed ignorance of the Southern environment, thus allowing African American tellers and audiences to tout their superiority over the benighted interlopers. The tales provide the rare opportunity for African Americans, who were so frequently identified both as possessing "folklore" and as being the objects of popular folk tales, to turn their storytelling prowess and folkloric lens on another group. To make the Irishmen the subjects of their folklore meant that African Americans were assuming authority over the cultural representations of white men, creating a context in which African Americans could comment on the foibles and follies of whites. Not surprising, the society's publication of the Irishmen tales elicited the criticism of *Southern Workman* readers, who apparently objected to the tales' translations of "certain oaths" related in the Irishmen tales. Bacon offered a conditional apology of sorts, stating, "In response to criticisms received . . . we would say that we are sorry that our desire to reproduce exactly for scientific purposes the stories as they are told in the South should have shocked the sensibilities of our reader."[34] She assumed the cloak of scientific objectivity in defending the society's imperative to publish folkloric materials whether or not they were aesthetically or socially acceptable to the audience, and then published two more Irishmen stories in the June 1899 "Folklore and Ethnology" column.

As Moton's situation illustrates, working within the context defined by the larger white scientific and intellectual community gave the Hampton folklorists access to a certain privileged position within the existing power structures. But even as they strove to be recognized as full and legitimate participants in the scientific endeavor, their racial identification with the subjects under study put them in a precarious position. Their work attests to what, for many, was the larger political agenda of redeeming black folklore by creating positive evaluations and representations. Some of the submitted materials document further counter-strategies by celebrating dissimulation as a form of resistance and by shifting the folkloric lens to consider stories and tales about white subjects. As much as their project anticipates 1920s engagements with black folklore, as Baker and Lamothe rightly assert, the work of the Hampton folklorists must also be understood in relation to the resistant engagements with black folklore undertaken by African American activists and intellectuals in the late nineteenth and early twentieth centuries.

At the end of the nineteenth century, black intellectuals were growing increasingly interested not only in the collection of black folklore by black folklorists, but also in the increasing political and cultural significance of black folklore representations. During this time African American intellectuals created what Henry Louis Gates refers to as the "culturally willed myth" of the "New Negro."[35] The New Negro was refined, educated, pious, cultured, clean, well-spoken, moneyed, and above all, "new." This fantasy of the fully modern black subject "was clearly intended to 'turn' the new century's image of the black away from the stereotypes scattered throughout plantation fiction, blackface minstrelsy, vaudeville, racist pseudo-science, and vulgar Social Darwinism." This new "'class of colored people,'" Gates explains, was defined in "marked contrast with their enslaved or disenfranchised ancestors." The "paradox of this self-willed beginning," as Gates identifies it, "is that its 'success' depends fundamentally upon self-negation, a turning away from the 'Old Negro' and the labyrinthine memory of black enslavement."[36] This disconnection, in turn, created a black subject dislocated from history, time, and place, yet left intact the plantation myths that reduced the masses of African Americans to mammies, sambos, jezebels, uncles, and savages.

The work of the Hampton Folklore Society, while part of the project of documenting the distance the New Negro had covered in becoming fully "civilized" and "American," also presented African Americans with the opportunity to reengage with a past that they might have come to interpret primarily through the plantation and minstrel stereotypes—the paradox Moton identified in his autobiography, for example. Indeed, from its inception in 1893 until its disbanding in 1900, many of the country's most prominent African American intellectuals established either formal or informal relations with the Hampton Folklore Society. Some of the most sustained involvement in the society's activities came from members of the American Negro Academy (ANA), founded by Alexander Crummell, named by Paul Laurence Dunbar, and counting among its members William Scarborough, J. L. Love, W. E. B. Du Bois, and Kelly Miller.

In general, the members of the ANA believed that through the acquisition of the white Western standards of Christian piety and classical learning, they had progressed to the level of civilization. Having realized the heights of civilization themselves, they were charged with a double mission to counter racist perceptions and practices and promote civilization among the masses of uncivilized blacks in the United States and Africa. The ANA's position to uplift the masses, as measured through the barometer of civilization, bears similarities to Armstrong's position on uplifting the masses through the cultivation of character. The ANA, however, stressed the attainment of science, arts, and literature as central to the uplifting of the race and argued against the absorption of blacks into white American civilization. Black folklore, particularly as located in or traced back to Africa, documented the progression of black civilization from barbarism to high culture, a progression paralleling the trajectory of white Western civilization. For members of the ANA, however, black folklore was more than just a marker of progress; it also served to maintain a modicum of cultural distinctiveness that legitimized Africa as a source of cultural integrity, and to establish a spiritual and cultural link to Africa.[37]

Alexander Crummell, in particular, viewed black folklore through both a civilizing paradigm characterized by an 1890s New Negro ethos and a black nationalist framework that saw black folklore as showcasing black cultural distinctiveness. In "Civilization, the Primal Need of the Race," an 1898 address to the ANA, Crummell argued that the Negro race needed to be uplifted through the cultivation of civilization among the masses by the educated and cultured men of the race. Crummell stressed the attainment of culture, arts, and literature as central to the uplifting of the race, but argued against the loss of black cultural distinctiveness as requisite for the full exercise of rights and privileges associated with dominant white male society. He declared that black people had a distinct contribution to make to civilization and humanity and that racial identity needed to be maintained. He further argued that it was incumbent upon cultured and educated black men to promote race pride and dignity.[38]

In an 1893 letter to Bacon expressing his support for the creation of the Hampton Folklore Society, Crummell explained that he had long sought to secure interest in and support for an "African Society" devoted to "the preservation of traditions, folk-lore, ancestral remembrances, etc." In his formulation, black folklore, issued forth from the ancestral source of Africa, provided black Americans with a lineage, culture, and tradition through which to locate black civilization. He expressed his hope that the Hampton folklore project would remind students of the "family ties" that connected them, not to the Anglo-Saxon but to their "kin over the water."[39] In his 1896 Hampton Institute Founder's Day address, Crummell took his message of race pride and identification directly to the Hampton students, imploring the students: "Don't forget that a *race* is a family. . . . Do not suffer any advantages, in the present or the future, to lead to forgetfulness of race feeling and race devotedness!"[40] For Crummell, this racial affinity should then inspire leading African Americans to go to work among their less fortunate brethren both in the United States and Africa to promote arts, culture, and Christianity.

In addition to Crummell, both Scarborough and John L. Love regularly addressed the Hampton folklorists, participated in their conferences, and contributed materials to their folklore collection. Love not only was active as a corresponding member of the Hampton Folklore Society, but he also established the Asheville Folk-lore Society in North Carolina. Scarborough, the third member of African descent of the American Philological Society and the first African American member of the Modern Language Association,[41] as well as a Wilberforce Professor of Classics, contributed folkloric materials to the Hampton collection and gave an address at the annual meeting of the Hampton Folklore Society in 1896. In this talk, Scarborough suggested that folklore consists of survivals or remnants of earlier stages of development, which are thrown off in the light of science, religion, and civilization or classical learning. He noted that folklore is "something to take pride in" and asserted that it reveals the "evolution of a race" from primitive to civilized. In discussing customs and superstitions, he noted the Negro of "to-day" had largely thrown off these "old observances," and that the student of folklore must look to Haiti, Africa, Bermuda, and among the Creole population in Louisiana, as well as the "isolated spots" in the United States to find examples of such outdated beliefs and practices. He offered an interpretation of Negro morphology and pronunciation as variants of standard English, noting the most "wonderful" aspects of Negro dialect are the "figures of speech," "hyperbole," "rhymes," and "picture words" molded by the "Old Negro" in response to his natural setting and environment. However, he asserted, these forms of speech and folklore were not to be found "among the Negro speech of today."[42]

In 1899 Scarborough published "The Negro in Fiction as Portrayer and Portrayed" in *Southern Workman*. The essay reiterates the ANA's position that black folk tradition, and the literature that incorporated such traditions, should advance its goals of creating and demonstrating the evolution of a distinctive African American civilization. Scarborough cited Albion Tourgee in arguing for works that could overcome the difficulty of "finding [oneself] always confronted with the past of his race and the woes of his kindred."[43] In working toward this goal, Scarborough and Crummell contributed and encouraged the Hampton folklorists to collect materials documenting African folklore and establishing a proud lineage for black Americans to claim their own evolutionary progress on a par with but distinct from that of white Americans of Anglo-Saxon descent.

In general, Anna Julia Cooper was in agreement with the ANA philosophy that African Americans had a distinct contribution to make to American society and culture. She was deeply suspicious, however, of the politics of race, class, and gender embedded in discourses of civilization, and she questioned what she saw as an uncritical acceptance on the part of some of her African American male contemporaries of the dominant values and standards by which "progress" and "success" were measured. In "Womanhood: A Vital Element in the Regeneration and Progress of the Race," first delivered in 1884 as an address to the black male clergy of the Protestant Episcopal Church, for example, she critiqued what she identified as the self-serving gestures of the "New Negroes" who evaluated success in terms of one's distance from the presumably unrefined masses. She noted that they were the ones who "exhaust their genius splitting hairs on aristocratic distinctions and thanking God they are not as others" and who demonstrated the heights to which they had risen by quoting "statistics showing the Negro's bank account and rent rolls."[44] For Cooper, it was not a matter of how to eke out success within the existing power structure, but rather how to expose the underlying assumptions and practices that maintained and perpetuated systemic inequality and injustice.[45]

Like her counterparts in the ANA, Cooper assumed an active role in the intellectual life and organizational activities of the Hampton Folklore Society. She submitted materials to the society's collection, corresponded with individual members, maintained a personal relationship with Alice Bacon, spoke at the 1894 Hampton Folk-Lore conference, established the Washington Negro Folk-lore Society, of which she became the corresponding secretary, and held an interim editorship of Hampton's *Southern Workman*, overseeing the monthly publication of the society's "Folklore and Ethnology" column.[46] Throughout her involvement with the Hampton Folklore Society, Cooper not only offered her services, but like Crummell, Scarborough, Love and others, also addressed the cultural and ideological significance of the society's work. While Cooper, like Armstrong, Bacon, and various members of the ANA, espoused a program of education and uplift, she saw education not as a means of reforming the individual, but as a catalyst for transformative social change.[47]

In her 1894 address to the Hampton folklorists, Cooper called into question the need to civilize the "folk," instead deploying the trope of the "folk" as a critique of civilization rather than as a barometer against which the "civilized" could measure their progress. She then went to work interrogating, or "de-naturalizing," the assumptions underlying the discourses of civilization, while also working to expose the biases encoded in the prevailing epistemologies employed to study and analyze black "folk" and black folklore. Cooper thus challenged the notion that the "folk" stand on the opposite end of a temporal and spatial divide, accessible only through the objectifying tools of the scientist. She validated an inherently personal and subjective epistemology rooted in memory and experience over the supposedly impartial and objective knowledge practices used to draw generalizations and conclusions about the "objects" of investigation. Finally, Cooper was equally concerned about perpetuating a value system that measured black cultural expressivity against standards dictated by white Western norms, and therefore she called for an African American literary tradition rooted in and responsive to the vernacular practices and everyday experiences of African Americans.

Cooper's suggestion that African American writers look to African American folklore as a source for black literary production was not a capitulation to Plantation Tradition mythology, as Scarborough might have assumed, but instead was an attempt to validate the plethora of experiences, creative expressions, and histories that had been largely misrepresented, distorted, and/or ignored in popular, scientific, and intellectual discourses. For Cooper, the politics of cultural representation were intricately tied to issues of equality, social justice, and democracy. As I argue in the final section of this chapter, Cooper envisioned a socially and politically engaged African American literary tradition, rooted in black folk culture. This kind of African American literary tradition would be part of an oppositional discourse that could challenge the conventions dictating black literary representation and increase agency for African Americans to determine the trajectory of their own literary production.

Following on the heels of Newell's address, Cooper began her 1894 talk at the Hampton Folklore Conference by challenging the cultural dominance assigned to white Western civilization. In this talk, she confronted the often-stated claims that African Americans were merely imitators of Western culture and thus incapable of originality and invention. While admitting that African Americans might be imitative, she observed that they certainly were no more so than every other nation "in the world's history." Just as Moton had reversed the commonly held belief that blacks were inherently imitative by suggesting that the most popular form of late-nineteenth-century entertainment, blackface minstrelsy, was based on white performers' imitations of African American musical performances, Cooper too suggested that imitation and borrowing was a central aspect of white artistic, intellectual, and scientific production. Just as "the Phoenicians imitated the Egyptians," and "the Greeks borrowed from the Phoenicians . . . the Norman who became the brain and nerve of the Anglo Saxon race," we are told, "was above all men an imitator." Cooper continued, quoting an unnamed source: "'Whenever,' says one, 'his neighbor invented or possessed anything worthy of admiration, the sharp, inquisitive Norman poked his long aquiline nose.'"[48] By beginning her talk to the Hampton folklorists, not with the black "folk" but with the "Anglo Saxon" imitator/investigator, Cooper located this Anglo Saxon both historically and physically. The white imitator/investigator is not allowed to remain the disembodied originator of culture but is located physically, by reference to bodily features and functions, and temporally, by refiguring the Anglo-Saxon as an heir to Egyptian culture rather than as the originator of Western civilization.

Having tackled one prevalent assumption, Cooper then turned her attention to dismantling the ideological foundations of social Darwinism that held white Western civilization as the height of all progress and advancement. Cooper granted that Anglo-Saxon civilization certainly "overpowers" other cultures, but her talk served as a warning to those enraptured by the "splendor of Anglo Saxon achievements." Instead of allowing Anglo-Saxon civilization to reign uncontested in its dominance, she redefined its preeminence in terms of rampant materialism, industrialization, and imperialism, stating: "Its stream of servants thread the globe. It has put the harness on God's lightning, which is now made to pull, push, pump, lift, write, talk, sing, light, kill, cure . . . securing with magic speed and dexterity fabulous wealth, honor, ease, luxury, beauty, art, power."[49] As Hazel Carby argues, "Cooper identified the intimate link between . . . domestic racial oppression and imperialism . . . [and] recognized the imperialist or expansionist impulse, with its ideology of racial hierarchies, as a supreme instance of patriarchal power." Carby further notes that Cooper "condemned the increasing imperialist expansion into Asia and the Pacific with its contemporary appeal to a manifest destiny to civilize the uncivilized as justification for 'consigning to annihilation one-third of the inhabitants of the globe.'"[50] Thus, in her address to the Hampton folklorists, Cooper tied the discourse of civilization to what Patricia Hill Collins identifies as a larger "matrix of domination" used to justify the exploitation and oppression of nonwhite and/or non-Western peoples both within the United States and around the globe.[51]

Continuing with what was certainly the most radical assessment of "civilization" with which the Hampton folklorists as a group had been presented, Cooper railed out against a system in which all achievement was measured in relation to Western ideals and values. She sarcastically remarked, "[T]o write as a white man, to sing as a white man, to swagger as a white man, to bully as a white man—this is achievement, this is success."[52] Thus, in her address Cooper began reconstructing an approach to folklore that was not bound within the current discourse lauding Western civilization as the standard by which all other cultures should be evaluated. Instead of aspiring to attain Western civilization, Cooper argued, "[E]mancipation from the model is what is needed," and implored African Americans to free themselves from the Anglo-Saxon standards by which their own traditions were judged primitive and lacking.[53] In this way Cooper distinguished her approach from an ANA position, asserting that African American vernacular traditions did not need to be stylized into "civilized" or Western forms but were aesthetically valid in their own right. Cooper further acknowledged, however, that there was tremendous pressure to re-present black vernacular traditions in the arts and popular culture only as they reinforced the public's preconceived notions, and she recognized that black folklore was considered valid only when "the approved style [is] affected."[54] Nevertheless, Cooper delivered an impassioned plea for the black folklorists to turn to their own culture for inspiration rather than rely on popular constructions of black folklore, and she implored them to collect and present folklore based on their own memories and experiences.

Asserting to her audience that folklore resides not in some far-off remote place but in "the whispered little longings of his soul," Cooper attempted to redefine the Hampton folklore project from a venture of objectively gathering and documenting items of folklore to a dynamic site of interaction and exchange. In this project, the students' memories of their communities' folklore and traditions could be recalled, reconstituted, narrated, and shared. Thus, Cooper's position directly contradicted the philosophy espoused by Armstrong. While Armstrong saw the rooting out of folk ignorance as a necessary process in the education of rural blacks, Cooper was adamant that the "so-called educated Negro, under the shadow of this over-powering Anglo-Saxon civilization," should not become "ashamed of his own distinctive features."[55] Cooper reminded her audience that they were not just talking about folklore, but family history. In this way, she impressed upon the Hampton folklorists that they were collecting their own and their communities' intimate, everyday traditions and customs, not just data to be analyzed by social scientists or relics of a primitive past that served as evidence of social progress. As Vivian May aptly demonstrates in her detailed reading of Cooper's oeuvre, Cooper was well aware that "scientific method and quantitative measures frequently mask prejudice and bigotry," and she understood that "abstraction, objectification and universalization, seemingly innocuous and neutral knowledge practices, are often both disingenuous . . . and harmful."[56] Rather than aspiring to what Cooper interpreted as an illusionary objectivity, she instead advanced an approach that would recognize, rather than disregard, the folklorists' social location and inherent subjectivity while validating, rather than dismissing, the everyday vernacular practices and ways of knowing of rural southern African Americans.

Cooper's proposal, however, meant, among other things, reconciling the "socialized ambivalence" that for many educated African Americans centered on their association or disassociation with black folk tradition.[57] As discussed above, for example, Hampton folklorist Robert Moton had stated that the treatment of black folklore by white minstrels had led many blacks to despise their own traditions. Moton explained that he had internalized the images of black folklore that circulated in the minstrel tradition; as a result, he initially shunned black folklore as embarrassing and degrading. Cooper passionately believed that if the students silenced and repressed their memories of their own family and community traditions, they allowed to persist the prevailing myths that obscured African Americans' humanity and erased the realities of the slave past. Folklore, for Cooper, functioned as an important "site of memory," challenging dominant claims to an authoritative or universal history.[58] This is not to say that memory, in Cooper's formulation, allowed unmediated access to some self-contained, pre-existing past, but rather that memory came to offer what Helen Lock identifies as "a powerful alternative means of negotiating with the past."[59] For Cooper, memory constituted an alternative way of knowing or "negotiating with" the past that functioned to open up space for those whose voices, stories, and histories had been co-opted, silenced, or suppressed.

Interestingly, Cooper's plea that the Hampton folklorists draw their folklore from their own remembrances anticipated the process that many would come to adopt in gathering folkloric materials. Directly following Cooper's 1894 address, society president Fred Wheelock opened the meeting for "the telling of Negro folk-tales."[60] After society member H. J. Patterson shared a tale he had heard in South Carolina, other members began to recall and recount tales they too remembered: "Mr. Patterson had hardly finished speaking when Mr. F.D. Banks, Vice President of the Hampton Folklore Society, came forward to tell a tale that was, he said, one of the very first that he remembered hearing in his childhood."[61] After Banks and several other members had come forth to share their recollections of folklore, another member, William Claytor, "was on his feet, and coming to front of the room." Claytor prefaced his contribution with the following remarks: "As I have been sitting here listening to these stories, quite a collection of stories have come back to me that I had once known and almost forgotten."[62]

Indeed, memory would become a defining aspect in the Hampton folklore collection. Daniel Webster Davis confirmed Cooper's assertion that the folklorists and their "informants" would likely find that the materials they sought were, when properly considered, a living part of their memories. Davis explained that he had a great deal of difficulty in collecting material on ring plays because many of the people he spoke with claimed that they "had forgotten the old ring plays." Once Davis had "recalled them to their memory," his informants began to share lively reminiscences of the plays they had once enjoyed.[63] In his 1897 poetry collection *Weh Down Souf*, Davis further contemplated issues of remembering and forgetting. One poem in particular, "Signs," depicts an educated young girl who attempts to cast off her traditional folkways to adopt a more modern and sophisticated manner. Yet, almost unconsciously, the girl enacts an old folk superstition by making a cross in the road when she has to turn around on her way to school and return home for something she forgot. The poem suggests the persistence of folkways even in the face of education and civilization and provides yet another example of Cooper's assertion that black folklore was not just an abstract concept but a part of the students' lives, connecting them with a not-so-distant folk past. Cooper clearly wielded a certain degree of influence within the society, and Bacon commented that Cooper's visits were "a source of great encouragement to us here and an incentive to do our own work as thoroughly and conscientiously as possible."[64]

In her closing remarks to the Hampton folklorists, Cooper asserted that the "vital importance" for African Americans in the "study of [their] own folk-lore" lay in the potential for the "songs, superstitions, customs and tales" of black folklore to serve as the basis for a distinctive, historically rooted, and socially engaged African American literary and artistic tradition. In her talk, she suggested that nineteenth-century Western notions of aesthetics—what she referred to as the "overpowering" model—were deeply racialized and gendered, and that rather than conform to creating art that is deemed valid within the conventions of the existing Western aesthetic, "emancipation" from this aesthetic model was what was needed. As Gene Bluestein argues, the Enlightenment "concept of cultural progress was predicated upon the eradication of myth and superstition from the minds of the peasantry. . . . Only after this liberation from the heritage of the past could the lower orders of society be raised to the level of educated and rational men."[65] In other words, as Cooper articulated in her address, "The whispered little longing of his own soul for utterance must all be a mistake. The simple little croonings that rocked his own cradle must be forgotten and outgrown and only the lullabies after the approved style affected. Nothing else is grammatical. Nothing else is orthodox."[66]

Cooper realized, however, that what is considered "grammatical," or aesthetically pleasing, has often been defined against that which is not grammatical or aesthetically pleasing, and in a U.S. and colonial context, those terms were almost always racialized and gendered. In identifying the "simple, common and everyday things," as that which "God has cleansed," for example, Cooper wrote against a prevailing nineteenth-century conception that "the folk" needed to be cleaned up as a prerequisite to becoming civilized. Further, Cooper suggested that it is in folk tradition where one finds the "fullest of poetry and mystery." Rather than sequester folk tradition and folk art to the past, available only as relics of survival for the men and women of the present to collect, Cooper called for a more organic relationship between African American literary production and various other forms of African American vernacular and creative expression.

While it may be charged that she engaged in a romanticization of the folk—redefining the black folk from unoriginal, uncivilized, and unclean to poetic, pure, and profound—Cooper's redefinition of the folk was part of an oppositional strategy that unsettled some of the most ubiquitously held and unquestioned assumptions about poor, rural African Americans in the late nineteenth century. Cooper's sophisticated analysis of race enabled her to valorize African American vernacular forms without adopting an essentialist understanding of cultural production. Instead, her aesthetic was an attempt to make room for the "voices of displaced, marginalized, exploited, and oppressed black people."[67] Indeed, according to Cooper's formulation, the "homely customs and superstitions" of the less formally accomplished African Americans would take their place alongside the heroic accounts of the more prominent members of the race.[68] While narratives showcasing African American achievement were valid, Cooper took the view that African American literature should not focus on narrating the achievements of its most accomplished members exclusively, but should also incorporate the everyday customs and practices of rural African Americans.

Thus, in her 1894 address to the Hampton folklorists, Cooper makes four distinct and significant contributions to the early studies of black folklore. First, she argues that concepts such as "civilization" and "folklore" must be understood as value-laden discourses that have everything to do with the creation and perpetuation of racialized, gendered, and classed hierarchies. Second, she critiques the biases often underlying the methods employed in scientific observations and analyses of "the folk." Third, she offers an alternative approach to accessing and representing group customs, traditions, beliefs, and practices, an approach that is self-conscious about the politics of representation and attentive to the social location and particularities of individuals. And finally, she validates folk and vernacular traditions as a site for the creation of a distinctive African American literary tradition and as a means of expanding the range of voices able to participate in the wider public discourse.

In her other writings, particularly "The Negro as Presented in American Literature," Cooper, who Mary Helen Washington identifies as a "literary critic . . . uncompromising in her denunciation of white control over the black image," expounded on the politics of representations as related to race and folklore in nineteenth-century American literature.[69] One of Cooper's primary complaints was that the parameters dictating African American literary representation had been laid out by white writers who both defined the conventions of black representation through their literary works and often exercised a great deal of influence over the literary marketplace, as was the case with William Dean Howells, who served as the editor of the *Atlantic Monthly* from 1871–81. Cooper felt that neither Howells, Joel Chandler Harris, George Washington Cable, Albion Tourgee, nor Harriet Beecher Stowe could "grasp and give out the whole circle of truth."[70] While she praised the causes to which Stowe, Cable, and Tourgee devoted their literary works, she lamented that white writers had become the arbiters of what was considered authentic about black life. And while conceding that their agendas might be well-intentioned, she was critical of the lack of range presented in their literary works, noting, for example, that Tourgee did not "create many men of many minds," hence, "[a]ll of his [literary] off-spring are little Tourgees—they preach his sermons and pray his prayers."[71] She saved her most damning criticism, however, for Howells, who she asserted could not "discern diversities of individuality, and has no right or authority to hawk 'the only true and authentic' pictures of a race of human beings." Cooper identified Howells's literary representations as a "kodak," noting that in his literary works, Howells purported to simply "push the button and give one picture from American life."[72]

In "Ethics of the Negro Question," Cooper similarly employed the phonograph as a metaphor to represent the politics of cultural representation: ". . . if one [African American] essay [were] to speak out an intelligible utterance, so well known is the place of preferment accorded to the mirroring of preconceived notions that instead of being the revelation of personality and the voice of a truth, the speaker becomes a phonograph and merely talks back what is talked into him."[73] Cooper's allusion to the phonograph recalls Bacon's search for the graphophone, and the American Folklore Society members' excitement at capturing an ostensibly authentic Negro folk song. Cooper, however, unsettled the notion that these supposedly objective technologies—the photograph, the phonograph, and by extension, the literary and scientific traditions that purport to reproduce reality objectively—are somehow free of partiality and bias. Instead, she asserted that every knowledge system and every form of representation is conditioned by a range of experiences, perspectives, locations, ideologies, and disciplinary conventions.

Again, highlighting the ways in which cultural representations, abstractions, and generalizations could support matrices of domination and oppression, Cooper delineates the dominant epistemological approaches to representing African American life and culture:

> Some have taken up the subject with a view to establishing evidences of already formulated theories and preconceptions. . . . Others with flippant indifference have performed a few psychological experiments on their cooks and coachmen, and with astounding egotism, and powers of generalization positively bewildering, forth with aspire to enlighten the world with dis-

> sertations on racial traits of the Negro. A few with really kind intentions and a sincere desire for information approached the subject as a clumsy microscopist. . . . Not having focused closely enough to obtain a clear-cut view, they begin by telling you that all colored people look exactly alike and end by noting down every chance contortion or idiosyncrasy as a race characteristic.[74]

In each case, Cooper notes how African Americans have become the objects of various discourses—scientific, literary, philosophical—and how, in turn, these discourses reduced African Americans to a few well-wrought traits and characteristics. This elimination of individuality, diversity, and humanity effectively served to erase and silence the range of African American voices and experiences. As Cooper explains, African Americans had been "sized up and written down by others" ad nauseam, yet remained the "great *silent* factor."[75]

As Vivian May asserts, realizing that African American "political, ethical and aesthetic standpoints were essential to realizing the full meaning of freedom," Cooper pushed for "the right of all humans to participate in the creating and defining of new paradigms of knowing and being that draw upon the race and gender-specific particularities of lived experiences, of cultural memory and of complex legacies of resistance."[76] In other words, recognizing a range of voices, but especially those that had hitherto been silenced or disregarded, allowed for the exchange of different viewpoints and perspectives. This range of voices was the vitalizing and necessary element in a responsive and healthy democracy.[77] As Karen Fletcher argues in her reading of Cooper's use of musical metaphor in *A Voice of the South*, harmony does not mean that all the voices sound the same, but that a range of chords are recognized.[78] Indeed, Cooper reminds her African American readers, "When we have been sized up and written down by others, we need not feel that the last word is said and the oracles sealed," explaining that what she hopes to see "is a black man honestly and appreciatively portraying both the Negro as he is and the white man, occasionally, as seen from the Negro's stand point."[79]

What is significant here is that Cooper saw a black literature—rooted in personal experience and collective memory and stylized through literary imagination—as not only representing aspects of African American experiences but also providing commentary on white American society. In Cooper's estimation, the function of African American literature was not to copy white American or European models, nor was it to create a distinct African American literary tradition to showcase the achievements of prominent African Americans. Instead, the folklore—the customs, beliefs, stories, and traditions—that this literature embodied conveyed a range of African American experiences, and as such, inherently critiqued what Cooper referred to as "the great gulf between its [America's] professions and its practices."[80]

In her own work Cooper modeled the literary aesthetic she articulated in various speeches and essays. As Elizabeth Alexander has shown in her analysis of the textual strategy Cooper employs in *A Voice of the South*, Cooper located herself as an active, visible agent within her texts. Her use of first person, her references to her body, her age, her hunger, the indignities she suffers, and her outrage create a "definite sense of source and agency" in her writing.[81] Referring to the impressive list of "colored women of America," from Frances Harper to Hallie Quinn Brown, which Cooper relates in "The Status of Woman in America," Alexander likens Cooper to a griot "who holds the whole tradition of her people in her head to be orally passed along."[82] Indeed, in several of Cooper's essays she becomes the storyteller, her personal experiences and observations mounting an ongoing critique of injustices rooted in race and gender prejudice. She places her personal stories in dialogue with dominant narratives supporting racial and gender oppression, creating a dynamic in which the dominant narratives are called into question by the first-person account of her intimate and everyday lived experiences. In "Woman versus the Indian," for instance, Cooper again called into question the widely held precepts drawing an evolutionary connection between "civilization" and race. In this essay, Cooper narrated her encounters in a Jim Crow train car, a car she noted, that was meant to separate those who are "known" persons of color from those who are "supposed" to be white. While reading her paper, Cooper is met by a "great burly six feet of masculinity" who demands that she exit the car. In recounting the interaction, Cooper renders the white male's voice in what is ostensibly rural Southern dialect, explaining that he "growls out" at her, "You better git out 'n dis kyar 'f yer don't, I'll put yer out." At this point, Cooper interjects, reporting her "mental annotation," ". . . *Here's an American citizen who has been badly trained.*"[83]

In relating this exchange, Cooper again locates through physical descriptors and orthography the traditionally disembodied white male figure. She employs understatement and sarcasm to reverse the traditional racialized and gendered roles. She is the model of decorum, rational and unexcited, while the white Southern man is ill-trained, poorly kept, and rude. Her ironic reversal exposes the arbitrariness of identifying African Americans as uncivilized and white Americans as the models of civilization. As her journey continues, she observes the inhumane treatment of young African American boys working on a chain gang. She marvels that this loosely veiled form of post-Emancipation slavery is allowed to persist "not in 1850, but in 1890, '91 and '92." After recognizing how the past continues to inform the present, Cooper makes "a note on a flyleaf of [her] memorandum, *The women in this section should organize a Society for the Prevention of Cruelty to Human Beings, and disseminate civilizing tracts, and send throughout the region apostles of anti-barbarism for the propagation of humane and enlightened ideas.*"[84] Again refocusing attention from reforming the individual to transforming an unjust social and economic system, Cooper suggests that missionary projects might be equally well-served by "civilizing" the white Southern citizens who allow the forced labor system to persist.

Sharing the observations made from the window of her Jim Crow car, Cooper placed her experiences within the larger context of racial and economic inequalities that thrived in the face of a supposedly civilized society. In addition to creating a polyvocal dialogical space, where her voice is able to interact with, comment on, and critique the dominant narrative, Cooper merges the written and oral forms. On the one hand, she creates an orally derived aesthetic by incorporating multiple voices and rendering her own thoughts in first-person narration. On the other hand, she highlights the place of written texts by noting that she is reading when the encounter takes place, making mental annotations—denoting a traditionally written form of demarcation—and writing on her memorandum that the women of the South should disseminate leaflets. In this account, Cooper does not privilege the oral over the written, but instead insists that the written must be infused with the orally derived perceptions, memories, and experiences. Thus, written or printed forms of communication can provide a space where traditionally underrepresented voices might gain a hearing. Cooper charges that her literate, female audience is responsible for hearing and registering the voices, cries, and complaints of her illiterate, less privileged sisters, stating, "Her cause is linked with that of every agony that has been dumb—every wrong that needs a voice." In other words, to return to her address to the Hampton folklorists, Cooper called for and demonstrated the workings of an African American literary aesthetic that could both participate in the larger discourse and remain responsive to alternative forms of knowledge and knowing.

Indeed, reconciling the relationship between memory, dominant ideologies, and folk forms has becomes a recurring trope in the African American literary tradition. In Toni Cade Bambara's 1980 novel *The Salt Eaters*, Velma, the protagonist, alludes to this process when she states, in terms reminiscent of Cooper's 1894 address, that she was determined not to "become anesthetized by the dazzling performance of someone else's aesthetic . . . but amnesia had set in anyhow."[85] In Bambara's story, it is only through oral and customary folk practices that Velma is restored to wholeness. As literary theorist Helen Lock asserts, "[M]any recent African-American written narratives have sought to propose an alternative approach to the past by foregrounding the functioning of oral memory both thematically and structurally: not to recall a fixed original or singular truth but to reconstruct and regenerate (inter) subjectively many kinds of truth."[86] Negotiating different forms of memory is the thematic and formal foundation of Ernest Gaines's *The Autobiography of Miss Jane Pittman,* for instance, as Gaines pits a history teacher's desire for an authoritative oral history of slavery against Jane Pittman's subjective and collective memory of her life and times. After the history teacher resigns to settling for a collectively recalled oral history, recounted and revised by Miss Pitman *and* her neighbors and relatives, he accepts that what he will present to the reader is the essence of Jane's story, even if not the verbatim narrative.

While Lock identifies the negotiation of memory as a central thematic and structural element of recent fiction, I would argue that as early as the 1880s and 1890s, Cooper's contemporaries, Charles Chesnutt and Paul Laurence Dunbar, drew on the black vernacular traditions of storytelling, masking, and conjuration as a way to juxtapose alternative versions of the past and introduce varying representations of reality.[87] While Chesnutt and Dunbar historically were often relegated to the confines of a form of minstrel realism by critics who are not specifically examining literature of the post-Reconstruction period, I would argue that both of these writers employed the content, themes, forms, and conventions characteristic of Southern black folk traditions to inaugurate a distinctive literary form that did not recapitulate, but instead signified and critiqued, the two dominant nineteenth-century popular forms: minstrelsy and Plantation Tradition literature. The aesthetic Cooper articulated is given creative and forceful expression, as writers from Zora Neale Hurston to Toni Morrison, from Toni Cade Bambara to Ernest Gaines, continually call on black folk tradition and memory as powerful sources for the creation of a history and past on which to build a more just future. But perhaps the works that responded most fully to Cooper's call were those of Dunbar and Chesnutt, her contemporaries who, through their literary works, sought to engage the social, artistic, and political significance of African American folklore.

4 Uprooting the Folk

Paul Laurence Dunbar's Critique of the Folk Ideal

In turning his literary and artistic attention to African American folklore, Paul Laurence Dunbar found himself, like many of the Hampton folklorists, in a precarious position. In assessing the state of literature by and about African Americans, William Scarborough remarked, "[W]e find Dunbar easily among the first of his competitors taking rank in the world of fiction as a portrayer of Negro life and character. Chestnutt [*sic*] follows in the same line." Still, Scarborough notes, "the demand is for the novelist who will portray the Negro not in the commonplace way that some have done, but one who will elevate him to a high level of fascination and interest." While Scarborough is hopeful that Dunbar or Chesnutt will assume the uplift mantle, he insinuates that both authors have followed too closely the "'suffering side'" of the race, producing "portrayals of the old fashioned Negro of 'befo' de wah'—the Negro that Page and Harris and others have given a permanent place in literature." While granting that Dunbar and Chesnutt occasionally give representation to the "higher aims, ambitions, desires, hopes and aspirations of the race," Scarborough quickly adds, "but by no means as fully and to as great an extent as we had hoped they would do."[1] In describing the role of the black novelist, Scarborough articulates an uplift agenda designed to produce respectable, middle-class images of African Americans to counter the derogatory and/or limiting stereotypes that had come to dominate representations of African Americans in various literary, scientific, and popular discourses. As Gene Andrew Jarrett points out, however, "mainstream (and usually white) literary critics . . . dismissed the relatively bourgeois and eloquent New Negro protagonists as unintelligible and unrealistic," while praising depictions, usually rendered in dialect, that captured the Negro's "simple," "sensuous," and "primitive" nature.[2] Writing between a New Negro uplift agenda on one side and a form of literary or ethnographic realism rooted, as Jarrett argues, in protocols of authenticity drawn from the minstrel and

Plantation Traditions on the other, Dunbar found himself in what Houston Baker refers to as a "tight space," forced to balance the racialized demands of the white mainstream literary marketplace with the diverse social and political agendas of a heterogeneous black middle class.[3]

Nevertheless, Dunbar chose to engage rather than ignore the past.[4] Dunbar's decision to engage the African American past, particularly through his representations of black folk and folklore both within and beyond the conventions of the plantation and minstrel traditions earned him divergent praise and criticism from the black and white literary establishments. Most often celebrated in his own time by white critics and reviewers for what were considered his authentic portrayals of rural African Americans in the ante- and postbellum South and for his so-called faithful rendering of African American dialect, these same critics were generally less impressed with Dunbar's standard English verse and his stories or novels set in non-Southern locales and/or featuring predominantly white characters.[5] For African American critics and reviewers, on the other hand, Dunbar served as an emblem of "race pride and achievement."[6] The upper echelon of the black literati was generally much more appreciative of Dunbar's Standard English verse than were white reviewers in the line of Howells.[7] In his Standard English poems Dunbar often recognized African Americans' rich cultural heritage, as in "Ode to Ethiopia," or praised prominent black Americans, as in "Douglass," his poem lauding the famed abolitionist. As Scarborough's comments make clear, however, the dialect poems for which Dunbar had received such abundant and lucrative praise from white critics and reviewers were greeted less enthusiastically by the New Negro members of the black middle class, who dismissed them as being more in line with the plantation tradition than representative of authentic black life.

Irrespective of the dichotomous reception by the black and white literary establishments, Dunbar's poems almost immediately entered into African American oral culture and vernacular tradition, where they remained with amazing staying power. His poems and songs were recited at gatherings of the A.M.E. Church on Eaker Street in Dayton, Ohio, and at high school and college assemblies.[8] He wrote the school anthem for the Tuskegee Institute, and in 1893, at the behest of Frederick Douglass, read his poem, "Columbian Ode," in front of twenty-five hundred attendees in the Haitian Pavilion at the World's Columbian Exposition's "Colored American Days."[9] In subsequent generations, his poems were memorized, passed on, and recited in homes, at religious and civic meetings, and in schools. Folklorist Darryl Dance found that several African Americans she interviewed, in over three decades of conducting fieldwork, "had not heard of Dunbar but recited verses from him that they had learned from family and friends." Henry Louis Gates, for instance, recalls that he "first heard Paul Laurence Dunbar's poetry as a child" from his father who was born in 1913 and "was fond of reciting long passages of poetry, to my brother and me." Similarly, Dunbar scholar Joanne Braxton acknowledges her mother, Mary Ellen Weems Braxton, "for reciting the poems of Paul Laurence Dunbar to me before I could read them to myself."[10] Dunbar's desire "to be able to interpret my own people through song and story," whether through the "broken tongue" of dialect or standard English verse, would come full circle as generation after generation would sing the songs and recite the poems Dunbar had written.[11] This circulation of Dunbar's poetry from and back to African American oral and vernacular tradition represents the efforts of generations of African Americans to pay homage to a black poet who achieved fame and notoriety by giving voice to African American themes and experiences and to recognize a tradition of black achievement in a realm (poetry) often thought to exclude African Americans.[12]

In "Negro Music," an 1899 article written for the *Chicago Record*, Dunbar explained the roots of his desire to engage creatively with African American folklore. In the article, he articulated a meaning-oriented and experiential approach to black folklore, admitting, "old plantation music [had] always possessed a deep fascination for me," and noting further that "there is an indescribable charm in it."[13] Moving away from a scientistic orientation, Dunbar recognized (as Douglass had years earlier) the deep, historically rooted, and experience-based meanings of African American "sorrow songs."[14] Following the aesthetic Cooper had articulated, Dunbar validates the inherent artistic and poetic qualities of African American folklore, identifying a "certain poetic sadness" within African American music, which he felt appealed strongly "to the artistic in one's nature."[15] Also like Cooper, he believed the inherent artistry of African American folklore resonated with, and could serve as the basis for, more formal African American creative expression. In a further departure from Newell's orientation, Dunbar identified African American songs and stories as part of an African American cultural heritage that had not yet become thoroughly Americanized, being still strongly informed by African cultural retentions. In fact, Dunbar credits his recognition of the poetic quality and artistry of African American folklore, not to minstrel performers or plantation writers, but to his chance encounter with performances of West African songs by "Dahomeyan" singers at the World's Columbian Exposition. Dunbar reflects:

> I heard the Dahomeyans singing. Instantly the idea flashed into my mind: "It is a heritage." . . . The Dahomeyan sings the music of his native Africa; the American negro spends this silver heritage of melody, but adds to it the bitter ring of grief for wrongs and adversities which only he has known. . . . If my hypothesis be correct, the man who asks where the negro got all those strange tunes of his songs is answered. They have been handed down to him from the matted jungles and sunburned deserts of Africa, from the reed huts of the Nile.[16]

Recognizing African American folklore as an African-inflected cultural heritage that could serve as a basis for creative literary expression, however, was fraught with difficulties. As argued in the preceding chapters, black folklore at the turn of the twentieth century was implicated in numerous intersecting discourses that hinged on the politics of racial and national identity. As I illustrate further in this chapter, the scientific approach to folklore studies provided a legitimizing frame for the folk ideals and/or caricatures emerging out of the reformist and Plantation Traditions, respectively. Furthermore, as an African American distinguished by critics for his "pure African blood," Dunbar, like the Hampton folklorists, was repeatedly placed in the position of native informant, charged with providing unfiltered access into the lives of black folk that would then validate his various audiences' preexisting ideals.[17] Faced with the strictures of the "tight space" constructed through these various intersecting discourses of folklore and race, I argue that Dunbar devised numerous strategies to negotiate the racialized politics of representing black folklore. Working from an alternative theorization of black folklore that shares more in common with Cooper's articulation than with the plantation writers with whom he is often associated, Dunbar enacted a black folk aesthetic that diversified and added complexity to the plantation images of black folks; brought attention to the scientific, popular, and literary conventions dictating representations of African American life; and introduced alternative geographies that disrupted the idealized picture of African Americans as an exclusively poor, rural Southern folk.

In this chapter I trace Dunbar's various strategies for representing black folklore by first examining how the discourses emerging out of folklore studies informed Dunbar's critical reception. I then locate Dunbar within the context of the Hampton community, showing how he sought to add nuance to the idealized and/or caricatured pictures of the black folk both through his work with the Hampton Institute and in his short stories. Reaching the limits of this artistic strategy—consistently being recast as a native informant or having his complex images glossed over in support of plantation stereotypes—I argue that Dunbar enacts a cultural critique through masking, a strategy articulated in his poetry and given full expression in his 1902 novel *The Sport of the Gods*. Through the novel's use of masking and dissimulation, Dunbar exposes and challenges the dominant discourses circumscribing the range of black cultural and literary representation. More than just mount a critique, however, Dunbar unsettles the prevailing paradigm that uncritically located an idealized folk and folklore in the rural South. Through his depiction of tensions within the Southern rural community, Dunbar disavows the entire notion of creating a representative black folk community and instead offers a pointed critique of the idealized notions of a monolithic black folk. He further challenges the construction of folklore as a Southern, rural phenomenon by introducing the urban North as an alternative geography in which to locate African American folk and folklore, thus providing one of the greatest affronts to the solidifying Jim Crow system: blacks who refused to "stay put" in the segregated South.

In his now infamous 1896 review of Dunbar's *Majors and Minors*, William Dean Howells hails Dunbar as "the first instance of an American Negro who had evinced innate distinction in literature." Howells notes that Dunbar's "brilliant and unique achievement was to have studied the American negro objectively, and to have represented him as he found him to be."[18] He identifies Dunbar's dialect poems as "divinations and reports on what passes in the hearts and minds of a lowly people."[19] On the contrary, Howells alleges (and other reviewers concurred, as evidenced in the *Southern Workman* reviews discussed below) that there is nothing particularly exceptional about Dunbar's Standard English poems, except that they are written by a black man. For Howell, Dunbar's dialect poetry provided unbridled access to, and indeed confirmation and authentication of, the black life Howells imagines to take place on the other side of the veil. Seemingly unaware that Dunbar's use of dialect is an engagement with written conventions that had already been established by white writers, Howells defines Dunbar's representations of black dialect as representative of black folks' "delightful personal attempts and failures for written and spoken language."[20] Howells's emphasis on objective, faithful reportage suggests that he was reading Dunbar's poetry through the prevailing folkloric frame as ethnographic reportage. Howells's assessment casts Dunbar in the role of native ethnographer or informant charged with providing "truthful" reports about the "Negro" as he is. In this way, Dunbar, much like Moton at the American Folklore Society meeting, ends up serving as both folk informant and authenticator for a pre-existing folk ideal—an ideal of the black folk as a Southern, rural, timeless people, an ideal that had been articulated by Armstrong in the reformist tradition, popularized in Plantation Tradition literature, and to some extent corroborated by the survivals approach promoted by Newell through the American Folklore Society.

Howells's appraisal was repeated in Hampton's *Southern Workman.* In 1901 alone, three reviews of Dunbar's works appeared in the page of *Southern Workman.* Susan Showers, a white member of the Hampton Folklore Society, reviewed *The Fanatics;* Helen Ludlow reviewed *Candle-Lightin' Time;* and *Southern Workman* published an unsigned review of *The Sport of the Gods,* with reviews of six additional works appearing between 1899 and 1907.[21] In *Southern Workman*'s lukewarm review of *The Sport of the Gods,* the reviewer praises what he/she reads as the novel's injunction for African Americans to remain in the South where they can be fortified by their religious beliefs and practices, rather than participate in the racy culture of the urban North. The reviewer then goes on to dismiss Dunbar's uses of the "condensed magazine 'novel'" form and criticizes the novel's "cynical tone."

On the other hand, the *Southern Workman* review of Dunbar's *When Malindy Sings* offers unqualified praise, stating Dunbar's "latest volume of verses is eminently satisfactory." Comprised of dialect poems and complementary illustrations (supplied by the Hampton Institute Camera Club) that depicted Southern settings and black Southern subjects, this book, the reviewer notes, provides an "illustration of Mr. Dunbar's insight into human nature and especially that found under the brown skin of his own people." The reviewer further comments that the characters who people the pages "are rollicking, pathetic, amusing, sad, sentimental, clever, weird, and altogether charming."[22]

Helen Ludlow's praise for *Candle-Lightin' Time,* Dunbar's 1901 photo-poetry book comprising of eight dialect poems and one Standard English poem with accompanying photographs by Leigh Miner, sums up the attitudes of many white mainstream reviewers toward the work of black authors and poets. Ludlow explains that Dunbar has "sufficiently proved his ability to sing in the white man's key [i.e., his use of Standard English verse in *Lyrics of Lowly Life*] . . . But we are glad that he has since devoted himself to dialect writing—especially in his verse. It is not that he can't do the other thing, but that his white brother can't do this" [i.e., write the dialect poems].[23]

While he certainly sought to give voice to the Southern rural communities he had learned about as a child, Dunbar was also committed to working in and across a number of literary traditions, forms, and genres. The literary assessments issuing from white mainstream critics discounted Dunbar's artistic reach, overlooking the artistry and irony Dunbar employed in representing black folk and folklore and forcing us to question exactly what picture of the folk Dunbar was authenticating for his white viewers. Kevin Young has suggested an important difference between "dialect" and African American vernacular, asserting that "dialect is a product of the Plantation Tradition, largely written . . . and African American 'vernacular' [is] something spoken [or] sung in an everyday voice."[24] Gates further identifies dialect as a "linguistic mask" used by black writers to create surface-level representations that might conform to reader expectations, while providing a smokescreen behind which to construct private meanings.[25] Thus, the reviewers' lauding of Dunbar's faithful renderings of dialect suggests that his representations were deemed faithful only to the extent that they confirmed the popular stereotypes issuing forth from the minstrel and Plantation Traditions.

Just as the white members of the Hampton community took an active role in engaging the cultural politics of representing black folklore, Dunbar, in his various formal and informal relations with the Hampton community, also entered into this ongoing dialogue about the politics inherent in the study, collection, and literary and cultural representations of Southern, rural African American life and folklore. Between 1901 and 1906, Dunbar published five works in *Southern Workman*.[26] In 1898 he performed at the Waldorf-Astoria with members of the Hampton Quartet at a benefit for the Hampton Institute.[27] His mother, Matilda, spent the summer of 1899 at Hampton, during which time the two maintained correspondence.[28] And in 1901 Dunbar entered into a more formal relationship with the institute when he accepted an invitation to give a reading as part of the strategy of Hampton's second president, Hollis Frissell, to stave off criticism of Hampton's allegedly anti-intellectual bent by showcasing the intellectual achievements of Hampton graduates and other prominent African Americans.[29]

Dunbar further engaged in a long-standing collaboration with members of the institute when he worked with the Hampton Institute Camera Club from 1899 to 1906 on the illustrations for six of his books of poetry.[30] Although the camera club was comprised predominantly of white faculty and staff from the Hampton Institute, Robert Moton was one notable exception, serving as "sole illustrator" for the poem "A Hunting Song," published in Dunbar's *Poems of Cabin and Field*.[31] As Ray Sapirstein has argued, the Hampton Institute Camera Club, aided by its proximity to and formal and informal relations with the Hampton Folklore Society, exhibited a knowledge and appreciation for folklore that allowed the camera club to add nuance and visual detail to their presentation of vernacular culture. Dunbar's illustrated poetry books provide a powerful counterpoint to the New Negro portraits. Instead of showing refined African Americans as emblems of middle-class respectability, they providing dignified and reverent depictions of African Americans in a variety of rural settings, at work and in leisure. Through collaboration with the Hampton Camera Club, and by extension with Moton and the Hampton Folklore Society, Dunbar, in his photo-poetry books, focused attention on average rural African Americans, thereby providing more complex and sincere images of African American "folk" than were typically presented in Plantation Tradition literature and minstrel shows.

Dunbar also employed this strategy in his short stories, peeling back the layers of plantation nostalgia to expose the complexities of the U.S. racial landscape. In their introduction to *The Complete Short Stories of Paul Laurence Dunbar*, Jarrett and Thomas Lewis Morgan assert a ". . . critical connection between Dunbar's short stories and the rest of his oeuvre," arguing that some of Dunbar's "most serious political interventions" occur in the short stories where "Dunbar complicates the simplistic caricatures of African Americans."[32] In "A Defender of the Faith," for instance, published in his final collection, *The Heart of Happy Hollow*, Dunbar moves the reader from the idyllic picture of the plantation South to a "coloured neighborhood" where the "inhabitants of the little cottages were so poor that they were constantly staggering on the verge of the abyss." Here, the narrator informs us, "life was no dream, but a hard, terrible reality, which meant increasing struggle."[33] In this story Dunbar creates a literal and figurative "window" through which he attempts to give the reader a view of African American life behind the plantation stereotype. The white reporter in the story, Arabella Coe, searches the street in this "coloured neighborhood" for a Christmas story until she happens upon an open window through which she observes a loud debate between members of an African American family concerning whether or not Santa Claus will visit their home for Christmas. Tom, one of the children engaged in the debate, reasons that Santa won't visit them because Santa has not answered his mother's prayers in the past, and that Santa only visits white people's homes, or at the very least, "col'red folks dats got the money."[34] While the narrator hints at the reporter's opportunistic perspective, once Coe is exposed to the realities that lie beyond what she assumes will be the window into picturesque black life, she is moved to provide gifts for the family as a sort of payment for the "Christmas story" she secures. In stories like "A Defender of the Faith," Dunbar moves the reader beyond the plantation types and stereotypical images of African Americans, providing more diverse and complex images of African American life. He also hints at the pointed ethical questions that underlie the economics of black representation, forcing the reader to consider whether the reporter's Christmas gifts are fitting compensation for the privilege of assuming authority over the representation of this poor black family.

While many of the short stories in his oeuvre maintain the plantation locale, Dunbar increasingly varied the settings with each subsequent collection. In his first collection, *Folks from Dixie*, most of the stories take place in the rural South, whereas in his last, *The Heart of Happy Hollow*, the settings shift from the rural South to more urban areas. As Jarrett and Morgan observe, Dunbar also tended to "frontload" his collections with stories that appeared to confirm his readers' expectations for plantation types and minstrel humor, while introducing more complex representations and critiques in later stories.[35] *The Strength of Gideon*, for example, begins with a story about the title character's unwavering devotion to his master's family. So devoted is Gideon that when everyone else leaves the plantation as the battles of the Civil War draw near, he remains steadfast in his promise to protect his master's wife and child after his master is killed. The next two stories in the collection likewise depict slaves' exaggerated commitments both to their former masters or mistresses and to maintaining the prewar glory of their plantations.

Later stories in the book, however, bring attention to the racial injustices precipitated by white society's misrepresentations of African Americans. "The Tragedy at Three Forks," for instance, portrays the utter racial injustice that pervaded Southern life to such an extent that the lynching of a black man is treated as a casual, foregone conclusion, whereas the eye-witnessed crime of passion committed by a white man is handled with restraint and an appeal to due process. Similarly, in "The Ingrate" Dunbar explores African American attempts to obtain justice within the context of duplicitous white actions. When a master teaches his slave to read, alleging selfless motives, the master's wife continually points out that the master is really driven by self-interest. The slave, however, dons the minstrel mask, playacting the expected role of docile and benighted servant only to achieve his greater ends of liberty, education, and just financial rewards.

Despite moments of deep social and political critique, and the inclusion of African Americans in a range of settings that exceeded the bounds of the plantation stereotype, Dunbar's reviewers continually reasserted a plantation frame in interpreting and evaluating his stories. One reviewer, for example, praised the "plantation tales [for showing] the Negro in his truest light—

fervid, credulous, full of rich, unconscious humor; lazy sometimes, but capable of dog-like faithfulness."[36] Furthermore, editorial strategies, such as illustrating his collections with images provided by E. W. Kemble, constantly undermined Dunbar's attempts to expand the range of African American literary and cultural representations. As Adam Sonstegard argues, Kemble's plantation images created a counternarrative to Dunbar's texts, shoehorning the diversity of Dunbar's stories into the plantation frame by illustrating characters that reify the plantation image and ignoring those that challenge it. The twelve images provided by Kemble for Dunbar's *Folks from Dixie* and *The Heart of Happy Hollow*, for instance, depict only characters who fit the plantation stereotype (with the possible exception of the illustration captioned "Jim," representing the defiant title character of "Jim's Probation," who is pictured with a slight sneer on his face and a rifle flung nonchalantly over his shoulder).[37]

In his short stories Dunbar sought to create characters that diversified existing portrayals of African Americans. Repeatedly, however, the literary establishment—reviewers, editors, illustrators—attempted to erase the diversity by reasserting a plantation frame that reified public perceptions of African Americans as plantation types. Recognizing the limits of his attempts to diversify portrayals of African Americans, I argue that Dunbar also entered into a "struggle over representation," bringing attention to the role of various discourses in constructing what Stuart Hall refers to as "racialized regimes of representation." Hall employs this phrase in reference to the ways in which multiple discourses intersect to construct representations of the "Other," and the role of those representations in the consolidation, maintenance, and exercise of power. Hall identifies multiple strategies for contesting such representations, including efforts to replace negative images with positive ones, a strategy common in New Negro approaches to racial uplift and one we see Dunbar utilizing in his short stories; reversing stereotypes, a strategy that entails reinterpreting as positive those differences perceived or represented as negative; and bringing attention to the very ways in which representational practices operate.[38]

Dunbar—and Chesnutt, as we will see in the following chapter—challenged popular depictions of African Americans by enacting these multiple strategies of resistance; but rather than simply replacing negative images with positive ones or attempting to jettison demeaning images by assimilating to or identifying with the dominant cultural representations, Dunbar sought to expose the racialized lens through which African Americans and African American cultural productions were viewed. In the late nineteenth century, the discourse and practice of folklore was a crucial component in constructing a "racialized regime of representation." Instead of relinquishing representational control of black folklore, however, Dunbar engages in a literary transformation of African American folklore, most specifically masking and dissimulation, as a way to mount a coded critique of these various discourses of folklore.

In his poetry and prose, as well as in his personal writings and letters, Dunbar employs masking as a way to expose the many intertwined discourses working in tandem to limit the range of African American cultural representation at the turn of the twentieth century. Through his literary transformations of masking, Dunbar engages a long tradition of masking as both black folk practice and African American literary device. In *African Voices in African American Heritage*, Betty Kuyk identifies masking as an African medium "for communicating with the spirit world," noting that masks are part of the ritual of both withholding and imparting knowledge.[39] Gates emphasizes the performative and functional aspects of masking, explaining, for example, that the Yoruba mask "remains only a piece of carved wood" until it is animated by both artist and audience; only when the wooden artifact is set in motion does it become functional, a "mask-in-motion." The mask is then used to negotiate coded meanings, enacted through "rhythms, movements, and tonal-specific harmonies."[40] Like Kuyk, Gates asserts that the mask, as facial covering and ritual performance, both conceals and reveals secret, interior meanings—meanings that can only be arrived at through initiation and participation in the masking ritual.

As an African cultural retention translated in a New World context, masking has played an important part in African American culture. As a result of slavery and segregation, African Americans historically have had to learn how to mask or conceal their true feelings. Realizing that laments of discontent, plans for freedom, or displays of self-assertion could bring swift retribution from white oppressors, masking became a vital social practice through which African Americans could conceal and protect their inner lives and desires. As Bernard Bell explains, the African American "struggle for survival led to a surface identification with the master's values and a subservient behavior pattern that exploited the disparity between white ideology and black reality."[41] Frederick Douglass depicts this quandary in his 1845 *Narrative of the Life of Frederick Douglass*, relating that a slave master disguised his identity and then asked one of the plantation slaves whether or not he was treated well by the master. The slave stated that he was not, and upon returning to the plantation, the slave was sold to a Georgia slave trader. Such deceitful practices by white members of the slaveocracy, Douglass explains, often compelled slaves, if questioned by a stranger, to state that they were treated well, confirming the assertions advanced by proponents of slavery that enslaved peoples were actually better off and happier in bondage than they would be in freedom.

In the African American literary tradition, as Craig Werner asserts, "writers drew on the folk tradition of masking to assert subversive ideas for black audiences while providing white audiences with seemingly innocuous surface meanings."[42] From its most overt representation in his poem "We Wear the Mask" to its more implicit appearance in "An Ante-Bellum Sermon," both published in 1895 in *Majors and Minors*, Dunbar continually reiterates the theme of masking the African American experience behind the face that "grins and lies." In "An Ante-Bellum Sermon," for example, Dunbar situates this masking technique within the context of a long tradition of African American dissimulation, demonstrating how biblical rhetoric was used to encode discussions of slavery and freedom within the black community. After relating Moses's escape from oppression in Egypt, the preacher facetiously reminds his audience, "I'm still a-preachin ancient / I ain't talkin' 'bout to-day," asserting, "I'm talkin' 'bout ouah freedom / In a Bibleistic way." Similarly, his poem "Goin' Back" appears to support the stereotypes perpetuated by the Plantation Tradition that an old black man, when seemingly betrayed by the North, would return south. There is slippage in the old man's story, however, that calls into question the sincerity of his desire to return South, even as he declares it. He begins, for example, by noting that this is "the same ol' tale that I have to tell." The poem then concludes with the advice, "don't mind the ol' man's tears, but say / It's joy, he's goin' back to-day."[43]

In his 1902 novel *The Sport of the Gods*, Dunbar utilizes masking to reveal, slowly and methodically, the extensive network of epistemologies that construct knowledge about African Americans. In an innovative double move, Dunbar critiques the various discourses constructing and romanticizing African Americans as an exclusively Southern rural phenomenon, but at the same time refuses to abandon African American folklore altogether, instead transforming masking as part of his literary strategy. In this way, Dunbar unsettles the idea of an authentic black folk, while still validating the longstanding use of masking as a valid and dynamic African American cultural practice. He critiques the idea of black folklore as something that exists within an objective, ethnographic frame—always revealing how so-called objective, ethnographic representations of black folk and folklore were part and parcel of romantic, sentimental plantation mythology—and instead presents black folklore as a vehicle for apprehending, challenging, and negotiating reality.

In *The Sport of the Gods*, Dunbar tells the story of Berry Hamilton, a butler who labored on the plantation of Maurice Oakley for thirty years prior to his emancipation from slavery. Once freed, Berry wanders helplessly, presumably during the Reconstruction period, before returning to his former master's plantation. Once Berry returns to his "proper" place, a not-so-subtle reference to the return of near-slavery conditions in the post-Reconstruction era, the text establishes parallel, separate spheres in which Maurice and Berry—once and again master and servant—coexist, not only harmoniously but profitably. The narrator explains, "[W]hen the final upward tendency of his employer began, his fortunes had increased in a like manner." Maurice and Berry even perform their marriage rites in sync, fulfilling Maurice's "laughingly" suggested prophecy: "There is no telling when Berry will be following my example and be taking a wife unto himself."[44]

Merging the fictions of the Plantation Tradition and the myth of separate but equal, Dunbar begins to show what is at stake in the idealized constructions of the folk in the Plantation Tradition, and how these construction are implicated in the racial discourse and practice of separate but equal. Indeed, while the Oakleys and the Hamiltons maintain separate households, and supposedly advance equality, the narrator offers textual clues suggesting the inherent flaws of this system. For example, the Hamiltons and Oakleys advance separately and "equally" only so long as the Hamiltons remain at a social and economic level far below and subservient to the Oakleys, content to receive the discarded things "handed down" from the Oakley household. When the Oakleys realize that 500 dollars has been stolen from their home, however, the myth of the contented former slave and the benevolent plantation owner is called into question. The theft can be read as an example of what Mikhail Bakhtin refers to as crisis or rupture in maintenance of a prevailing system that offers or threatens the emergence of "novel" narratives.[45] Possibly recognizing the threat that this crisis portends, Maurice withdraws a convenient explanation from his storehouse of fictional narratives about the Negro to swiftly and effectually suppress any rupture in the social order that this crisis might provoke. The text underscores the threatening potential of this crisis by showing the degree to which the white Southern community mobilizes to comply in the mythmaking necessary to suppress this potential crisis.

The first branch of the community to comply with Maurice's fiction is the law. As circumstantial as the evidence against Berry is, the law, after a weak show of resistance, accepts Maurice's fictional narrative as the premise for its so-called investigation. Later, a group of Southern "gentlemen" gathered at the Continental Hotel serve as a perverse think-tank, postulating theories to reconcile the narrative of the contented Negro with that of the Negro who, of course, stole the money from his former master. In this scene the men combat the potential crisis in epistemology that would ensue if they were to recognize they had no ready explanation for why a contented slave would steal the money by inserting other ready-made fictions about the Negro. Consistent with Dunbar's textual practice of casting dominant narratives with a difference, the text provides the example par excellence of the need to deal with ruptures in so-called Southern racial logic in a manner that allows no narrative gaps or questioning. When the Colonel, one of the Southern "gentlemen" gathered at the hotel, hesitantly asks, "Well, do you think there's any doubt of the darky's guilt?" the narrator comments, "He was the only man who had ever thought of such a possibility. They turned on him as if he had been some strange, unnatural animal." The crowd responds in a crescendo of disbelief:

> "Any doubt!" cried Horace.
>
> "Any doubt!" exclaimed Mr. Davis.
>
> "Any doubt?" almost shrieked the rest.
>
> "Why, there can be no doubt. Why, Colonel, what are you thinking of? Tell us who has got the money if he hasn't? Tell us where on earth the nigger got the money he's been putting in the bank? Doubt? Why, there isn't the least doubt about it."[46]

In this scene, the crowd effectively suppresses any consideration of an alternative narrative ("The Colonel saw, or said he did"), and thus averts the crisis in epistemology that might have ensued if the crowd were to entertain the Colonel's query. It is, however, the narrator who proposes an alternative narrative—a narrative that never comes to bear in either the law's or the community's verdict but serves the purpose in the text of undermining the validity of the dominant narrative. What the Colonel could not say, the narrator does: ". . . Berry had no rent and no board to pay. His clothes came from his master, and Kitty and Fannie looked to their mistress for the larger number of their supplies . . ." and therefore Berry lacked a motive for the theft.[47]

In *The Sport of the Gods*, Dunbar unmasks the idealized depictions of the black emerging from the Plantation Tradition as an integral part of the larger cultural discourse on the legal, political, and social ramifications of the "race problem." Berry's fate, for instance, could be read as a veiled critique of the concessions to social segregation and second-class citizenship endemic in the Washingtonian emphasis on industrial education and black economic advancement enabled through the political and financial support of Southern white democrats and white Northern patrons.[48] Berry's misperception that his utilitarian ideology and industriousness can secure his rights and liberty is, ironically, partly responsible for his imprisonment. He believes in the tenets of what George Frederickson refers to as the "new paternalism" of the 1890s: "the claim that the Negro was now making progress with the help and encouragement of Southern whites and that this process constituted a continuation of the harmony and racial development of the slave era." In reality, however, this new paternalism amounted to little more than a gesture made by Southern whites to provide moral guidance and industrial education for Southern blacks. Frederickson reminds us, "At best it was an effort to prepare the blacks more adequately for scratching out a living at the lower levels of a capitalist society; at its worst it openly capitulated to racial discrimination to such an extent that even this modest goal was endangered."[49]

In contrast to the white community, however, the black community is powerless to articulate an operative response to the crisis. When Oakley and the sheriff arrive at the Hamilton cottage to "question" Berry about the theft, they encounter a "Berry" who is still acting out the plantation fiction upon which he has created his world. He is still the smiling "darky," who grins and laughs for the white audience:

> "Shall I question him," asked the officer, "or will you?"
> "I will. Berry, you deposited five hundred dollars at the bank yesterday?"
> "Well, suh, Mistah Oakley," *was the grinning reply*, "ef you ain't the beatenes' man to fin' out things I evah seen."[50]

Unlike most blacks in the South during the nadir, Berry, who is at this point a romantic construct of the Plantation Tradition, "seemed not to understand" at all what it meant to have the owner of the plantation, "his man," and an officer arrive at his house. When Oakley states the accusation, Berry is rendered powerless in his attempt to tell a story that differs from the prevailing one. He must defer Oakley and the detective to his wife. Oakley and the detective, however, disregard Fannie's comments and order the arrest of her husband and her dismissal. In a surprising show of resistance, Fannie takes a strong and vocal stance against the white men: "'I won't go,' cried Fannie stoutly; 'I'll stay right hyeah by my husband. You shan't drive me away f'om him.'"[51] Fannie is thus the first to challenge the Plantation Tradition by acting completely out of line with what was acceptable behavior for "darkies." Berry, perhaps inspired by his wife's show of defiance, is the next to break from the mode of expected behavior, shouting, "'Den, damn you! Damn you! Ef dat's all dese yearhs counted fu', I wish I had a-stoled it.'"[52] These shows of defiance, however, are readily ignored, and by the end of the interrogation and after Fannie's misinterpreted supplication to Mrs. Oakley, Fannie and Berry are rendered powerless in their attempts to tell a story that differs from the prevailing one.

Additionally, the blacks in the town, instead of uniting with the despairing family, make offhand remarks about the Hamiltons' own accountability and are rendered virtually silent in the face of a white power structure they know not how to challenge. The A.M.E. church and Berry's lodge handle the crisis by expelling the threatening element from their community, and even Berry's friends "were afraid to visit him and were silent when his enemies gloated."[53] The Hamiltons, having aligned themselves with the white aristocrats in their attempts to get their piece of the pie, certainly share in the responsibility for their treatment by the blacks in the town. The narrator, however, makes it unclear if things would have been any different if the Hamiltons were accepted members of the black "community." In what might be one of the most disparaging diatribes on the privation of a black community forged under the oppression of slavery and servitude, the narrator presents a strong case for just the opposite:

> [I]n the black people of the town the strong influence of slavery was still operative, and with one accord they turned away from one of their own kind upon whom had been set the ban of the white people's displeasure. If they had sympathy, they dared not show it. Their own interests, the safety of their own positions and firesides, demanded that they stand aloof from the criminal. Not then, not now, nor has it ever been true, although it has been claimed, that negroes either harbour or sympathise with the criminal of their kind. They did not dare to do it before the sixties. They do not dare to do it now. They have brought down as a heritage from the days of their bondage both fear and disloyalty. So Berry was unbefriended while the storm raged around him.[54]

To reinforce this point, the narrator questions the allegation that the Hamiltons' relationship with their peers warranted such harsh treatment from the blacks. The Brown family, for instance, defends their treatment of the Hamiltons by asserting that Berry's daughter Kit "wouldn' speak to my gal, Minty, when she met huh on de street." The narrator dismisses this justification, stating "the fact of the matter" was that "Minty Brown was no better than she should have been, and did not deserve to be spoken to. But none of this was taken into account by either the speaker or the hearers. The man was down; it was time to strike."[55]

In an otherwise astute reading of *The Sport of the Gods,* Lawrence Rodgers asserts that Dunbar's migrant characters would have fared better had they developed meaningful relationships with their Southern black folk community.[56] Rodgers's reading of the text is informed by a contemporary critical paradigm that idealizes the Southern, rural black community as the home of an authentic and nurturing blackness. Rodgers's assumptions about a healing and powerful Southern folk community, however, are not supported anywhere in Dunbar's text. In "Narration and Migration: *Jazz* and Vernacular Theories of Black Women's Fiction," Madhu Dubey discusses the problematic dichotomies of south/rural/folk and north/urban/literate which, she asserts, have been employed in discussing black cultural and literary history. She cites Lawrence Levine, who identifies a "'tendency to regard folklore and the oral tradition as rural phenomena almost exclusively,'" and she goes on to state, "the most significant development in recent migration studies is its revision of the tendency . . . to restrict black oral tradition to the rural South."[57] Rodgers's reading seems to be rooted in a version of this critical paradigm, privileging the South as the home of black community, tradition, and culture. The text, however, seems ambivalent at best about this prospect, instead locating in the South plantation stereotypes, a legacy of individuals and families broken by slavery and a historically divided and contentious community. Nowhere does the text suggest that the Hamiltons would have fared better had they maintained an alliance with what it represents as an antagonistic and petty group of individuals. The Hamiltons fail in the South because they have bought into a damaging set of conventions perpetuated by a white power structure that seems to allow black economic gain, but in actuality is supported by a social, political, and legal presupposition of black inequality.

Dunbar may certainly be held accountable for the gross exaggeration of the barrenness of the South in terms of its ability to produce strong, resilient communities and of the ability of Southern African Americans to nurture a vital and supportive community. It is problematic that the text offers no empowered Southern black community or meaningful mode of resistance within the South, and thus the white power structure is able, swiftly and effectively, to utilize a storehouse of fictions about the "Negro" to re-imprison a black man so recently "freed" from slavery, separate him from his family, kick him off his land, and claim the earnings of all his post-emancipation, Reconstruction labors. It is necessary, however, for contemporary critics to recognize the complexities in Dunbar's representations of the black community in the South and to examine this as an area for critique, rather than gloss it over by inserting a contemporary paradigm valorizing the rural South as the home of an authentic black community.

Indeed, I argue that Dunbar's representation of the Hamiltons and their black neighbors is a critique of the idealized and romanticized depictions of "authentic" black folklore in various literary, popular, and folkloric discourses, rather than an attempt to comment on the vitality of Southern black folk culture. The text utilizes the Southern terrain to explore the crisis that ensues when romantic ideals and constructs are challenged by harsh realities. Berry, as a romantic construct of the Plantation Tradition and an emblem of the industrious Negro who knows his place, is the first to fall when he is reminded that the system he has bought into works only so long as it suffers no disturbances, real or imagined. Oakley also falls victim to a failing system predicated on the sentimental ideals of Southern honor and chivalry. Even after the reality of the theft is thrust upon him, Oakley still tries to preserve the veneer of Southern honor and the respectability of his family name (his efforts, of course, reveal the constructed nature of these ideals and insinuate the hypocrisy of "Southern honor"). Thus the Southern narrative signals the limitations of romantic or sentimental fiction as literary mode for black characterization and advances an acerbic assessment of the rise of the "new paternalism" as a viable option for anchoring race relations in the New South.

This is not to say, however, that the text, in its pre-migration narrative, does not do important cultural work; it does. For instance, it gives voice to the very real predicament of blacks in the South at the turn of the century. In a 1902 article from the *Independent*, a black woman writes about the hypocrisy and self-fulfilling prophecies of the white power structures that controlled representation of Southern blacks:

> I am a colored woman, wife and mother. I have lived all my life in the South, and have often thought what a peculiar fact it is that the more ignorant the Southern whites are of us the more vehement they are in their denunciation of us. They boast that they have little intercourse with us . . . but still they know us thoroughly . . . The Southern say we negroes are a happy, laughing set of people, with no thought of tomorrow. . . . The Southerner boasts that he is our friend; he educates our children, he pays us for work and is most

> noble and generous to us. Did not the Negro by his labor for over three hundred years help to educate the white man's children? . . . The Southerner says "the Negro must keep in his place" . . . A self-respecting colored man who does not cringe but walks erect, supports his family, educates his children, and by example and precept teaches them that God made all men equal, is called a "dangerous Negro;" "he is too smart;" "he wants to be white and act like white people." . . . Whenever a crime is committed, in the South the policemen look for the Negro in the case . . .[58]

These are the very issues at the heart of *The Sport of the Gods*, and part of the cultural import of the text is that it provides a literary representation of the kind of oppression faced by Southern rural African Americans.

While the text does not offer a narrative alternative for blacks in the South, the ruptures in the prevailing discourses permit a space out of which the rest of the Hamilton family is able to escape and test their endurance in the North. After finding their life in the South destroyed by the false accusation of theft (the money was stolen by Maurice's own half-brother) and the imprisonment of their father, Berry's wife and children set off for New York.

At the turn of the century, New York occupied a paradoxical space in the minds and lives of African Americans. It re-inscribed the narratives created during slavery of the North as an earthly promised land in which persecuted blacks could find not only refuge but also economic and social opportunity to realize the American dream. Upon arriving in the urban locales, however, many of the transplanted blacks were sorely disillusioned by the dismal living conditions they were subjected to, the persistent unemployment, and Northern versions of racism. In *Black Manhattan*, James Weldon Johnson describes the harsh conditions in New York at the turn of the century, while also recognizing the new opportunities the city offered. The New York race riot of 1900 serves as Johnson's point of reference in asserting that "the general spirit of the race was one of hopelessness or acquiescence. The only way to survival seemed along the road of sheer opportunism and of conformity to the triumphant materialism of the age." Johnson explains: "this fourth of the great New York riots involving the Negro was really symptomatic of a national condition. The status of the Negro as a citizen had been steadily declining for twenty-five years; and at the opening of the twentieth century his civil state was, in some respects, worse than at the close of the Civil War."[59]

Elsewhere in *Black Manhattan*, Johnson recognizes the opportunities that New York offered for blacks, who were so often systematically silenced and robbed of opportunities for self-expression: "[I]t was in places such as these [i.e., the clubs and stages represented in *The Sport of the Gods*] that early Negro theatrical talent created for itself a congenial atmosphere of emulation and guildship. It was also an atmosphere in which new artistic ideas were born and developed."[60] Johnson was hardly naïve enough to assert that these arenas offered unqualified opportunities at self-expression. Indeed, he recognized the degree to which an audience's acceptance of black artistic creation was limited by the stereotypes forged on these same stages. Johnson asserts that some of the most persistent stereotypes about blacks ("lazy, shiftless, unreliable . . . irresponsible child, a pathetically good-humored buffoon, a ridiculous caricature of a civilized man") "have, for the greater part, been molded by what may be termed literary and artistic processes," and he identifies the minstrel stage as a central site in the production of these stereotypes.[61]

Writing from the vantage point of 1934, Johnson would have seen the African American theatre emerge from the minstrel tradition through black versions of minstrelsy. And while the African American minstrel tradition still constituted a highly circumscribed medium, black actors were able to add nuance and subversive content to the stage images they inherited from their white predecessors. Johnson, however, would also have seen black minstrel performances and coon ditties give way to more expressive and complex representations of black culture with the rise of jazz, the blues, and other performing arts, and therefore in 1934 he was able to surmise how coon ditties and vaudeville acts secured the stage and the mixed audience that would lead to greater opportunities for black artistic self-expression. Dunbar, however, did not have the advantage of that perspective when he was writing *The Sport of the Gods* in the first years of the 1900s, nor would he ever gain the years to evaluate the period from a historical distance. The paradox Johnson retrospectively identifies in the 1930s is the same paradox out of which Dunbar wrote the Northern narrative of *The Sport of the Gods.*

In the second half of Dunbar's novel, the Hamiltons head for the North, lured by the fantasy they identify as New York: "[T]hey had heard of New York as a place vague and far away, a city that like Heaven, to them had existed by faith alone. All the days of their lives they had heard of it, and it seemed to them the centre of all the glory, all the wealth, and all the freedom of the world. New York. It had an alluring sound."[62] Escaping the constructs that imprisoned them in the South, however, proves more difficult than following the trajectory of yet another narrative myth. Thus, even as the crisis in the South affords new possibilities in the North, as the Hamiltons painfully discover, New York is as fraught with intricately manufactured snares as the South. While unwilling to advance an idealized picture of the North as a twentieth-century promised land and deeply critical of the "decayed and rotten morals" oozing through the streets of New York's Tenderloin district, in the Northern narrative of the text Dunbar dislocates the folk from the Southern locale and gives representation to African Americans who are geographically and imaginatively out of bounds. As Anand Prahlad argues, the urban African American disturbs the discourse of folkness that gets institutionalized with the founding of the American Folklore Society, which reflected "a romanticization of the rural and quaint 'folk.'"[63] Through the Northern narrative of *The Sport of the Gods*, Dunbar challenges this prevailing discourse of folkness, introducing new narrative possibilities, a new cast of Northern-style characters, and a new geographic setting in which to locate an alternative African American cultural identity.

In *The Sport of the Gods*, Dunbar presents the Banner Club as a cross-racial underworld frequented by those interested in "the Sporting life." While critics have generally concurred with the narrator's assessment that "the place was a cesspool," the Banner Club has its redeeming qualities.[64] It is at the Banner Club, for instance, where the Hamilton siblings, Joe and Kit, meet characters such as Sadness, William Thomas, and Hattie Sterling, club patrons who try to teach the Hamilton children the new strategies necessary for their survival in the North. While Joe and Kit adopt these strategies with only limited success, the blame for their shortcomings does not lie solely with the moral depravity of the club and its patrons.

Joe, for instance, transports his romantic ideals to New York, where he clings to them in the face of very unromantic urban elements. His attempts to transplant this Southern romantic framework prove woefully inadequate for navigating the Northern terrain, and his romantic posturing makes him an inviting victim for various kinds of exploitation. After a year in New York, Joe is still unable to discern the inner working of the Banner Club. Even after Sadness provides him with a thinly veiled exposé, taking Joe behind the mask of New York nightlife and telling him the truth about Skaggs, the white Northern reporter who takes it upon himself to tell the Hamiltons' story for his aptly named newspaper, the *Universe*, Joe still projects his illusions onto the unsavory Northern urban environment. When he enters into a relationship with Hattie, the streetwise, opportunistic chorus girl, he tries to situate her within his sentimental designs. He cannot see the inherent contradiction in trying to merge his romantic fantasy with Hattie, who on the one hand represents commodified sexuality and on the other hand can never be the passive heroine of his romance. When Hattie confronts Joe with the reality of this situation, shaking him out of a drunken stupor and telling him he'll have to find a "another baby" to be the object of his fantasies, she destroys the last vestiges of his romantic world. Joe retaliates by killing the false icon of his doomed romance, and is arrested and put in jail.

While Kit's portrayal is less than flattering, she relinquishes romantic attachments to the past and therefore fares better than her brother. Kit survives in New York, but only as she assumes a functional role in performing the fictions of the North as a show girl. She distances herself physically and emotionally from her family, and she demonstrates her mastery in employing the "mask" by "selflessly" offering money for Joe's lawyer, but "when Joe confessed all, she consoled herself with the reflection that perhaps it was for the best, and kept her money in her pocket with a sense of satisfaction."[65]

While the Southern migrants' dismal fates in the North have been read as Dunbar's injunction for blacks to stay in the South even at the nadir of Southern race relations, their destinies are less determined by their geographic location than they are by the characters' inabilities to navigate the various representational discourses they encounter. In the North, with the ostensible absence of direct white oppression, the characters' fates lie in their attempts to cling to and reinvent the romantic fictions by which they are bound, in Joe's case, or, like Kit, to comply too readily with the exoticizing and gendered fictions of the stage. If Dunbar had limited *The Sport of the Gods* to these recent migrant characters, the text would seem unrelenting in its determinism. The novel imparts its naturalistic tendencies by representing these characters' declines in relation to their environments, which in this case are the various ensnaring fictional landscapes. What seems brutally unfair, however, is the narrative's simultaneous indictment of the characters' blind but zealous corroboration with this "natural determinism."

What redeems the text from such harsh evaluation, however, is the new brand of Northern-style characters who are more experienced and savvy at negotiating the forces of their environments and able to wrest some control from the various conflicting fictions. Hattie, for example, is a bold, assertive, defiant figure, and although she falls victim to Joe's sentimental designs, through her character Dunbar introduces a new alternative for female characterization in the African American literary tradition. It is also Hattie's apprenticeships of Kit that enables the Hamiltons' economic survival in New York. Sadness is one of the few characters who makes a sincere and concerted effort to instruct Joe on the evils of city life. He is articulate, his powers of perception are keen, and he is the character most alert to the racial politics of artistic production.

Dunbar's own experiences with the racial politics influencing representations of and by African Americans in the arts and literature are especially instructive in reading the text's use of masking in the Northern section of the novel. In a succinct example of the continued pressures of the white literary marketplace in defining African American literary and cultural representations, William Dean Howells writes about Dunbar's *Majors and Minors* in a way that recalls the letters of authentication white abolitionists supplied for slave narratives. First, Howells establishes that Dunbar's volume of poetry was indeed written by a real live Negro: "The face which confronted me when I opened the volume was the face of a young Negro . . . the black skin, the wooly hair, the thick out-rolling lips, and the mild, soft eyes of the pure African type." Howells then states that the "Majors" (written in Standard English) are more generic with nothing, except that they are written by a Negro, "specially notable." He goes on to "establish" the validity of "Minors" (the dialect poems), asserting that the reader will find in them authentic representations of the Negro:

> It is when we come to Mr. Dunbar's Minors that we feel ourselves in the presence of a man with a direct and fresh authority to do the kind of thing he is doing . . . ["The Party"] show[s] what vistas into the simple, sensuous, joyous nature of this race Mr. Dunbar opens . . . he has been able to bring us nearer to the heart of primitive human nature in his race than anyone else . . . Mr. Dunbar's race is nothing if not lyrical, and he comes by his rhyme honestly . . ."[66]

Likely feeling obliged to display some kind of gratitude for the popularity Howells's review brought the young poet, Dunbar writes a letter thanking Howells for his "more than kindness." Embedded in the letter's exaggerated humility and inflated pathos, however, is Dunbar's manipulation of the mask by overacting the provincial part Howells has scripted for the black poet:

> . . . That I have not written you sooner is neither the result of willful neglect or lack of gratitude. It has taken time for me to recover from the shock of delightful surprise. My emotions have been too much for me. I could not thank you without "gushing" and I did not want to "gush" . . . I feel much as a poor, insignificant, helpless boy would feel to suddenly find himself knighted. I can tell you nothing about myself because there is nothing to tell. My whole life has been simple, obscure, and uneventful. I have written my little pieces . . . but it seems hardly by my volition. The kindly praise that you have ac-

corded me will be an incentive to more careful work. My greatest fear is that you may have been more kind to me than just . . ."[67]

It is said that upon reading Howells's review in *Harper's*, Dunbar knew not whether to laugh or cry. Later he would align with the latter sentiment, writing to a friend in 1897, "One critic says a thing and the rest hasten to say the same thing, in many cases using identical words. I see very clearly that Mr. Howells has done me irrevocable harm in the dictum he laid down regarding my dialect verse."[68] Alice Dunbar-Nelson, too, found Howells's patronizing review objectionable and expressed her displeasure with the degree to which Howells had influenced readings of Dunbar's poetry: "Say what you will, *or what Mr. Howells wills*, about 'feeling Negro life esthetically, and expressing it lyrically,' it was in the pure English verse that the poet expressed *himself*."[69]

In *The Sport of the Gods*, Dunbar introduces a variant of Mr. Howells' will through the character of Skaggs, the white Northern reporter who writes the story of the Hamiltons for the *Universe*. While Houston Baker champions Skaggs as the "energetically improvisational" blues hero of the text who can "both solve the 'crime' of the Plantation Tradition and provide a more adequate artistic perspective to take its place in an American universe of fictive discourse," reading Skaggs in light of Dunbar-Nelson's comments suggests an alternative interpretation of the white reporter.[70]

In the Northern section of the text Dunbar presents Skaggs as the hero but unmasks the motives behind his supposedly benevolent acts. When Joe first meets Skaggs at the Banner Club, for example, Skaggs is operating behind a mask akin to those associated with African American tradition. He creates a narrative of his life that legitimizes his association with the blacks at the club; in other words, he justifies his "slumming." Even as Skaggs attempts to employ the mask, however, the narrator and then Thomas peer behind it. The narrator first explains, "It was the same old story that the white who associates with negroes from volition usually tells to explain his taste," and then goes on to "tell the truth about the young reporter." Thomas, too, reveals Skaggs's inadequacy at wielding the mask, commenting, "Skaggsy's a good fellah, all right, but he's the biggest liar in N' Yawk."[71] Captivated by the rag-time dancers, Skaggs demonstrates his own inability to see behind the mask employed by African Americans, reading their performance as "'the poetry of motion.'" Sadness replies cynically, "'Yes . . . and dancing in rag-time is the dialect poetry.'"[72] As Sadness's comments reveal, Skaggs mistakenly identifies rag-time dancing as an unmediated depiction of authentic blackness, failing to recognizing that rag-time dance, like dialect poetry, is a conscious performance of and play on existing convention and expectations. Reading the performance as poetry-in-motion rather than as what Gates refers to as the mask-in-motion, Skaggs mistakes the performance as an authentic window into black life behind the veil.

Skaggs's fumbling attempts to utilize the mask to get "in" with the blacks at the club, while being completely blind to the masking that the blacks themselves are doing, would be comical if the text did not also show the power he exerts over African American representation. Governed by his ambitions, Skaggs is shown to be completely insensitive to the realities of black life. Skaggs, after securing Berry's release from the Southern jail, and upon seeing the broken and disillusioned Berry Hamilton emerge, announces, "[T]his is a very happy occasion."[73] He then gives Berry Fannie's address but fails to inform him that she has remarried and his son is in jail. Thus the text represents Skaggs as one who, regardless of his insensitivity to the realities of this black family, writes the story of the Hamiltons for the *Universe* and precipitates Fannie's and Berry's return to the South, where society is more or less falling apart around them. Thus the new perspective Skaggs offers is little more than another veiled exploitation of a pathetic image of blacks. He replaces the stereotype of blacks as a thieving, untrustworthy lot with that of the helpless victim. The *Universe,* for example, spreads its headlines across New York: "A Burning Shame! A Poor And Innocent Negro Made To Suffer For A Rich Man's Crime. Great Expose by the *Universe*! A *Universe* Reporter To The Rescue!"[74]

Additionally, just as the white racist system in the South played an active role in the "fate" of the Southern blacks, Skaggs and the *Universe* are conflated with "Will" or "fate" in the North. Thus, in the North, Skaggs, empowered by this mythical *Universe,* takes the place of Southern paternalism in controlling black representation, recasting the detrimental, confining, and inaccurate fictions about blacks. The text, therefore, does not simply tie the Hamiltons' fate to some unidentifiable, disembodied force, but instead conflates this "fate" or "will" with Skaggs and his *Universe.* The white hegemony of the North is doubly sinister in its omnipresence and ubiquity, as well as in its attempts to remain invisible. However, there are characters like Thomas and Sadness, masters of masking, who are endowed with the double vision to see Skaggs's designs and try to impart this new way of seeing to others. Additionally, only one as masterful at masking as the narrator could present Skaggs as the hero, while unmasking him as the villain. Finally, considering Alice Dunbar-Nelson's comments on "what Mr. Howells wills," one wonders if Dunbar, too, was not masking his critique, not only of Howells's will, but also of a tradition that privileges the testimony of whites in "authenticating" black texts.

In his seminal study, *Black American Writing from the Nadir,* Dickson Bruce identifies *The Sport of the Gods* as "a sensitive man's inner history of the triumph of racism in American society."[75] Bruce's assertion not only brings attention to the dismal state of race relations in the American South at the turn of the century, it also proves instructive in understanding the "triumph of racism" in the Northern section of the narrative. While much attention has been devoted to reading the Northern narrative of *The Sport of the Gods* in relation to either urban naturalism or as an expression of Dunbar's own instinctive distaste for the evil influence of city life, these assessments downplay the degree to which racism and racist representations remain prominent features in the Northern narrative as well. For example, in Rodgers's reading, he asserts, "having cleared a geographic space, he [Dunbar] sends them [Hamiltons] to a setting that is relatively *free of white racial stereotyping* and is instead informed by urban naturalism."[76] While the existence of white hegemony is not as visible as it is in the South, it is certainly still omnipresent in the North. Indeed, the illusion of placidity and equality among the races is sustained only so long as white society allows that illusion to persist. When threats to white supremacy emerge (as with the theft) or when white ambitions surface (as with Skaggs's desire to get a good story), the power structures that control not only blacks' representation, but also their freedom, become more apparent.

In *The Sport of the Gods,* Dunbar unmasks the politics at work in the various conflicting fictions defining African American literary and cultural representations at the turn of the twentieth century. He illustrates how the concept of the "folk" was wed to the conventions of the Plantation Tradition, and disrupts the construction of the folk as a Southern rural phenomenon by taking his narrative North and introducing characters that exist outside the traditional bounds of existing constructions of black "folk." While exceedingly skeptical about the opportunities New York offers, the text stakes out new terrain in which to locate alternative African American identities; and while critical of constructions of an idealized black folk or folk culture, whether located in the North or the South, the text still validates African American cultural practices through the narrative use of masking as a way to reveal concealed knowledge about the literary and cultural constructions of race.

5 "The Stolen Voice"

Charles Chesnutt, Whiteness, and the Politics of Folklore

When in the late 1880s, Chesnutt made the conscious, deliberate, and as yet, unaided decision to employ conjuration as the basis for his first three conjure stories, he had already identified himself as a purposeful writer.[1] As expressed in his journals, Chesnutt hoped to secure a profitable niche among the reading public while altering his audience's attitudes about race. Chesnutt's decision to draw on elements of black folklore in his fiction to reach a wider reading audience was not surprising, for even while the status of blacks had continued to deteriorate since the end of Reconstruction, public interest in black folklore had steadily increased. As Bruce Jackson succinctly states: "the interminable love affair between the American reading public and the image of the antebellum South was taking hold at just about the same time the Negro was demoted from freedman to serf. A chattel is not a fit subject for literature, but a serf, it seems, is."[2]

Accordingly, writers such as Joel Chandler Harris, Albion Tourgee, and George Washington Cable, the first a member of the American Folklore Society and the latter a member of the Chicago Folklore Society, capitalized on the newly discovered storehouse of folklore materials to craft literature that would satisfy public interest and earn the authors popular acclaim. The success of these authors convinced Chesnutt that black folklore could provide the appropriate medium through which to reach a wider audience. In an 1880 journal entry Chesnutt commented on the success of *A Fool's Errand*, remarking that Tourgee's book is about the "manners, customs, modes of thought" of the South. Chesnutt further observed that "nearly all of [Tourgee's] stories are more or less about colored people, and this very feature is one source of their popularity." Chesnutt then posed his now famous question, "why could not a colored person write as good a book about the South as Judge Tourgee has written?" As his early journal entries show, Chesnutt realized there was a piqued public interest in folklore and that being "a colored man, who has lived among colored people all his life," placed him in an advantageous position to translate for mass consumption the folkways of Southern blacks.[3]

While recent scholars have done commendable work reading his literary texts in relation to contemporary white writers and dominant literary conventions,[4] Chesnutt was also part of a wider movement among African Americans that saw growing interest by blacks in the preservation of their own traditions.[5] In this chapter I propose to read Chesnutt not only in relation to white mainstream writers' engagements with black folklore, but also within the context of African American theorizing about the social, cultural, and political significance of black folklore. Exemplified in the work of the Hampton Folklore Society, African American intellectuals and cultural workers in the late nineteenth century exhibited a keen interest in black folklore. On a very tangible level, the Hampton Folklore Society provided wider access to Southern black folklore that was hitherto undocumented and unpublished. Chesnutt, like Dunbar, would have had access to the full range of Hampton materials through their primary publication outlet, *Southern Workman*, where the Hampton Folklore Society, from 1893 to 1905, regularly published materials from its folkloric collections, member papers, and society proceedings. Chesnutt's short stories "Lonesome Ben" (1900) and "The Partners" (1901), as well as his essay "The Free Colored People of North Carolina" (1902) and the conjure tale "Tobe's Tribulations" (1900), were all published in *Southern Workman*, where *The Conjure Woman* and *The Marrow of Tradition* were also reviewed in 1899 and 1901, respectively.[6] As Chesnutt's letters and journal entries indicate, he paid careful attention to the sources that published and reviewed his writings. In various letters to his daughters, for example, he directs their attention to reviews of *The Conjure Woman* and in one letter he notes, "one of my stories, 'Tobe's Tribulations,' a bullfrog conjure story came out in *Southern Workman* this last week."[7] Thus it is likely Chesnutt encountered at least some of the Hampton Folklore Society's materials and reports published in the "Folklore and Ethnology" column of *Southern Workman*.

On a less material level, Chesnutt shared with many of the Hampton folklorists such critical challenges as how to negotiate their relationship to a black folk from whom they may have felt separated by class, geography, and/or education. Like many members of the Hampton Folklore Society, Chesnutt spent years teaching at remote country schools in the South. At age 15, he curtailed his own schooling and began teaching to supplement his family's income. In 1877, Chesnutt was appointed first assistant and teacher of the State Normal School in Fayetteville, North Carolina. Two years later he journeyed to Washington, D.C., in search of more challenging and profitable work. Disappointed that he was unable to secure a job as a stenographer, a field in which he had been self-training for the previous three years, Chesnutt returned south and accepted a post as principal of the Normal School.[8]

Because teaching jobs were one of the few vocations available to educated blacks, Chesnutt's career path at this point was quite traditional. In many ways, his experiences mirror those of his contemporaries at Hampton, as well as scores of other educated blacks working to "uplift" the less fortunate of the race. While Chesnutt and the folklorists at Hampton initially may have been motivated by this impulse to educate and uplift, both gradually realized that their role as teachers among rural black Southerners put them in a unique position to collect what was recognized, either immediately or retrospectively, as black folklore.

As Robert Moton describes in his autobiography, however, before he could seriously attend to the collection and study of black folklore, he had to first recognize and then overcome the images of the black folk in the popular media that had led him to despise his own traditions. He explains, "this meant a readjustment of values that was not particularly easy for a raw country lad."[9] Through various incidents in his autobiography, Moton narrates the process through which this "readjustment of values" took place. Participation in the Hampton Folklore Society, for example, offered him an opportunity to consider black folk traditions as a member of a larger group devoted to the collection and preservation of black folklore. Additionally, in many of the meeting between the AFS and the HFS, Moton acted as an ambassador of black folk culture, performing and providing commentary on various black folk traditions.

Chesnutt's journal entries from 1870 to 1888 show a similar shift in his relationship to black folklore. In his early 1870 entries, Chesnutt is outraged at the persistence of superstitious beliefs and practices among the rural blacks in Fayetteville and Charlotte, North Carolina: "Well! Uneducated people are the most bigoted, superstitious, hard-headed people in the world! These folks down stairs believe in ghosts, luck, horse shoes, witches, and all other kinds of non-sense, and all the argument in the world couldn't get it out of them."[10] Critics such as Wiley Cash and Richard Brodhead reference aspersions such as these to argue that Chesnutt's education led to a sense of difference from which he viewed uneducated rural blacks as "profoundly other" (Brodhead's phrase). Cash further asserts that Chesnutt sought to distance himself from blackness and to move away from folklore in each of his subsequent literary works.[11] These readings, however, reduce the complex negotiations that Chesnutt and scores of other educated African Americans engaged in as they sought to address dominant cultural stereotypes, their own socialized ambivalence, their various cultural and social or political projects, and their relationship to African Americans with less formal education and mobility than themselves.

Granting that both Chesnutt's and Moton's education created a rift between them and the communities in which they taught, it was, however, the stereotypical portrayals of black folklore in the minstrel tradition and plantation literature that caused both men to regard black folk traditions with distanced humiliation and condescension. There was also awareness, particularly for Chesnutt, that caricatures of the black folk as ignorant and primitive buttressed segregationists' claims that blacks were inherently inferior to whites.[12] Both men, however, were encouraged by the interest expressed on the part of certain dominant white cultural institutions to reconsider the value of black folk traditions. For Moton, that attention came from the American Folklore Society and arrived in the form of support for, as well as a vested interest in, "Negro" folklore. Chesnutt, on the other hand, was inspired by the sympathetic and profitable portrayals of black folklore that characterized the works of Harris, Tourgee, and Cable.

Thus, in many ways, the interest expressed by these white academic and intellectual institutions provided a viable space for the serious consideration and treatment of black folklore. Nevertheless, both Moton and Chesnutt had to learn to negotiate these dominant cultural interests with their own divergent goals and objectives, and both found ample strategies for an alternative engagement with black folklore articulated in the work of their African American contemporaries. Moton, for example, rejected the decontextualized amassing of black folklore and instead brought attention to contextualizing frameworks as a way to suggest the deeper meanings and social functions of black folklore. He also negotiated his supposed position as native informant by introducing into the Hampton collection tales that inherently critiqued that position, documenting the resistant, subversive, and dualistic qualities of black folklore.

Like Dunbar, Chesnutt called on the subversive aspect of black folklore as a way to engage and challenge the prevailing literary discourses of his day. Also like Dunbar, Chesnutt devised a literary strategy informed by an African American cultural form to expose and subvert the protocols of authenticity influencing African American literary and cultural representation.[13] For Dunbar, that form was masking, and while Chesnutt drew on numerous forms of folklore, including masking and storytelling, his most overt literary engagement with African American folklore came in the form of conjuration.

In a 1976 essay Robert Hemenway, one of the first scholars to take seriously the sophisticated role of folklore in Chesnutt's literary works, suggested that literary scholars and folklorists needed to work across disciplinary lines to arrive at more productive analyses of folklore's function or "transformation" in literary texts. On one hand, Hemenway admonishes folklorists, traditionally scientifically oriented and taxonomically driven, to be more attentive to the aesthetic functions of folklore particularly as advanced in literary works. On the other hand, he illustrates for literary scholars the importance of identifying folklore as it may have existed in oral tradition as a way to interpret the significance of literary adaptations and variations to traditional folkloric materials. In reading *The Conjure Woman*, for example, he identifies Chesnutt's use of recognizable folkloric items and his approximation of folk speech as efforts to "authenticate the atmosphere of the stories," but he acknowledges this as a rather rudimentary use of folklore.[14] Instead, Hemenway focuses attention on Chesnutt's more sophisticated transformations of folklore, which he argues worked to propel characterization, advance plot, and reveal characters' perspectives through their various attitudes toward black folk beliefs. Hemenway's study was inspired in part by Alan Dundes's "identification and interpretation" model, in which Dundes proposed a dialectical relationship where folklore in literature could be read for how it contributed to the literary project, not just for whether or not it had existed in oral tradition.[15]

Since Dundes's foundational essay and Hemenway's important study, numerous works have offered insightful analyses of Chesnutt's adaptations of folklore. Moving beyond the identification and interpretation model, for example, Karen Beardslee demonstrates an approach to reading folklore in literature stressing the ways in which Chesnutt's *The Conjure Woman* treats the theme of folklore and how this treatment "shapes what we are to come away with upon finishing the story." In particular, Beardslee focuses on how folklore in various literary texts facilitates individual characters' journeys to psychic wholeness and healing, emphasizing the folk tales' ability to "transmit information, maintain hope and teach proper modes of behavior."[16] Beardslee highlights the significance of folklore in negotiating the individual's relationship with tradition and to negotiating the connection between self and community.

Other scholars assert that Chesnutt not only transforms the conventions of conjure into an effective literary device, but that he simultaneously illustrates the vitality of African cultural retentions within New World forms of cultural expressivity, while suggesting the power of African American folklore to serve as a site of memory that can, in turn, introduce an alternative story of the African American past. While these aspects of his fiction have been treated convincingly by literary scholars, exemplified in Eric Sundquist's reading of Chesnutt's representation of the cakewalk in relation to African cultural retentions and William Andrews's analysis of the conjure tales as providing a history of African American life during slavery, what I want to suggest is that we also read Chesnutt's engagement with black folklore in the context of the emergence of African American and American folklore studies.[17] Chesnutt is not only validating African American folklore as an effective literary device, as an emblem of one's relationship to broader communal traditions, or even as an alternative source for history or cultural identity; instead, like Moton, Chesnutt is also challenging the conventions emerging from folklore studies and the new social scientific ways of perceiving and representing African American "folk" and folklore.

In his 1899 folklore-inspired collection of interconnected short stories, *The Conjure Woman*, Chesnutt transforms the principles of conjure and ritual to challenge the conventions of the Plantation Tradition, to critique the dominant folkloric/ethnographic approaches to representing black cultural traditions, and to suggest a subjective, process-oriented approach to representing African American folklore. In carrying out each of these projects, Chesnutt remains attentive to the racialized politics of representing folklore, and whether he shows folklore in process or as a functional component of his literary strategy, he never neglects to intimate the ways in which black folklore has been implicated in constructing the post-Reconstruction racialized discourses of segregation and difference. By 1905, in *The Colonel's Dream*, Chesnutt pursues yet another strategy for exposing the insidious ways in which the discourses of folklore operated to sustain the structures of white supremacy and African American oppression when he turns his attention to exposing the forms of white folklore that allowed the various fictions of race, like those exemplified in Plantation Tradition literature or embodied in the "logic" of the separate but equal ruling, to persist.

In his literary works, Chesnutt exposes the biases inherent in supposedly objective knowledge practices associated with the social sciences, revealing how the objectifying gaze often operates as part of a system of domination and oppression. Chesnutt's works also critique the dominant nineteenth-century approach to folklore collection, known as the item- or text-centered approach, or what Bronislaw Malonowski referred to as collecting "mutilated bits of reality."[18] As Alan Dundes explains, the text-centered approach was informed by "[t]he theoretical assumption that folklore was limited to a survival and reflection of the past." Dundes notes that within this theoretical framework, "there was no point in bothering to attempt to collect the present context of folklore. A past-oriented folklore collector would tend to regard his informants as relatively unimportant carriers of precious vestigial fragments."[19] Further, according to Dan Ben-Amos, the text-centered approach, which viewed folklore as "a collection of things . . . completed products or formulated ideas," required "a methodological abstraction of objects from their actual context."[20] The text-centered approach allowed supposed experts to extract folkloric items from various sources, collate and classify them, and then use the materials as evidence to make various observations and assertions. Two primary drawbacks of this approach are that assertions are based not on observing folklore in process, but instead on abstract reasoning and deductive logic, and that the onus for interpreting the materials lies solely in that hands of the collector, with the so-called informant serving as the passive carrier of an extractable folkloric treasure.

I argue that, in addition to all the other vitally important cultural work Chesnutt performs in *The Conjure Woman*, his text—read in the context of African American folklore studies—also poses a challenge to the text-centered approach to interpreting African American cultural traditions, offering instead a process-oriented, performance-based approach to understanding African American folklore. As Ben-Amos explains, in a process-oriented approach, folklore is seen "not as an aggregate of things, but a process—a communicative process," and within this framework, "the narrator, his story, and his audience are all related to each other as components of a single continuum, which is a communicative event."[21] This process-centered approach is informed by what Mikhail Bakhtin refers as a "dialogical interaction," in which meaning is dynamic and relational, constructed in the context of exchange and interaction.[22] Importantly, however, as Regina Bendix reminds us, once we understand folklore as a communicative interaction or event, we must not be lulled into believing that the process-centered formulation can grant access to an unmediated authentic folklore experience.[23] Instead, the collection and representations—even the very label of folklore—are always informed by a complex politics of cultural representation.

While one can never re-create the lived context in which customary or oral practices circulate, in *The Conjure Woman* Chesnutt utilizes the contextualizing framework to suggest that folklore is an event, a process based on interactions and dialogical exchange. In Chesnutt's formulation, interracial, cross-cultural understanding and knowledge come not through the objective observer who collects bits of materials taken to be "authentic" representations that merely confirm what the collector believes he already knows about the Other; rather, it is through exchange and interaction that folklore opens up the possibility of increasing cultural understanding and inspiring personal transformation and social change. Thus, the interaction and exchange between the characters provides us with a literary rendering of a process-centered approach. Chesnutt, however, keeps just enough of a wink in his storyteller's eye to remind the audience that even the folkloric event is still very much informed by self-conscious performances of various cultural identities.

Chesnutt's 1901 essay "Superstitions and Folk-lore of the South" serves as an entrée into several of the recurring issues centered on the racialized politics of folkloric representation that are highlighted in *The Conjure Woman* and *The Colonel's Dream*. In the essay Chesnutt constructs himself as an interviewer-ethnographer investigating and reporting on the "latter-day prevalence of the old-time belief in . . . 'conjuration.'"[24] Through the negotiation of his own subject position, Chesnutt advances an understanding of folklore that is not arrived at through questioning and interrogation; instead, he constructs folklore as a shared process and interactive experience reflecting the ideas and belief systems not only of those being represented but also of those doing the representing. In this way Chesnutt highlights the subjectivity of the interviewer, introducing to the essay a form of self-reflexivity about his own role as an informant and participant in the culture that he has been charged with representing.

Within the essay, Chesnutt assumes a dramatis personae, interacting with the various conjure doctors and reflecting on the origins and significance of conjure as a basis for both his own literary transformations of black folklore and for African American cultural production more generally. Through his interviews with "a half a dozen old women, and a genuine 'conjure doctor,'" Chesnutt "discover[s] that the brilliant touches, due, I had thought, to my own imagination, were after all but dormant ideas, lodged in my childish mind by old Aunt This and old Uncle That . . . awaiting only the spur of imagination to bring them to the surface again." Just as his own knowledge of conjure lies dormant beneath the surface of his conscious memory, Chesnutt explains that the beliefs and practices associated with conjure have been driven underground by "education" and "the scornful sneer of the preacher," from which, he explains, "it is difficult for the stranger to unearth them."[25]

Chesnutt's access to and rapport with the people who carry these traditions, and their willingness to share their guarded beliefs and practices with him, marks his position as an insider. Rather than assume the objectifying position of the supposedly impartial observer, however, Chesnutt constructs his interactions as personal and subjective, informing his perspective on his own past and creative process.

In the second half of the essay, Chesnutt relates an encounter with Uncle Jim Davis, a "professional conjure doctor," who Chesnutt visits in hopes of obtaining a charm to bring good luck and to keep him from losing his job. As a professional man of letters who availed himself of all plausible avenues to achieve financial success, Chesnutt, in this tongue-in-cheek example, accepts the aid of the conjure doctor to exert a level of supernatural control over the circumstances that dictate his job security—circumstances that were too often over-determined by external forces. While he assures the reader that the charm and the rabbit's foot he has procured should keep him "reasonably well protected," he concedes that he "shall omit no reasonable precaution which the condition of my health or my affairs may render prudent."[26] In this interaction, Chesnutt maintains his pose of interested skepticism but nevertheless becomes a willing participant in the proceedings. He does not remain on the outside looking in, but instead becomes an active participant in the conjure practices. He does not, however, conceal his own reservations, instead allowing the reader to see how his own perceptions might influence the representations of conjure he presents in his essay.

After relating the transaction, Chesnutt recounts a conjure tale involving "the fate of a lost voice." In the tale of the stolen voice, the conjure doctor takes on increasing significance as the traditional but limited arbiter of social justice. In the story, a woman's voice is so beautiful that it lures away another woman's man. In response to this rebuff, the "jilted woman," through proxy, manages to "steal" the first woman's voice. The woman whose voice is stolen appeals to the conjure doctor for justice. The doctor intercedes and identifies the "guilty person," but he is unable to restore the stolen voice to its rightful owner. In unmistakable legalese, Chesnutt relates that the conjure doctor sought out the woman who had stole the voice and "charged her with the crime, which she promptly denied." Chesnutt further explains that after "being pressed," the woman "admitted her guilt," at which time the doctor "insisted upon immediate restitution." As the story of the stolen voice continues, Chesnutt reveals that the conjure doctor, unfortunately, wields only limited powers. When the doctor insists that the voice be returned to its rightful owner, the woman who stole the voice "expressed her willingness, and at the same time her inability to comply—*she had taken the voice but did not possess the power to restore it.*" In response to this affront, the conjure doctor places a spell on the woman that is to remain until the voice is restored. Chesnutt concludes the story, relating that the case of the stolen voice "is still pending."[27]

In the first part of the essay Chesnutt establishes conjure as a dynamic site of African cultural retentions. As Sundquist argues, "By locating elements of his stories in the childhood tales told him by elders of the generations of slavery, Chesnutt . . . made the remembrance of slave culture a foundation for modern African American culture."[28] In relating his interactions with Aunt Harriet and Uncle Jim Davis in the second section of the essay, Chesnutt suggests that knowledge of cultural practices such as conjure comes through dialogical interaction and exchange rather than through supposedly objective forms of interrogation and/or observation. Chesnutt's interactions with Aunt Harriet and Uncle Jim not only illuminate their practices and beliefs as related to conjure, but also change the way Chesnutt understands his own experiences and creative processes, suggesting that dialogical interactions have the potential to evoke self-reflection and a resultant shift in perspective.

In the final section of the essay, the story of the stolen voice could be read allegorically as a commentary on the appropriation of the black voice and black cultural representation. While Plantation Tradition writers such as Joel Chandler Harris and Thomas Nelson Page may have been lured by the sweet sounds they associated with the plantation South, and blackface minstrels like Thomas Rice and Dan Emmett may have been excited by the transgressive and energetic qualities they associated with black folklore, it would be unreasonable to expect that these entities would be able to "restore" to the public discourse the voices of African Americans.

In "Charles Chesnutt and the WPA Narratives," John Edgar Wideman argues that, from the colonial period through the late nineteenth century, the black voice in American literature was characterized as comic and childlike. He further contends, "[N]egro dialect . . . was a way of pointing to difference . . . [and] *difference* in the dialect tradition clearly signaled deficiency." Wideman asserts that Chesnutt chose not to avoid "incriminating dialect"; rather, he became a "major innovator" of another strategy: the framed narrative. Wideman explains that this tale-within-a-tale approach allows Chesnutt to blend "literary and oral traditions without implying that the black storyteller's mode of perceiving and recreating reality is any less valid than the written word. . . . Chesnutt's frame displays the written and spoken word on equal terms or at least as legitimate contenders for the reader's sympathy."[29]

Sandra Molyneaux, in her reading of Chesnutt's conjure tales, also argues that dialect-speaking caricatures have "stolen" the African American voice. Like Wideman, Molyneaux focuses on how Chesnutt's use of oral tradition recovers the African American voice by restoring dignity and purpose to black oral traditions and by revealing how orally transmitted traditions kept history alive and promoted social cohesion.[30]

While both Wideman and Molyneaux focus their readings on Chesnutt's use of black oral tradition, the role of conjure is of equal consequence. If the black voice was what needed to be freed from dominant cultural representations, then conjure was the vehicle through which Chesnutt sought to liberate it. Like black folklore generally, conjure constituted contested cultural terrain. As Yvonne Chireau explains in *Black Magic: Religion and the African American Conjuring Tradition*, "conjure practitioners, it is believed, were 'the most powerful and significant individuals on the plantation.'" Chireau further notes, "although accepted by some whites, conjuring traditions thrived within the slave quarters."[31] Within the quarters, conjure doctors were seen as powerful individuals to be both feared and respected. They had the power to confront domination by white slaveholders, protect runaways, keep couples from being separated, heal the sick, facilitate communication with the spirit world, intercede in interpersonal relationships, and inspire or thwart romances.[32] Even blacks and whites who disparaged conjure practices were often reluctant to disavow them altogether. In his seminal text *Slave Religion*, Albert Raboteau shares a story about Jacob Stroyer, who stated that, though he was skeptical of conjure practices, because "the majority of the people believed it" he was not willing to discount it entirely, as "they ought to know better than one man."[33]

In one of the most famous examples of the mysterious powers of conjure, Frederick Douglass, who similarly professed not to believe in conjuration, still engaged in its practices, accepting a "root" from Sandy, a well-known conjure man, that subsequently served to protect Douglass in his battle with Covey, his ruthless overseer. Many of the slavery and post-emancipation accounts of conjure stressed African origins. Douglass, William Wells Brown, and other informants from coastal Georgia and the Sea Islands variously described conjure doctors as "African-born," "pure-African," and/or "genuine African."[34] Raboteau explains: "the prevalence of the idea that conjure was African in origin and that Africans were especially powerful conjurers indicates that slaves thought of hoodoo as their own . . . separate tradition. Whites might be susceptible to conjure, but almost never were they conjurers."[35]

In the Reconstruction and post-Reconstruction years, conjure became a highly contested emblem in the debates over blacks' ability to assimilate or advance in post-slavery U.S. society. On one hand, Northern missionaries and educators, such as Samuel Armstrong, saw conjure as a remnant of slavery that would be stamped out in the face of proper education and religious instruction. Southerners, on the other hand, often stressed the resurgence of conjure practices and its innate connections with Africa as a way to argue that such ignorant and superstitious practices were held in check by slavery, but with emancipation former slaves had reverted back to primitive African ways. Among the black middle class, conjure was often seen as a symbol of outdated beliefs from which blacks must distance themselves in efforts to achieve middle-class respectability. Despite pressure on every side to disavow conjure as a relic of the past, conjure remained a potent force in the black community and perhaps more significantly, it became a powerful symbol of an alternative, often oppositional black cultural identity.

In his five-volume collection on hoodoo, Voodoo, and conjure, Harry Hyatt states, "To catch a spirit, or to protect your spirit against the catching, or to release your caught spirit—this is the complete theory and practice of hoodoo."[36] Documented repeatedly throughout the Hampton collection, the highly symbolic rituals of conjuration offered rural blacks (and occasionally whites) a way to influence aspects of their daily lives that otherwise seemed beyond rational control.[37] The conjure doctor was skilled at reading the traditional signs, and as he or she presided over the conjure rituals, his or her power to effect change was mirrored in his or her manipulation of symbolic icons. She or he was a master of verbal and nonverbal persuasion; by influencing a person's beliefs, he or she could influence an individual's health, behavior, or general well-being.

The methods of the conjure doctor varied from place to place, sometimes requiring the mixture of a potion, other times the ceremonial burying or digging up of bottles or roots. But more significant than any formula or incantation was the degree to which the parties involved were willing to place their faith in the power of the conjure doctor: "Never mind what you mix . . . it will be powerful or feeble in proportion to the dauntless spirit infused by you, the priest or priestess."[38] In one instance a patient reports seeking the assistance of a conjure doctor in finding a cause and remedy for her chills. After the doctor is paid for his services, the conjurer prepares a "walking boy," or a bottle in which the doctor surreptitiously places a living creature so that it will roll around on the floor, thereby directing the conjurer to the source of the chills. The patient explains that she knows the doctor has animated the bottle and that the ceremony is done to impress her, but she states, "[A]s I had good faith in the 'doctor,' the chills vanished."[39] As this example from the Hampton collection shows, conjure required a willingness to suspend disbelief and to accept the conjure ritual as constitutive of a symbolic rather than mimetic approach to reality.

For Chesnutt, conjure was an ideally suited medium through which to carry out his project of altering his audience's perceptions about race, while inspiring a sense of fairness and justice in his readers. In *Re-Situating Folklore*, Frank de Caro and Rosan Jordan explain that writers and artists can "re-situate" folklore into a literary or artistic context by "imitat[ing] or otherwise adapt[ing] not a particular text but the conventions that inform a series of related texts."[40] Conjure, as a process or event that is inherently participatory and serves as a basis for individual and collective transformation, offered stylistic conventions that were congenial to Chesnutt's project of presenting an alternative way of constructing, perceiving, and responding to reality. Thus, Chesnutt culls from the principles of conjure an aesthetic that recognized the value of dialogical interaction, that interpreted folklore as a process rather a static item, and that presented representational strategies as subjective rather than objective.

In each of *The Conjure Woman*'s seven interconnected tales, Chesnutt creates a framed narrative in which the first narrator, John, a white Northern businessman and entrepreneur, recounts observations gathered during his foray into Southern land speculation. During the course of each of the stories a second narrator, Uncle Julius, a black Southern "retainer" and Chesnutt's signifying allusion to Harris's Uncle Remus, takes over the narrative to relate to John and John's wife, Annie, a conjure tale set in the antebellum South. Through this narrative frame we learn that John's perspective is thoroughly circumscribed by the conventions of various fictions emerging from both the Plantation Tradition and the prominent folkloric and pseudoscientific discourses of the day. Although John is presented as the outsider, he continually assumes responsibility for representing this Southern rural community. John perceives himself to be an astute observer of the human species, but as the text reveals, his observations are colored by popular myths about the "ole plantation" and the objectifying frameworks through which he views Julius. While Julius frequently manipulates the minstrel mask to reveal the distinction between the mask and the man, John continually misses the point. Julius's minstrel performances, however satirical, only further confirm John's preexisting ideas about African Americans. While Chesnutt's characterization of Julius works to expose the various conventions that defined the parameters of African American identity in the postbellum era, John's continual inability to recognize Julius's performance suggests *The Conjure Woman* can be read as a meditation on the inherent dangers of donning the minstrel mask to challenge the minstrel tradition. Instead, Chesnutt tests a different literary strategy, incorporating conjure as a way to introduce an alternative worldview.

Prior to recounting the first of his seven conjure tales, Julius acknowledges that he does not expect Annie and John to believe his stories, explaining, "I would n' spec' fer you ter b'lieve me 'less you know all 'bout de fac's." As Janie, the protagonist of *Their Eyes Were Watching God*, explains to her friend Phoeby, "'[T]ain't no use in me telling you somethin' unless Ah give you de understandin' to go 'long wid it," Julius too realizes the need to provide a context for his audience before he can expect them to comprehend the meaning of his story.[41] In a conscious layering of symbols, Julius begins his conjure initiation of John and Annie with a tale about conjure's profound power to effect individual, communal, and social well-being. Julius knows the power of this ritual lies, in part, in his ability to give a convincing performance.[42] Therefore, Julius does not just tell the story, but instead seems to be "living over again in monologue his life on the old plantation." As Julius is taken back to the old days, he begins his tale by reaffirming popular constructions of the black folk, stating, "[E]f dey's an'thing a nigger lub, nex' ter 'possum, en chick'n en watermillyums, it's scuppernon's." This early description echoes the images of blacks prevalent on the minstrel stage. Julius uses these images to capture his audience's attention, and by first confirming their expectations, he lowers their resistance to the rest of his story.

The first story, "The Goophered Grapevine," is one of the most frequently analyzed and anthologized of all Chesnutt's short fiction. Chesnutt states that the origin of the story was a folk tale he had heard from his father-in-law's gardener, and in 1895 the Hampton Folklore Society documented a folk belief that, like "The Goophered Grapevine," tied a man's physical attributes to the vitality of a grapevine.[43] As promised, in this opening story Julius imparts the history of the plantation to the newcomers. The old ex-slave's history, however, conforms to popular myths of the "ole South" at only the most superficial levels. In *To Wake the Nations* Eric Sundquist asserts that, through conjure and storytelling, Julius brings "'de old times' of slavery forward into the post–Civil War present and splinter[s] the prevailing structure of plantation mythology."[44] The story Julius tells disrupts the myth of the benevolent plantation owner and posits Julius's combination of "memory" and "imagination" as valid sources for an alternative history of life on the plantation, a history that exposes the greed and exploitation that drove an insatiable desire for higher rates of return and increased profits on the part of both Southern slaveholders as well as Northern entrepreneurs.

By including references that parallel the current circumstances, Julius also makes clear that his story is not a history that can be neatly contained in the past. Julius creates the Northern Yankee in "The Goophered Grapevine" to represent John, and he hopes that John will learn from the destruction that the Northern Yankee brought to the plantation and decide not to buy the land. As John tells us, however, he "bought the vineyard, nevertheless, and it has been for a long time in a thriving condition, and is often referred to by the local press as a striking illustration of the opportunities open to Northern capital in the development of Southern industries."[45] John later learns that Julius too had generated "respectable revenue" from cultivating the neglected vines, and John guesses that perhaps Julius's story was intended to dissuade John from purchasing the vineyard. While John is able to glean the most overt motive for Julius's story, he misses the more subtle commentary on the ills of exploitation. For just as the slave master in the conjure tale reaped an inordinate return on his "investments," John hires Julius and assumes that Julius's employment as a coachman more than compensates for Julius's loss of the vineyard.

Though Julius is unable to accomplish his primary objective of thwarting John's purchase of the plantation, he exerts a least a semblance of control over his current circumstances by securing employment with John, and in this way he can continue "conjuring" Annie and John. In fact, Annie's response betrays the first sign that Julius's conjure may be working and that he may be able to effect a change in her perceptions. For as Julius tells us, when he concluded the story Annie "doubtfully, but seriously," inquired whether or not the story was true.

By the introduction of the second story, Julius has surreptitiously taken on the role of guide and, as such, assumes responsibility for introducing Annie and John to the new and unfamiliar terrain. In the second tale in the collection, Julius relates the heart-wrenching story of Sandy, a fieldhand whom Mars Marrabo lends out to several of the neighboring plantations. While Sandy is being "lent out," his wife is sold to a speculator. When Sandy eventually takes up with a new wife, he resolves not to be lent out again. Driven by the experiences of being lent out and the fear of being separated from his family, Sandy implores his new wife Tenie, who is also a conjure woman, to turn him into a tree so that he will not be sent away from her again. She complies, but even this desperate act does not free Sandy and Tenie from hardship. When Marrabo decides to build a new kitchen, he sends his men to chop down the large pine tree, which, of course, turns out to be the tree into which Sandy has been transformed. The wood is then used to build Marrabo's new kitchen, but the kitchen is eventually torn down and the wood from the kitchen is used to build the very schoolhouse that John and Annie are considering tearing down to build their new kitchen. Julius explains that Tenie was so overcome when she discovered the tree had been cut down that she spent her final days closed up in the schoolhouse, grieving the loss of her husband, and eventually died of a broken heart.

John's wife Annie responds to the extreme actions that individuals were driven to take in order to preserve their families during slavery, exclaiming, "What a system it was . . . under which such things were possible. . . . Poor Tenie!" Annie, whom John describes as being "of a very sympathetic turn of mind," is receptive to the affective nature of the stories and sympathizes with Tenie as a woman, a wife, and a person. John, to the contrary, is stuck questioning the impossibility of a man being turned into a tree, and "in amazement," asks his wife, "[A]re you seriously considering the possibility of a man's being turned into a tree?" Later John continues questioning his wife's credulity, half-asking, half-stating, "You would n't [*sic*] for a moment allow yourself . . . to be influenced by that absurdly impossible yarn which Julius was spinning to-day?"[46] As the frame of the narrative reveals, John possesses the type of abstract reasoning Cooper critiques in "The Negro as Presented in Literature," in which she argues that "it is only when we ourselves are out of tune through our pretentiousness and self-sufficiency, or are blinded and rendered insensate by reason of our foreign and unnatural 'civilization' that we miss her [nature's] meanings and inadequately construe her multiform lessons."[47] John's rational and literal belief system requires a verifiable and concrete representation of the past. His mode of understanding remains on the logical and unemotional plane of reason, and it inhibits him from sympathizing with the characters in the tale or from seeing how Julius's story might provide him with the "truth" of the plantation past and the reality of the present moment.

Julius's conjure does, however, succeed on two levels. First, as we come to find out, Julius's object was to forestall the destruction of the schoolhouse so that he could use it for his church meetings. Not surprisingly, Annie decides that she is no longer interested in using the wood from the school but prefers her kitchen be built from all new lumber. Thus Julius is able to save his church's meeting place. Second, Annie has become a willing initiate. She has agreed to suspend disbelief and accept Julius's stories as symbols that point to a deeper reality—a reality that cannot be expressed mimetically, but that must be apprehended through the interpretation of symbols and metaphors. As Robert Hemenway argues, the key to understanding the relationship between the characters "is not the trickster scheme, since Julius's tricks are often transparent, but . . . their [the characters'] attitudes toward the folk belief of 'conjure.'"[48] Through Annie's willingness to participate in the conjure ritual, Julius is able to introduce her to a new understanding of the past and thereby convince her to adopt a different course of action in the present.

At the beginning of the third story, John continues to employ his ethnographic lens as a way to understand Julius. He observes that Julius displays a deft familiarity with everything related to the history and care of the land John has recently acquired. Again, however, he misconstrues the nature of Julius's knowledge and familiarity, suggesting that Julius's "simplicity" accounts for his understanding of the vast topography and that his habit of considering himself the "property" of another accounts for his personal attachment to the land. In his assessments of Julius, John has proven that his impressions are unreliable. Nevertheless, John continues to evaluate Julius and the plantation environment with such cool self-assurance, and is so thoroughly invested in his own perceptions, that he presents his observations as though they were undisputed facts. In yet another brilliant layering of narrative perspective, Chesnutt's characterization of John allows the reader to view John as the unaware observer; thus Chesnutt resituates the folkloric lens to consider not just Julius's customs and habits, but to also reveal the customs, traditions, and practices that permeated dominant white cultural groups and were also used to maintain racially based separation and hierarchy. "Mars Jeems' Nightmare" pointedly illustrates how the stereotypes that worked to assign certain racialized characteristics to blacks were, in large part, a by-product of the popular white imagination, thereby exposing the degree to which the white imagination was implicated in popular constructions of the black folk.

In framing the story, John explains that he "discharges" Julius's nephew Tom because of his "laziness, his carelessness, and his apparent lack of any sense of responsibility."[49] As readers we have already been taught that John's perceptions are not only unreliable but that they are structured by the popular stereotypes of blacks. John judges Tom on the basis of his unreliable impressions and draws a stereotype from the Lost Cause tradition to characterize Tom as lazy and shiftless. As the frame of the story reveals, Tom has not been dealt with fairly. While Julius cannot make John switch places with Tom, he can teach John the meaning of the folk saying, "[I]t's best not to judge a man until you've walked a mile in his shoes." Julius then imparts to John and John's wife Annie a tale about Mars Jeems, a plantation owner who works his slaves so mercilessly that the slaves appeal to Aunt Peggy to "wuk her roots" on him. Aunt Peggy prepares a powerful conjure mixture that induces Jeems to have "a bad dream" in which he becomes a slave and is made to experience firsthand the brutality and humiliation of slavery.[50]

As Eric Sundquist explains: "[I]n the momentary imaginative space of this story, Mars Jeems is made a slave. Whipped and brutalized in recompense for the history of his own plantation brutality . . . Mars Jeems' nightmare . . . is a recapitulation of both the physical and cultural denigrations of slavery."[51] In one particularly telling scene, the overseer encounters the transformed Mars Jeems. Put off by what he perceives as the new slave's uppity mannerisms, the overseer insists that the new slave call himself Sambo. In this scene, Chesnutt implies that the caricature of the pretentious slave putting on airs is really the product of a performance by the Southern landowner. The overseer, however, insists that the new slave perform the role not of the uppity negro, but of the docile and submissive Sambo, representing yet another stereotypic black identity, one created and enforced by the overseer. This scene reveals the degree to which the stereotypes of the black folk were not rooted in reality, but instead were products of a racist system meant to limit the scope of African American representation. As a result of what is interpreted as his insolent behavior, the new slave suffers the humiliation of being whipped and sold without any mode of recourse—a not-so-subtle mirroring of John's decision to fire Tom. When Mars Jeems is finally turned back into the plantation owner, his harsh attitude toward the slaves has softened. Julius punctuates the tale with an explicit statement of the moral: white folks who are strict and hard are liable to have bad dreams, but those who are kind and good are sure to prosper in the world. Again, having figured things out, John sarcastically remarks that the moral of the story is obvious and declares, "I am glad, too, that you told us the moral of the story; it might have escaped us otherwise."[52]

At the end of Julius's tale it is John's wife Annie, not John, who rehires Tom. She has understood the meaning of the tale, and increasingly, Julius and Annie form an "in" community based on their shared knowledge and understanding of the stories' deeper meanings. John's literal and rational approach bars him from participation in Julius's and Annie's more subtle and emotive community, and his know-it-all attitude makes his ineptness at gleaning the inner meanings of the various situations all the more comical. Chesnutt transforms a stereotypical image from the minstrel stage that characterized blacks as utilizing elaborate rhetoric without understanding the meaning and implications of their own words. Increasingly, John, not

Julius, becomes the comic figure; John's boisterous professions only further reveal his own ignorance of the subtleties that characterize each situation. In an ingenious twist of characterization, the real minstrel figure in the stories turns out to be John, not Julius.

Through "Mars Jeem's Nightmare," Chesnutt exposes the constructs that were used to characterize Julius, and blacks in general, during the post-Reconstruction era. He critiques the degree to which authority for representing the black folk and black folk culture had been co-opted by white "outsiders" and, through his characterization of John as an entrepreneur, reveals the white Northerner's investment in these constructs. Just as Thomas D. Rice's Jim Crow performances were not a true delineation of black folk life but instead a product of the Irish immigrant's imagination, so Julius turns out to be a plantation type only in the limited perspective of the Northern industrial capitalist.

At this point in *The Conjure Woman*, Chesnutt has posited memory as an alternative source for plantation history; established the various aspects of conjuration as powerful elements of his literary strategy; and exposed the more insidious mechanisms at work in post-Reconstruction racialized discourse. As Sandra Molyneaux argues, "[E]ach story both responds to the preceding and anticipates the next, and the whole moves forward in a recursive pattern that gathers the chaotic past into a hopeful future."[53] While I would qualify Molyneaux's assertion about a "hopeful future," I agree that the tales, taken as a whole, form a ritual performance in which the characters have a chance to learn from and apply what was presented in the previous tale to their future situations. The next story, "The Conjurer's Revenge," does just that, giving John and Annie further opportunities to grasp the lesson that Julius is trying to teach them.

"The Conjurer's Revenge" is probably the least appreciated of *The Conjure Woman* stories. Many critics argue that this tale represents a lapse in Julius's character, securing only his individual needs and failing to address the needs of the larger community. Karen Beardslee contends that it is the one story where Julius is out for his own self interest: "Julius has made known another side of himself—the shrewd, self-serving side." Arlene Elder comments that the tale relies on "trickery to accomplish a totally material gain," and she concludes that "Julius momentarily loses his identity for cheapening his art." William Andrews views "The Conjurer's Revenge" as an "aesthetic failure," because Julius fails to reach his white audience.[54] I argue, however, that this tale can be considered a "doubling back" in the ritual performance—a necessary review of lessons John has still not learned.

In this story, Chesnutt pits opposing forms of knowledge against each other. When John decides he wants to buy a mule, Julius tells him a story about Primus, a slave who had been turned into a mule by a conjure doctor who mistakenly believes Primus stole his shirt. Realizing his mistake, the conjurer, in his dying breath, attempts a ritual to transform Primus back into a human. With the exception of Primus's foot, which remains a mule's hoof, the conjure is successful. Julius concludes the tale with a nonchalant recommendation that John not carry out his plan to buy the mule, since Julius could not bear to drive what could be one of his transformed relations. Instead, Julius notes that there is a worthy horse for sale in town. After making his inspection of the horse and negotiating down the price, John decides to buy the horse. "But alas for the deceitfulness of appearances," John exclaims when the horse dies a short time later. John is again dismayed when he notices Julius wearing a new suit of clothes "that very next Sunday" and surmises that Julius and the horse salesman were in cahoots on the sale.

This tale is significant because it shows, as John exclaims, the "deceitfulness of appearances." In the concluding frame of the tale, Julius explains that he is "tellin' nuffin but de truf," and even though he did not see the conjurer perform this transformation, he knows that the story is true because he "be'n hearin de tale fer twenty-five yeahs."[55] Julius is trying to teach John that oral tradition often conveys "truths" not contained in standard histories or obvious appearances. The lesson that John still needs to learn is that what he reads in his "missionary reports" and what he sees with his own two eyes do not necessarily bring him closer to the truth. Assuming the role of conjurer, Julius tries to change the way John perceives the world. While Julius secures material gains through the telling of the tale, he does so not out of selfishness but instead to reach John where he would seem to be most vulnerable, his wallet.

In "Sis' Becky's Pickaninny" Julius gives John a chance to put into action the lessons he has learned about the "deceitfulness of appearances." In the tale, Kunnel Pen'leton trades a slave mother, Becky, away from her child to acquire a race horse. Kunnel alleges, "Well, I doan lack ter, but I reckon I'll haf ter."[56] Then, under the guise of protecting Becky's feelings, he tricks her into leaving her son behind so that he does not have to witness the painful breakup. Aunt Peggy eventually intervenes and turns Becky's son into a mockingbird so that he can visit his mother and whistle songs to comfort her. After several painful years, Becky and her son are reunited, and the conjure woman lifts the spell so that they can live out their days together. Not surprisingly, the concluding frame reveals John still unable to see beyond the surface of the tales. John again assumes his role as privileged observer, offering a precise explanation of the function of the rabbit's foot and the value it holds for slaves and free blacks. But again, John's sense of having "figured things out" leaves him blinded to the item's deeper meaning; he concludes, "your people will never rise until they throw off these childish superstitions and learn to live by the light of reason and common sense."

Alternately, we learn that Annie, who has been in ill health, finds the story satisfying. She responds to her husband's disbelief, "'[T]he story bears the stamp of truth, if ever a story did.'"[57] In the concluding frame, Annie and Julius begin working in concert. When John persists in questioning the role of the rabbit's foot, which was conspicuously absent from Julius's tale, Julius refers John to Annie, "I bet young missis dere kin 'splain it herse'f." Annie obliges, "I rather suspect . . . that Sis' Becky had no rabbit's foot," and Julius concludes, "Ef Sis' Becky had had a rabbit foot, she nebber would 'a' went th'oo all dis trouble."[58] The final scene of the story reveals that Annie has taken Julius's rabbit foot into her possession, and from that day forward, her physical condition begins to improve. Annie has allowed herself to undergo the conjure ritual, and it restores her to health. The conjure works on Annie because she is willing to believe in it. Her attitude toward black folklore has been changed, and she and Julius, if not friends, have developed a relationship based on mutual respect.[59] In contrast to "The Conjurer's Revenge," "Sis' Becky's Pickaninny" models the type of audience reception Chesnutt hoped to achieve with his readers. Chesnutt employs conjure as a literary device to mediate relations between his characters and as a vehicle for their change—the characters' transformations serving as a metonymy for the larger transformations Chesnutt hoped to produce within his audience.

Following the second-to-last story, "The Gray Wolf's Ha'nt," *The Conjure Woman* culminates with "Hot-Foot Hannibal." In the concluding tale, Chesnutt reiterates several of the themes treated in the previous stories. As with all the preceding stories, Julius's tale is meant to influence the ideas and actions of the white characters in the narrative frame. "Hot-Foot Hannibal," for instance, relates the courtship woes of a young white couple. Mabel, Annie's sister from the North, and Malcolm, a younger Southern "gentleman," have placed their impending union in jeopardy by succumbing to petty games and jealous rivalries. Julius, therefore, shares a conjure tale about a love triangle that ends in disaster for a young slave couple.

In the conjure tale, Hannibal, a conniving plantation hand, tries to lure a young slave girl named Chloe away from her beau, Jeff. By creating a tar baby–like decoy, Hannibal convinces Chloe that Jeff has been unfaithful. Although the story speaks to the recurring theme of not being able to rely solely on what an individual perceives with his/her eyes, it also comments on the capricious couple's lack of respect for the power of the black folk customs they attempt to employ. While they obtain a charm from Aunt Peggy that puts a hex on Hannibal, once the conjure is successful they forget to return to charm to Aunt Peggy as instructed. Additionally, Chloe commits another fatal faux pas by appealing to the slave master's system to redress a community wrong. When Chloe discovers what she believes to be Jeff's infidelity, she reports him to the slave master and sets in motion a series of events that leads to Jeff's being sold downriver and his eventual suicide.

Throughout the story, Chloe has the chance to utilize the power of black folk traditions, both in the form of conjure and by reading the cultural signs. The well-known tar baby folk tale should have reminded her about the "deceitfulness of appearances" and warned her about the prevalence of trickery and the power of illusion. But Chloe is a "jealous" woman who turns not to the power of black folk tradition, but to the slave master's system, a system predicated on the denial of her freedom and humanity. As with all of Julius's stories, the conjure tale relates an incident from the past to provide commentary on a current situation. In the concluding narrative frame, Mabel has learned from Chloe's hardships and she decides to put aside her jealousy and reunite with Malcolm. When the young couple offers to take Julius on as their new coachman, Julius declines, and instead decides to remain with Annie and John.

Critics generally read this story as a reflection of Julius's selflessness in uniting the young white couple and his willingness to stay with Annie and John. Molyneaux, for instance, argues that Julius "contents" himself to stay on with Annie and John, continuing to try to effect a change in their perceptions. Peter Caccavari proffers a more sentimental reading, suggesting that the tale is about Julius's ability "to sympathize with a white Southerner and to see the love of white couples to be the same as that of black couples."[60] Instead, I view the last tale as the culmination of a ritual developed through Julius's progression of tales, each one building upon the previous until the final story ends with the reunion of the North and the South at the expense of the slave past. While Annie's potential for change saves *The Conjure Woman* from the more pessimistic ending of a naturalist-informed text, like *The Sport of the Gods*, and it is true that "Hot-Foot Hannibal" is the only conjure tale that leaves unclear what Julius's motives are or what he has to gain, the final tale, more than anything, provides Chesnutt's closing commentary on the deteriorating racial conditions for African Americans in the post-Reconstruction South. In "The Ethics of the Negro Question," Anna Julia Cooper writes that

"Northern capital is newly wed to Southern industry and the honeymoon must not be disturbed . . . [and] the negro is being ground to powder between the upper and the nether millstones."[61] Chesnutt's final story illustrates this point, for while the young white couple may be happily married and building a life together in their new Southern home, Julius's conjure tales continue to haunt the landscape. Stories of broken homes, broken black bodies, slave mothers separated from their children, lost loved ones, suicide, trauma, pain, and desperation form an ominous backdrop for the white couple's amiable reunion. Mixed with an old storyteller-conjurer's weary humor, the tales, taken as a whole, embody the age-old blues adage "laughing to keep from crying."

In each story, Chesnutt employs black folklore to expose the many intertwined literary, cultural, and pseudoscientific conventions that set the parameters of black representation, but he also goes beyond simply exposing the politics of cultural representation. In *Chesnutt and Realism*, Ryan Simmons asserts that central to Chesnutt's literary work is "the conviction that understanding reality rightly requires action; no one who truly saw reality for what it was could stand by and do nothing."[62] Chesnutt engages in narrative experimentation, creating a conjure aesthetic to explore how he might persuade his audience to understand and respond to the racial situation differently. Thus Annie's decision to act completes Julius's conjure ritual and models for Chesnutt's readers the proper response to what he hopes will be their new understanding of American racial realities.

While *The Conjure Woman* may constitute Chesnutt's more optimistic statement about the power of folklore, properly perceived, to effect change, in *The Colonel's Dream* Chesnutt explores the strictures that inhibit the adoption of new perspectives. In "Who Has the Right to Say? Charles Chesnutt, Whiteness and the Public Sphere," Matthew Wilson argues that Chesnutt increasingly came "to realize that right reason would have no effect whatsoever on American racism, that the ideology of whiteness was the fundamental problem in trying to ameliorate American racism."[63] While Chesnutt had already started experimenting in *The Conjure Woman* with exposing the role of John's objectifying gaze in constructing representations of the "other," it is in his 1905 novel, *The Colonel's Dream*, that Chesnutt turns his full literary attention to explicating ideologies of whiteness as a means of revealing the performances of race that kept African Americans in a subservient position in the post-Reconstruction years. Though not as frequently or overtly associated with folklore as *The Conjure Woman*, Chesnutt, in *The Colonel's Dream*, not only exposes the conventions emerging from folklore studies and the new social-scientific way of perceiving and representing African American folk and folklore, but also shows what was at stake in the perpetuation of these conventions and reveals how they could underlie a seemingly progressive, liberal reform agenda. Chesnutt identifies the fictions that asserted black inferiority and dictated racial separation as a kind of white folklore of race, and in *The Colonel's Dream* he works to expose the interrelationship between constructions of race, the anti-modern romanticism latent in the formation of folklore studies, Plantation Tradition mythology, and turn–of-the-century revival of medieval romance. By turning his literary lens on what could be considered white forms of folklore and the discourses that constructed whiteness, Chesnutt, in his last published novel, attempts to make his white readers aware of the ways in which their own folklore informed and was informed by the various racialized discourses of the period.

In *The Colonel's Dream*, Henry French, a former officer in the Confederate army, has relocated to New York following the Civil War. After ten years of building a profitable bagging firm, French and his partner sell off the firm, securing a sizeable profit. Though a staunch believer in the principles that enabled his profitable ventures in New York, a life dictated by reason, hard business sense, disciplined investing, and calculated risk—in other words, a life dictated by the mechanical and unforgiving rhythms of modernity—has taken its toll on French. As the business deal is consummated, French collapses. At the counsel of his physician, French, a widower, decides to return south with his son Phil to their ancestral abode. Though a Southerner by birth, French must reconcile the progressive, modern, "enlightenment" ideas he has acquired in the North with the realities of the antebellum past and postbellum present. By invoking the ideals embodied in the medieval romance and by resuscitating the myths associated with the Plantation Tradition, French is able to bring his enlightenment ideology with him to Clarendon and begin his project of instilling his progressive agenda in his new Southern locale. In her discussion of childhood, chivalric order, and the medieval romance, Jeanne Fox-Friedman explains that in late-nineteenth-century America, "modern society believed medieval men and women to be free of the artifice and over-refinement that they saw as plaguing contemporary society." As Fox-Friedman notes, however, "This medievalism . . . was no mere sentimental refuge from the perceived evils of modernity; rather, the robust nature of medieval life was to be the instrument by which modern America would re-energize its quest for progress."[64]

When French first arrives in Clarendon, he hears a young untrained "coloured girl" singing lyrics from Michael William Balfe's popular 1843 opera,

The Bohemian Girl. Repeated at various intervals throughout the novel, the lyrics "I dreamt that I dwelt in marble halls / With vassals and serfs at my side" create a running refrain. As the ethereal lyrics tell us, Colonel French's dream of a New South is really a return to an imaginary old South reconfigured through enlightenment reason, plantation mythology, and medieval romance. His new world vision requires the just and reasonable rule of a gracious master, the reign of right reason, and benevolent motives. Even more to the point, it requires a status quo in which some are willing and happy serfs and vassals, while others are gracious and loved kings and queens. Chesnutt, however, underscores the degree to which the Colonel's dream is enabled by an active forgetting of the realities of the antebellum South. French, we are told, views the land of his childhood "through the golden haze of memory."[65] His faded remembrances and nostalgic recollections allow him to relish the South as an ahistorical utopia where things are simpler, where a man can still be a hero, a woman saved, and a villain vanquished; where reason prevails and all functions efficiently and profitably. It is only through his insistent forgetting of the realities of the antebellum South, facilitated by the myths of the "ole plantation," that French is able to blindly impose his progressive, enlightenment version of the medieval romance on the denizens of this Southern locale.

In the first half of the narrative French dwells in cemeteries, lingers at family gravesites, and muses over headstones and monuments. When he encounters Peter, his family's former house slave, pruning the branches away from the French family plots, he is delighted to have found a living relic to serve as witness to his family's former glory. When French meets Laura, an old family friend, they stroll along with Peter "following the party at a respectful distance." As Laura, French, and French's son, Phil, cross a bridge into an enchanting knoll, Peter, "seeing himself forgotten, . . . walked past the gate . . . and went, somewhat disconsolately, on his way."[66] For French, his edenic antebellum past is momentarily realized. As French sallies forth into the garden of his plantation dreams, however, Peter, unbeknownst to the Colonel, is rounded up to serve in the convict labor system—Peter's forced enslavement an aspect of the new South French deigns not to notice.

The following day, when French is finally confronted by Peter's situation, he buys Peter's time, and in effect restores the master/slave relationship. Later in the day, when he learns that Nicholas, a "mulatto" barber who has done quite well for himself, has purchased and is living in the French family mansion, he buys back his former home as well. French enacts what T. J. Jackson Lears identifies as an antimodern quest to embrace "premodern symbols" and in turn adapt those symbols for modern ends. As Lears explains, antimodern seekers "longed to rekindle possibilities for authentic experience, physical or spiritual—possibilities they felt had existed once before, long ago."[67] French, in effect, is attempting to restore/create the antebellum South of his imagination by repossessing symbols of the past to ease his own modern anxieties; the authenticity, vigor, and vitality he associates with the past serve as a panacea for the sterile and inauthentic present. Indeed, French does not want anything to disrupt his fantasy. When Laura's niece Graciella and her friends begin belting out the "latest New York 'coon songs,'" French's dream is disturbed. The narrator reports, "[I]t was the first discordant note," and French reasons silently, "In a metropolitan music hall, gaudily bedecked and brilliantly lighted, it would have been tolerable from the lips of a black-face comedian," or, he surmises, "a plantation song of olden times . . . would have been more pleasing."[68] Later in the novel French charges Peter with hunting down a "real" ole time fiddler for his housewarming party, one whose performances will be consistent with the authentic antebellum experiences French expects from the South. Through these various musical references, Chesnutt unveils the degree to which French's ideas about authenticity are determined by the degree to which the performances conform to his plantation fantasies.

In discussing the antimodern turn and the development of folklore studies, Roger Abrahams explains that modern Americans ". . . had come to feel alienated from a society committed to mechanizing and rationalizing all aspects of life. As counterpoints to this modernism, they idealized earlier epochs (the Middle Ages in particular) and simpler societies (such as that of the American Indian). All these they saw as times and cultures exhibiting more energy and imagination and encouraging a wider range of vigorous experiences."[69] Abrahams notes as emblematic of this turn that American Folklore Society founder William Wells Newell and the society's first president, Francis James Child, both exhibited intense interest in recovering medieval culture as part of their folklore projects. Thus this valorizing of an earlier time and romanticizing of simpler people was one of the driving impulses in the development of early folklore studies. French shares these characteristics with the founding practitioners of earlier American folklore studies, and one can read in *The Colonel's Dream* a critique of this impulse to collect the supposed authentic survivals of an idealized past.

At exactly the midpoint of the novel, just as French begins to shift from dwelling in memories of the past to attempting to reform the present, Peter takes control of the narrative, to tell a tale about "de Black Cat an' de Ha'nted House." The tale is intended to teach French's son Phil about the power of black folk culture, and the story serves the larger purpose in the narrative of sounding a warning against dwelling in an idealized and self-created past. While fishing, Peter and Phil notice a black cat. Peter suggests that they find a new spot, commenting, "She'll be comin' down heah terreckly tellin' us ter gho 'way fum her fishin' ground's.'" Phil, however, protests, noting, "[C]ats can't talk!" At this point, Chesnutt allows Peter to shift his minstrel mask: "'Law,' honey,' said the old man, with a sly twinkle in his rheumy eye, 'you is de sma'tes' little white boy I ever knowed, but you is got a monst'us heap ter l'arn yit, chile.'"[70] Peter then commences to tell Phil about a black man named Jeff who accepts a deal with Mistah Sellers to spend one night in a haunted house in exchange for one dollar up front and four more in the morning. Jeff fares well until he is awoken around eleven o'clock in the evening, and notices a black cat sitting up on the table:

> "Jeff look' at de black cat, an' de black cat look' at Jeff. Den de black cat open his mouf . . . an' sezee—"
>
> "'Good evenin'!'"
>
> "'Good evenin' suh,' 'spon' Jeff, trimblin' in de knees, an' kind'er edgin' 'way fum de table."
>
> "'Dey ain' nobody hyuh but you an' me, is dey?' sez de black cat, winkin' one eye."
>
> "'No, suh,' sez Jeff, as he made fer de do', '*an' quick ez I kin git out er hyuh, dey ain' gwine ter be nobody hyuh but you!*'"

When Peter concludes the tale with a chuckle, Phil reveals that he has missed the humor, and the coded meaning, of the story:

> "Is that all, Uncle Peter?" asked Phil.
>
> "Huh?"
>
> "Is that all?"
>
> "No, dey's mo' er de tale, but dat's ernuff ter prove that black cats kin do mo' dan little w'ite boys 'low dey kin."

When Phil persists in asking why Jeff did not remain to talk to the cat, noting that he would like the chance to talk with a black cat, Peter responds in disbelief, "Whoever heared er sich a queshtun! He didn' wan' ter talk wid no black cat, 'ca'se he wuz skeered. Black cats bring 'nuff bad luck w'en dey doan' talk, let 'lone w'en dey does. . . . Keep away f'm 'em, chile, keep away f'm 'em. Dey is some things too deep fer little boys ter projec' wid, an' black cats is one of 'em."[71]

Phil, of course, misses the warning in Peter's story, and instead, naïvely clings to his desire to engage this powerful emblem of black folk culture. Despite the twinkle in Peter's eye and the mischievous wink of the cat's eye, Phil, like his father, misreads Peter's performance as an example of quaint bygone days, rather than as a warning that it is dangerous to occupy houses haunted by ghosts, even if those ghosts are products of their own imagined past.

After underscoring the power of black folk culture, Chesnutt gives us a view into two sets of conflicting customs; those of French, the paternalistic aristocrat, and of Fetters, the former overseer turned ruthless landowner. In French we see a man trying to reconstruct the sentimental, surface-level customs he associates with his plantation life: the titles, the etiquette, the dress, the dinners, the dances that are all ways for him to recapture the authentic, simpler, more honorable life he believes to be embodied in these re-collected antiquities. Fetters, on the other hand, abides by a different set of Southern customs: the unspoken rules of race relations that keep blacks in subservient position and where racism and white supremacy trump progressive ideals of collective uplift. It is through his interactions with Fetters that the Colonel learns there are customs that run deeper than the superficial titles and dining etiquette he reveres, customs that govern race relations and are more deeply ingrained than any law and not beholden to his chivalric code. Chesnutt, however, exposes French's retreat into the customs and traditions of a supposed simpler, nobler era as part of the white folklore that allows the less savory customs and traditions dictating racial relations in the New South to persist.

In the second half of the narrative, French undertakes a series of missteps that reveal not only how naïve he is regarding the realities of Southern race relations, but also how his supposed ignorance of the racial realities is, in fact, complicit in perpetuating racial oppression and violence. Like his son, French, too, is unable to heed the warnings of those around him, and in turn he receives a gruesome initiation in the customary politics of postbellum race relations in the New South. French's medieval romance, for instance, is exposed as a biased, non- egalitarian system in which the select few impose their righteous will on their benighted subjects and display true courtesy only toward those within their charmed circle, while the rest are disregarded or subjugated. Chesnutt rereads and rewrites chivalry as chauvinism, recognizing, as Cooper had articulated years earlier, that ". . . the much lauded chivalry of the Middle Ages meant what I fear it still means to some men in our own day—respect for the elect few among whom they expect to consort."[72]

As Dean McWilliams points out, when a close friend of the French family, a fellow white man, is in trouble, French sells out Bud Johnson, a militant black man who has been a victim of the convict labor system and is facing certain lynching for his fatal retaliation against his captors. McWilliams explains that French somehow fails to realize that his white friend will have a better chance of securing a fair trial than will Bud Johnson, and hence he is unable to understand why Fetters will not acquiesce to his honor-based appeals for Bud's release.[73]

After Peter dies trying to save Phil, who falls in harm's way as he pursues a black cat across the path of an oncoming train, French assumes that his son's sentimental attachment to Peter will justify crossing the most final of color lines. He believes that he can bury Peter alongside Phil in the white cemetery. He is mistaken. As we have already been told, the men in the town wanted "no part nor parcel" in French's "sentimental folly."[74] When the town digs up Peter's body and lays it at French's doorstep, the colonel retreats. Confronted with the intractability of racism in the New South, French retires his progressive agenda and returns to New York.[75] French's constant misreading of the New South's emotional landscape suggests not only the degree to which his plantation mythology, his medieval romance, and his enlightenment reason are inadequate in addressing the racism and prejudice in the New South, but also indicates, as Charles Mills explains through what he terms an "epistemology of ignorance," that French does not understand his own role in creating the social system he comes to detest. Mills explains: ". . . *on matters related to race, the Racial Contract prescribes for its signatories an inverted epistemology, an epistemology of ignorance, a particular pattern of localized and global cognitive dysfunction . . . producing the ironic outcome that whites will in general be unable to understand the world they themselves have made.*"[76] French seems to understand not at all that the prejudice, racial hierarchy, and class antagonism that stymie his attempts at liberal reform in the South are products of his own—and his plantation aristocracy ancestors'—making.

In *The Colonel's Dream*, Chesnutt turns his attention to exposing folklore as an operative component in constructing the fictions of race. His text engages the impulses underlying, at least in part, the institutionalization of the study of folklore and, like Dunbar, he refocuses attention on the degree to which representations of African American folklore are informed by various dominant cultural discourses. Furthermore, I assert that in *The Colonel's Dream*, Chesnutt does something quite extraordinary by turning his literary and ethnographic gaze on unveiling white forms of folklore, including both the conscious enactments of idealized customs and traditions associated with the myth of the Ole South and the less romanticized, but perhaps more deeply entrenched, customs and traditions that dictated race relations in the New South. Thus, *The Colonel's Dream* stands as a stunning achievement, showcasing the complex ways African American writers engaged the increasingly restrictive "regimes of representation" that worked to construct, maintain, and perpetuate the system of racial difference that took root during the inaugural years of Jim Crow segregation.

Conclusion

By repositioning African American folklore and literary projects in relation to each other, I have shown how both undertakings sought to push beyond the bounds of the dominant popular and scientific discourses. Although disparate in their ideologies and approaches, the intersecting interests and activities of the Hampton folklorists and black intellectuals and cultural workers resulted in experimentation with various forms and strategies. The literary and ethnographic innovations that grew out of this joint engagement centered on excavating what had become ingrained, and often naturalized, protocols for depicting African American culture. In enacting this aesthetic, these folklorists and authors dislocated black folklore from the expected paradigms that had come to define popular and scientific approaches. They brought attention to the role black folklore played in the politics of racial representation, both problematizing idealized, romanticized, and/or caricatured notions of black folklore and challenging the decontextualized amassing of folkloric artifacts and materials.

Unwilling to throw the baby out with the bath water, however, they recontextualized folklore, situating it between a dual gesture of validating the hidden, communal, and/or oppositional meaning of black folklore while drawing attention to the racialized politics of authenticity that threatened to reduce and essentialize black cultural representations. They introduced an alternative epistemology that emphasized a dynamic, contextual, process-oriented approach to black folklore; highlighted the role of memory and imaginative recreation over a vaunted, but unattainable objectivity; and, through Chesnutt in particular, they turned the folkloric lens on white customs and traditions, revealing the folklore, myths, and legends that sustained a white supremacist power structure in both the South and the North. In sum, these authors and folklorists realized that popular, literary, and ethnographic representations of black folklore were intimately tied to larger racial politics, and that it was not enough simply to present different images—they also had to present an alternative way of seeing and interpreting black folklore. Thus they drew attention to the constructions of folklore and race without relinquishing the vital histories and perspectives embodied in African American folklore. The approach they enacted in the late nineteenth century anticipated an alternative, oppositional black folk aesthetic characterizing a number of African American literary and folkloric works produced throughout the twentieth century and into the twenty-first.

Zora Neale Hurston most overtly engaged the politics of folklore and the constructions of racial representation as she sought to negotiate the position of author, "folk informant," folklorist, and ethnographer. Her unconventional approach to collecting and documenting folklore put her at odds with her mentor Franz Boas, who as early as 1927 attempted a course correction with the willful young folklorist. In a letter to Hurston, he admonished her to "please try to pay particular attention to the points here mentioned," which included a request that she document more accurately the forms and structure of the folkloric materials she observed, rather than the content, and that she pay attention to discovering the European origins of the tales told by the planters.[1] As late as 1939, however, Hurston pushed back against her mentor's scientific and objectifying approach to collecting and documenting folklore. In a recorded interview, Hurston responded to Herbert Halpert's question, "how do you learn most of your songs?" by explaining, "I just get in the crowd with the people and they singin' and I listen as best I can, then I start a joinin' in with a phrase or two . . . I keep on till I learn all the song, the verses, then I sing them back to the people until them tell me I can sing them just like them . . . then I carry it in my memory."[2] Her emphasis on the process-oriented, dynamic exchange that characterized her fieldwork and her unorthodox reliance on memory ran counter to the scientific approach emerging out of the late nineteenth century that emphasized a taxonomy of collecting, classifying, and categorizing.

Throughout her career, Hurston continually challenged the epistemological and representational strategies emerging from anthropology and folklore studies; she experimented with numerous forms, from ethnography, to drama, to documentary film, to fiction and autobiography, in an effort to work within and against the scientific frameworks she inherited from anthropology. In her 1935 hybrid text, *Mules and Men*, Hurston explained that the scientific framework acquired through her formal studies in anthropology had given her a lens through which to recognize the academic value of her, her family's, and her community's long-held folkloric customs, stories, and beliefs. She explains, "it was only when I was off in college, away from my native surroundings, that I could see myself like somebody else and stand off and look at my garments. Then I had to have the spy-glass of Anthropology to look through at that."[3] As was the case with some of the Hampton folklorists, however, acquiring this scientific lens represented something of a double-edged sword. The "spy-glass" metaphor suggests a firmly scientific perspective in which the objectifying gaze is actually magnified. It further implies that Hurston had become the object, not only of an external and disembodied gaze, but also of her own internalized scientific gaze through which she was then able and perhaps compelled to see herself as a specimen for study.

Working within and against the epistemological strictures of the scientific frame, however, Huston, like her counterparts in the late nineteenth century, continually brought attention to the folkloric lens through which African American culture was viewed. As she moves from the introduction to the body of the *Mules and Men,* she uses literary conventions to expose the limits of traditional ethnographic representations of black folklore. By creating herself as a character within the text, for example, she adds an element of self-reflexivity, bringing attention to the role of the folklorist and highlighting her use of imaginative re-creation in creating the ethnographic report. In other words, in *Mules and Men* Hurston refuses to adopt the disembodied, all-knowing gaze of the scientifically trained anthropologist/ethnographer, and instead brings attention to ways in which folkloric representations are filtered through, and indeed created in, the dynamic interactions between the folklorist and the people whose traditions are being studied and represented.

Like Hurston, Ralph Ellison thought deeply about the significance of African American folklore, contemplating how folklore functioned to negotiate African Americans' varied relationships to larger American society. In a 1955 interview Ellison identified "Negro folklore" as "an especially courageous expression," noting "it announced the Negro's willingness to trust his own experience, his own sensibilities as to the definition of reality, rather than allow his masters to define these crucial matters for him." Like Cooper before him, Ellison recognized an alternative tradition of African American folklore studies, arguing that African American folklore must be understood within a specific context, as a dynamic product of a particular set of social and cultural factors and in relation to dominant cultural, social, and political discursive and material practices (i.e., "within a larger culture which regarded it as inferior"). He proposes that folklore both shapes and is shaped by individual and collective identities ("his own experiences"), and he insists that

African American folklore functions in the formation of black subjectivities, suggesting that folklore indicates an interiority at work in constructing and interpreting "reality." In effect, Ellison validates black folklore as a culturally specific phenomenon that takes shape within the larger dominant culture, and yet is not reducible to the "master's" values and conventions. Instead, he identifies African American folklore as a contingent, but distinct, oppositional cultural form rooted in the experiential and the particular rather than the disembodied and universal.

In his various writings Ellison leveled his critique not at the scientific hermeneutic through which black folklore was often apprehended, as Hurston did, but instead exposed the ways in which cultural representations of black folklore—in film, in literature, and in music—were part of a white mythology that served as the very basis of the nation's ideas about itself. He referred to depictions of black folklore within this framework as part of "the endless sacrificial rites of moral evasion" needed to maintain the myth of American democracy in the face of racial segregation and continued racial inequalities. According to Ellison, dominant cultural representations of black folklore participated in "molding the attitudes, the habits of mind, the cultural atmosphere and the artistic and intellectual traditions that condition men dedicated to democracy to practice, accept and, most crucial of all, often blind themselves to the essentially undemocratic treatment of their fellow citizens."[4] "Whatever else the Negro stereotype might be as a social instrumentality," Ellison asserted, "it is also a key figure in a magic rite by which the white American seeks to resolve the dilemma arising between . . . his acceptance of the sacred democratic belief that all men are created equal and his treatment of every tenth man as though he were not."[5] Like Chesnutt, Ellison sought to expose how representations of black folklore in the dominant discourse had themselves become part of the national folklore used to justify a mythology of white racial superiority and black inferiority.

In his 1944 short story "Flying Home," Ellison provides a succinct literary example of how dominant representations of black folklore could serve to indoctrinate subconscious ideas about one's place in American racialized society. At the same time, however, Ellison also integrates the structure and elements of folklore and ritual as part of a literary strategy that leads to his protagonist's ultimate liberation. In the story, Todd, a young African American pilot, believes he can soar beyond the confines of the Jim Crow South by excelling in aviation and serving heroically in the segregated services of the U.S. military. When his plane hits a buzzard and he crashes into a field in the middle of the state of Alabama, the futility of his attempts to rise above U.S.

racial constructs by succeeding within the Jim Crow system bursts upon him. Although an older black man named Jefferson rescues him, Todd initially rejects Jefferson's help. He cannot rely on Jefferson because he understands him only through the dominant cultural stereotypes of the black folk. Todd is so invested in the dominant cultural mythology about race that the racist ideas about blacks have become his ideas. Todd thinks to himself, "'humiliation was when you were always a part of this old black ignorant man. Sure, he's all right. Nice and kind and helpful. But he's not you.'"[6] Todd sees Jefferson only as a smiling "darky," a direct descendent of the Uncle Remus style plantation stereotype.

Jefferson, however, assumes the role of healer, mentor, and guide, taking Todd through the ritualistic process in which Todd's old ways of knowing and seeing are exorcised. Through the telling of the "Flying Fool" folktale, Jefferson comments on Todd's situation while also affirming the potential pedagogical and oppositional function of black folklore. When Todd realizes the "Flying Fool" folktale is a not-so-coded commentary on his own situation, he is overcome with anger at the realization that *he is* the flying fool. Todd's near fatal flaw was that he bought into a white racist society's ideas about blackness. He accepts and then tries to escape white misperceptions about blacks rather than realizing the destructiveness of these ideas. Ultimately, however, Todd's recognition of how his identity has been inscribed allows him to see both himself and Jefferson differently, revising his understanding of the black folk past and recognizing a shared sense of humanity between himself and Jefferson.

In "Flying Home," Ellison explores the ways in which folklore operates as part of a complex American racial politics, both constructing national mythology and negotiating the individual's relationship to that mythology. Folklore comprises both the "magic rites" initiating individuals into the rugged U.S. racial system and the "courageous expressions" that expose and resist the invisible customs and practices structuring those race relations. Like Hurston, Dunbar, and Chesnutt, Ellison enacts an oppositional black folk aesthetic that is as much about exposing what is at stake in the various constructions of black folklore as it is about reconstructing black folklore as the site for creating an alternative black subjectivity.

Most recently, Colson Whitehead, in his 2001 novel *John Henry Days*, takes up the question of how the folk past is interpreted in the commercial, Internet-infused present, suggesting the numerous ways African American folklore has been commodified and essentialized in our contemporary consumer culture. Nevertheless, black folklore remains an important component in the main character's, J. Sutter, negotiation with his own identity and with the past. Signaling the contingent and multiple nature of folklore, Whitehead begins *John Henry Days* with fourteen, at times widely divergent, variants of the John Henry story collected from informants of varying subject positions and geographic and temporal locations. Variously described as "black as a kittle in hell," "a white man," and "Jamaican, yellow-complected, tall and weighted about 200 pounds," the indeterminacy of even John Henry's racial identity suggests that despite attempts over the last century to locate the "real" John Henry, what we are left with is a multitude of often conflicting accounts.[7]

As these opening epigraphs indicate, one of the primary concerns of Whitehead's novel is the process through which black folklore is constructed, represented, and consolidated. Indeed, the construction of John Henry in these epigraphs presages Whitehead's construction of the legend within the novel through the inclusion of numerous fragmented vignettes relating different characters' interpretations of John Henry as inflected through their different motives and experiences.

At the center of the novel is the John Henry Days celebration—a three-day event to commemorate the unveiling of the John Henry postage stamp and its induction into the U.S. Postal Service's Folk Heroes series. As the narrative vignettes reveal, the event's participants all utilize John Henry to construct and reify meanings about themselves, their town, their history, and their identities. Their relationship to and reconstruction of the myth is equally inflected through their economic and social agendas—whether they construct and claim John Henry in an effort to revitalize the careers of town officials, to earn local businesses a little extra money through the three days of increased traffic, or to reap a modest increase in the value of the stamp. What Whitehead makes clear is that the town's constructions of John Henry, not unlike French's constructions of Peter in *The Colonel's Dream*, are products of the town's efforts to create its own romantic and heroic past.

Initially J. Sutter distances himself from the hero of what seems to be an over-determined folk tale, reinterpreted and reinvented to such an extent as to make it almost meaningless. However, the narrative of John Henry fighting to assert his humanity against the encroaching mechanization of the industrial age, as well as the second life of the story, encapsulated in the legend of John Henry being trapped within an endless cycle of co-optation, commodification, and commercialization, speaks to J. Sutter at a deeper level than even he is initially aware. Caught in a futile, and ostensibly fatal, battle against the increasing abstraction, commodification, and commercialization of his own life's work and labor—where his role as a journalist in the new Internet media is measured only in terms of "useable content" and word counts—J. Sutter comes to realign his relationship to this hero of black folk tradition, not through the superficial and entrepreneurial lens of the event promoters and publicity hounds, but through his own personal interrogations about what John Henry has meant to one black family.

For Whitehead, the folktale, legend, myth, and ballad of John Henry becomes a vehicle to comment on the ways in which folklore is constructed and to what ends. Even from Whitehead's post-structuralist, postmodernist stance, however, there is something in the John Henry story that speaks to the hidden truth of J. Sutter's precarious position as a black man trying to prove, like Todd in "Flying Home," that he can overcome a dehumanizing, racialized, and exploitative system if only he can master and dominate that system. So while Whitehead employs the John Henry story to point to the inherent constructedness of folklore and the folk past, the story also becomes a vehicle for the main character's own evolving subjectivity. J. Sutter's recognition of the ways in which John Henry has been constructed leads him to his final realization that perhaps there is more to this story than dominant constructions would have him believe.

Negotiating between the racialized politics of folkloric representation and the desire to recover and validate the often concealed and coded meaning of black folklore has been an ongoing project in African American literature. As I have shown, this quandary occupied nineteenth-century African American authors and folklorists in ways no less sophisticated or urgent than it would engage generations of subsequent writers and cultural workers. Rather than being confined to the existing protocols within which these nineteenth-century writers and folklorists found themselves, however, they drew inspiration and alternatives through their intersecting interests and challenges. While they may not have drafted overt manifestos like their successors in the Harlem Renaissance or even constituted a coherent movement like that associated with the Blacks Arts writers and artists of the 1960s and 1970s, the story of their intersecting interests and their uneven efforts to move the fledgling field of black folklore studies beyond the boundaries laid out by the white folklore establishment and to construct an African American literary aesthetic that valued without essentializing African American folklore deserves a foundational place in both black folklore studies and African American literary history.

NOTES

Introduction

1. While the origins of African American folklore studies are sometimes identified with Joel Chandler Harris's *Uncle Remus: His Songs and His Sayings* or William Francis Allen, Charles Pickard Ware, and Lucy McKim Garrison's *Slave Songs of the United States* (see Sw. Anand Prahlad, "Africana Folklore: History and Challenges," *Journal of American Folklore* 118, no. 469 (2005): 254–55 [253–70]), more frequently Newell's statement is taken as the inaugural moment in the formalized, systematic, and institutionalized study of American folklore generally and black folklore specifically. See John Roberts, "African American Diversity and the Study of Folklore," *Western Folklore* 52 (1993): 158–62 [157–71].

2. Founded by Josephine St. Pierre Ruffin in Boston in 1890, the Society for the Collection of Negro Folklore predates the Hampton Folklore Society by three years. Unfortunately, little is known about the short-lived society except that Ruffin was the driving force of the organization and that it faltered and died once Ruffin turned her attention more fully to her work in the black women's club movement. See Mitchell Kachun, "Society for the Collection of Negro Folklore," in *Organizing Black American: An Encyclopedia of African American Associations*, ed. Nina Mjagkij (New York: Garland, 2004), 536.

3. Audrey Smedley, *Race in North America: Origin and Evolution of a Worldview* (Boulder: Westview Press, 1999), 29.

4. See Brad Evans, *Before Cultures: The Ethnographic Imagination in American Literature, 1865–1920* (Chicago: University of Chicago Press, 2005), 15–16.

5. George Frederickson, *The Black Image in the White Mind: The Debate on Afro-American Character and Destiny, 1817–1914* (1971; reprinted Middleton, Connecticut: Wesleyan University Press, 1987); George Stocking, *Race, Culture and Evolution: Essays in the History of Anthropology* (1968; reprinted Chicago: University of Chicago Press, 1982); Simon Bronner, *American Folklore Studies: An Intellectual History* (Lawrence: University Press of Kansas, 1986); Prahlad, "Africana Folklore"; Roberts, "African American Diversity and the Study of Folklore."

6. By calling for a recognition of the "deep structures" of racial discourse, I am evoking the works of John Ernest and David McBride, both of whom admonish critics to recognize the intertwined layers of apparatus that underlie our current and historical racial discourses. See Dwight McBride, *Why I Hate Abercrombie & Fitch: Essays on Race and Sexuality* (New York: New York University Press, 2005), 174; John Ernest, *Chaotic Justice: Rethinking African American Literary History* (Chapel Hill: University of North Carolina Press, 2009), 5.

7. In a significant intervention in previously prevailing models of folklore studies, Alan Dundes's 1973 anthology, *Mother Wit From the Laughing Barrel*, incorporated nineteenth- and twentieth-century African American writings on black folklore, including a commentary and contribution by Hampton folklorist Frank Banks. To incorporate African American voices, however, Dundes stated that he had to expand his definition of who and what counted as folklorists and folklore. As he explained, most of the materials in the anthology were written by "non-folklorists" and published in a "bewildering variety of journals." Appropriately, his selections include works from figures as diverse as Eldridge Cleaver, Zora Neale Hurston, Charles Chesnutt, and A. Phillip Randolph. See Alan Dundes, "Preface," in *Mother Wit from the Laughing Barrel: Readings in the Interpretation of Afro-American Folklore*, ed. Dundes (Jackson: University Press of Mississippi, 1990), xii.

8. Barbara Christian, "The Race for Theory," *Cultural Critique* 6 (Spring 1987): 52 [51–63].

9. According to Shuman and Briggs, "folklorists have continued to work against the discipline's romantic origins and have disavowed uncritical antiquarian efforts to preserve the past." See Amy Shuman and Charles Briggs, "Introduction," *Western Folklore* 52, no. 2 (1993): 109, 118 [109–34].

10. Folklorists and scholars from 1893 through the present have drawn from the Hampton materials to supplement other collections, yet there exist only a handful of extended examinations of this organization. Reprints or excerpts from Hampton Folklore Society materials originally published in *Southern Workman* or the *Journal of American Folklore* appear in works by the following authors: Newbell Puckett, Lawrence Levine, Bronner, Dundes, Bruce Jackson, and Daryl Dance. The Hampton Folklore Society, however, has been almost entirely absent from traditional histories of the discipline of folklore studies. William McNeil's lengthy dissertation on folklore studies prior to 1910 does not mention the folklore society at Hampton even in the chapter on African American folklore; and Susan Dwyer-Shick's dissertation, "American Folklore Society and Folklore Research in America, 1888–1940," similarly does not include a discussion of the Hampton Folklore Society. See: Newbell Niles Puckett, *Folk Beliefs of the Southern Negro* (Chapel Hill: University of North Carolina Press, 1926); Lawrence Levine, *Black Culture and Black Consciousness* (New York:

Oxford University Press, 1978); Simon J. Bronner, *Folk Nation: Folklore in the Creation of American Tradition* (Wilmington, Delaware: Scholarly Resources, 2002); Alan Dundes, *Mother Wit from the Laughing Barrel*; Bruce Jackson, *The Negro and His Folklore in Nineteenth Century Periodicals* (Austin: University of Texas Press, 1967); Daryl Cumber Dance, *From My People: 400 Years of African American Folklore* (New York: W. W. Norton, 2002); William McNeil, "A History of American Folklore Scholarship before 1908" (diss., Indiana University, 1980); Susan Dwyer-Shick, "The American Folklore Society and Folklore Research in America, 1888–1940" (diss., University of Pennsylvania, 1979).

11. Melvin Wade, "The Intellectual and Historical Origins of Folklore Scholarship by Black Americans: A Study of the Response to the Propaganda of Racial Superiority at Hampton (Virginia) Institute 1893–1939," unpublished manuscript (Hampton, Virginia: Hampton University Archives, 1982).

12. Elaine Lawless, "'Reciprocal' Ethnography: No One Said It Was Easy," *Journal of Folklore Research* 37, no. 2/3 (May–December 2000): 199 [197–205].

13. Adrienne Lanier Seward, "The Legacy of Early Afro-American Folklore Scholarship," in *Handbook of American Folklore*, ed. Richard Dorson (Bloomington: Indiana University Press, 1983), 48–56; Prahlad, "Africana Folklore"; Cassandra Stancil, "An Early Model for the Study of African-American Folklore: Carter G. Woodson and the *Journal of Negro History*," *New York Folklore* 18, no. 1–4 (2000): 103–17; Gerald L. Davis, "Thomas Washington Talley: Early Twentieth-Century African American Folklore Theorist," *New York Folklore* 18, no. 1–4 (2000): 91–102.

14. See Lee Baker, *Anthropology and the Racial Politics of Culture* (Durham, North Carolina: Duke University Press, 2010); Daphne Lamothe, *Inventing the New Negro: Narrative, Culture and Ethnography* (Philadelphia: University of Pennsylvania Press, 2008); Ray Sapirstein, *Out from behind the Mask: The Illustrated Poetry of Paul Laurence Dunbar and Photography at Hampton Institute* (diss., University of Texas, Austin, 2005); Donald Waters, *Strange Ways and Sweet Dreams: Afro-American Folklore from the Hampton Institute* (Boston: G. K. Hall, 1983).

15. In *Chaotic Justice*, John Ernest articulates this dynamic in relation to nineteenth-century antebellum literature (and I would argue the same holds true for postbellum, pre-Harlem African American literature as well): "Too often this body of literature is identified simply as the beginnings of a literary tradition that eventually discovers its force in the Harlem Renaissance and is fully realized in the unprecedented authority that some of the most prominent African American writers enjoy today" (7). Carla Peterson reiterates this claim in "Commemorative Ceremonies and Invented Traditions," suggesting that Toni Morrison fails to recognize her own works' commonalities with "the task post-bellum–pre-Harlem novelists had set for themselves nearly one hundred years earlier: to record the experience of slavery and the

inner life of the enslaved by means of memory and imagination." See Carla Peterson, "Commemorative Ceremonies and Invented Traditions: History, Memory and Modernity in the 'New Negro' Novel of the Nadir," in *Post-Bellum, Pre-Harlem, African American Literature and Culture, 1877–1919*, ed. Caroline Gebhard and Barbara McCaskill (New York: New York University Press, 2006) 54 [34–56]).

16. In *Authentic Blackness*, for example, J. Martin Favor examines how black writers "during the period between the world wars" created alternative versions of black identity as a way to challenge the predominance of the privileged "folk" identity they had inherited from the previous generation of black writers. David Nicholls's *Conjuring the Folk* also analyzes constructions of the folk by black writers, examining how these writers "between the wars" mediated their representations of the folk from their positions within modern, metropolitan spaces. This important work is taken up in such illuminating studies as Martha Nadell's *Enter the New Negroes*, Anne Carroll's *Word, Image and the New Negro*, and Lamothe's *Inventing the New Negro*, though each of these works locates the bulk of their analyses midway through the first half of the twentieth century. See J. Martin Favor, *Authentic Blackness: The Folk in the New Negro Renaissance* (Durham: Duke University Press, 1999); David Nicholls, *Conjuring the Folk: Forms of Modernity in African America* (Ann Arbor: University of Michigan Press, 2000); Martha Nadell, *Enter the New Negroes: Images of Race in American Culture* (Cambridge: Harvard University Press, 2004); and Anne Carroll, *Word, Image and the New Negro: Representation and Identity in the Harlem Renaissance* (Bloomington: Indiana University Press, 2005).

17. Henry Louis Gates Jr., "The Trope of a New Negro and the Reconstruction of the Image of the Black," *Representations* 24 (Autumn 1988): 131 [129–55].

18. Caroline Gebhard and Barbara McCaskill, ed., *Post-Bellum, Pre-Harlem, African American Literature and Culture, 1877–1919* (New York: New York University Press, 2006), 9.

19. See Houston Baker, *Blues, Ideology, and Afro-American Literature: A Vernacular Theory* (Chicago: University of Chicago Press, 1984); Henry Louis Gates Jr., *Figures in Black: Words, Signs, and the Racial Self* (New York: Oxford University Press, 1987); and Gates, *The Signifying Monkey: A Theory of Afro-American Literary Criticism* (New York: Oxford University Press, 1988).

20. Gates, *Signifying Monkey*, xxii.

21. *Ibid.*, xxvi, xxi.

22. *Ibid.*, xxii.

23. *Ibid.*, xxii, xix.

24. Favor, *Authentic Blackness*, 4.

25. Evie Shockley, *Renegade Poetics: Black Aesthetics and Formal Innovation in African American Poetry* (Iowa City: University of Iowa Press, 2011), 6.

26. *Ibid.*

27. Robin Kelley, "Notes on Deconstructing the Folk," *American Historical Review* 97, no. 5 (December 1992): 1408 [1400–1408].

Chapter 1

1. Historian James Grossman asserts that Rayford Logan, C. Vann Woodward, and subsequent historians and scholars, incorrectly attribute the phrase "stateways cannot change folkways" to William Graham Sumner, and though Sumner expresses this sentiment, including in this 1906 study *Folkways*, Grossman claims that Sumner actually stated, "legislation cannot change mores." See James Grossman, "Did They Really Say That: Getting Our Quotations Right," *American Historical Association Today*, http://blog.historians.org/news. 19 April 2012. Web. 10 April 2013. The origins of the erroneous attribution may have come from Gunnar Myrdal's *An American Dilemma*, in which Myrdal paraphrased Sumner's position with the phrase "stateways cannot change folkways." See Gunnar Myrdal, *An American Dilemma: The Negro Problem and Modern Democracy*, vol. 2 (New York: Harper and Row, 1962), 1049. See also William Graham Sumner, *Folkways* (New York: Blaisdell, 1906).

2. T. F. Crane, "Recent Folk-Lore Publications," *Nation* 12 (12 June 1890): 475 [475–76].

3. F. S. Bassett, "The International Folk-Lore Congress of the World's Columbian Exposition, Chicago, July, 1893/Address by Lieutenant F. S. Bassett" http://en.wikisource.org/w/index.php?title=The_International_Folk-Lore_Congress_of_the_World%27s_Columbian_Exposition,_Chicago,_July,_1893/Address_by_Lieutenant_F._S._Bassett&oldid=2511450. Accessed 17 March 2011.

4. For a complete list of the society's charter members, see "Members of the American Folk-lore Society," *Journal of American Folklore* 1, no. 1 (April–June 1888): 94–96. For more on the popularity of folklore studies in the late nineteenth century and on learned national organizations generally, see Simon Bronner, *American Folklore Studies: An Intellectual History* (Lawrence: University Press of Kansas, 1986), 15–19.

5. Newell, "First Annual Meeting of the American Folk-lore Society," *Journal of American Folklore* 3, no. 8 (January–March 1890): 5 [1–16].

6. William Wells Newell, "On the Field and Work of a Journal of American Folk-Lore," *Journal of American Folklore*, 1, no. 1 (April–June 1888): 3 [3–7].

7. Bronner, *American Folklore Studies*, 17.

8. Newell, "Introduction," *Journal of American Folklore* 2, no. 4 (January–March 1889): 2 [1–2].

9. Jon Cruz, *Culture on the Margins: The Black Spiritual and the Rise of American Cultural Interpretation* (Princeton: Princeton University Press, 1999), 191.

10. Newell, "Additional Collection Essential to Correct Theory in Folk-Lore and Mythology," *Journal of American Folklore* 3, no. 8 (January–March 1890): 25–26 [23–32].

11. Newell, "Theories of Diffusion of Folk-Tales," *Journal of American Folklore* 8, no. 28 (January–March 1895): 7 [7–18].

12. See Brad Evans, "The Failed Genealogies of Culture," in *Before Cultures: The Ethnographic Imagination in American Literature, 1865–1920* (Chicago: University of Chicago Press, 2005), 1–23.

13. Newell, "Myths of Voodoo Worship and Child Sacrifice in Hayti," *Journal of American Folklore* 1, no. 1 (April–June 1888): 17–18 [16–30].

14. Newell, "Theories of Diffusion of Folk-Tales," 16.

15. Cruz, *Culture on the Margins*, 191.

16. *Ibid.*, 198–199.

17. John Roberts, "African American Diversity and the Study of Folklore," *Western Folklore* 52 (1993): 161 [157–71].

18. Newell, "On the Field and Work," 6.

19. *Ibid.*, 5.

20. *Ibid.*

21. Newell, "Folk-lore," in *Johnson's Universal Cyclopedia*, Vol. 3 (New York: A. J. Johnson, 1893–97), 453.

22. Newell, "On the Field and Work," 1.

23. Roberts, "Grand Theory, Nationalism and American Folklore," *Journal of Folklore Research* 45, no. 1 (2008): 48 [45–54].

24. Newell, *"Third Annual Meeting of the American Folk-lore Society,"* *Journal of American Folklore* 5, no. 16 (January–March 1892): 2–3 [1–8].

25. Lee J. Vance, "The Study of Folk-Lore," *Forum* 22 (1896–97): 249.

26. Newell, "Third Annual Meeting," 1.

27. For more on the influence of evolutionary paradigms on early folklore studies, see Hugo Freund, "Cultural Evolution, Survivals, and Immersion: The Implications for Nineteenth-Century Folklore Studies," in *The American Folklore Society: 100 Years*, ed. William Clements (Washington: American Folklore Society, 1988), 12–15.

28. See A. R. Wright's description of Alfred Nutt's 1898 presidential address. In this address Nutt explained his interpretation of folklore as "elements of culture surviving among the less advanced sections of the community, but discarded by the more advanced." This sentiment had been stated similarly by previous British Folklore Society presidents, including Lawrence Gomme in 1893 and Edward Clodd in 1895. See A. R. Wright, "Presidential Address: The Folklore of Past and Present," *Folklore* 38, no. 1 (March 1927): 13–39.

29. Rosemary Zumwalt, *American Folklore Scholarship: A Dialogue of Dissent* (Bloomington: Indiana University Press, 1988), 16.

30. Roger Abrahams, "Rough Sincerities: William Wells Newell and the Discovery of Folklore in Late Nineteenth Century America," in *Folklore in American Life*, ed. Jane Becker and Barbara Franco (Lexington, Massachusetts: Museum of Our National Heritage, 1998), 67–68 [61–75].

31. Newell, "The Importance and Utility of the Collection of Negro Folk-lore," *Southern Workman* 23, no. 7 (July 1894): 131 [131–32].

32. *Ibid.*

33. *Ibid.*, 132.

34. Bronner, *AFS*, 20.

35. *Ibid.*, 9.

36. Newell, "The Necessity of Collecting the Traditions of the Native Races," *Journal of American Folklore* 1, no. 2 (July–September 1888): 163 [162–63].

37. Mel Watkins, *On the Real Side: Laughing, Lying and Signifying* (New York: Simon and Schuster, 1995), 84.

38. Most accounts in both nineteenth-century reports and twentieth-century scholarship relate a singular encounter between Rice and either Jim, the black holster/stable groom, or Cuff, the levee luggage man. See refutation of this encounter in Lhamon, *Cain*, 154, and for additional variants of this legend see Watkins, *On the Real Side*, 84; Robert Tolls, *Blacking Up: The Minstrel Show in Nineteenth Century America* (New York: Oxford University Press, 1974), 28; Eric Lott, "Love and Theft: The Racial Unconscious of Blackface Minstrelsy," *Representations* 39 (Summer 1992): 41–44.

39. The white actor George Nichols reported that he had learned Jim Crow in New Orleans in 1830 from Picayune Butler, a black street performer (Lhamon, *Cain*, 181); in *Step It Down*, Bessie Jones tells of having played "Knock Jim Crow" on the Georgia Sea Islands as a child during the early twentieth century (Bess Lomax Hawes and Bessie Jones, *Step It Down: Games, Plays, Songs and Stories from the Afro-American Heritage* [New York: Harper and Row, 1972], 55).

40. Lhamon, *Cain*, 195.

41. Lhamon observes that the early Jim Crow, as portrayed by Rice, "moved like a free man, crowed like a dandy cock, enjoyed the liberty of every public conveyance." According to Lhamon, he broke out of bondage and embodied quick reversals of social order and individual fortunes. See W. T. Lhamon, *Jump Jim Crow* (Cambridge: Harvard University Press, 2003), 36.

42. Quoted in Lhamon, *Jump Jim Crow*, 169.

43. *Ibid.*

44. In fact, blackface minstrels, resentful of implications that they had any black blood in them, began publishing portraits of themselves not in blackface alongside their minstrel characters. This was done, Tolls explains, to establish their identity as performers and as white men. See Tolls, *Blacking Up*, 40.

For a detailed history of the transition from blackface minstrelsy to black minstrel performances, see Karen Sotiropoulos, *Staging Race: Black Performers in Turn of the Century America* (Cambridge: Harvard University Press, 2006).

45. Tolls, *Blacking Up*, 35.

46. Watkins, *On the Real Side*, 86.

47. White-owned companies, such as the Callander Company, dominated the black minstrel industry. They virtually monopolized markets, had the most exposure, and made the most money, and "they illustrated that when blacks became marketable as entertainers, it was white men who reaped the profits." See Tolls, *Blacking Up*, 211.

48. See for example, "The Old Cabinet: Simplicity," *Scribner's Monthly* 16 (May–October 1878): 435 [434–5].

49. Tolls, *Blacking Up*, 201–2.

50. Quoted in Ibid., 200.

51. For an historical reconstruction of the World's Columbian Exposition in Chicago (1893), see Julie Rose, "The World's Columbian Exposition" http://xroads.virginia.edu/~MA96/WCE/title.html, accessed January 2004; and Bruce Schulman, "Interactive Guide to the World's Columbian Exposition" http://users.vnet.net/schulman/Columbian/columbian.html, accessed January 2004. For an extended examination of the relationship between racial discourse, gender and the discourse of civilization see Gail Bederman, *Manliness and Civilization: A Cultural History of Gender and Race in the United States, 1880–1917* (Chicago: University of Chicago Press, 1995).

52. "Through the Looking Glass, *Chicago Tribune* (1 November 1893), 9.

53. Bederman, *Manliness and Civilization*, 38.

54. See Ida B. Wells and Frederick Douglass, "No 'Nigger Day,' No 'Nigger Pamphlet!'" *Indianapolis Freeman* (25 March 1893), 4; Bederman, *Manliness and Civilization*, 38–40; Karen Sotiropoulos, *Staging Race: Black Performers in Turn of the Century America*, 26–28.

55. Anna Julia Cooper, "The Negro as Presented in American Literature (1892)," in *The Voice of Anna Julia Cooper*, ed. Charles Lemert and Esme Bhan (Lanham, Maryland: Rowman and Littlefield, 1998), 138 [134–60].

56. Tolls, *Blacking Up*, 271 (italics added). Ironically, Newell claimed that "the importance of the study of popular traditions, through recognized by men of science, is not yet understood by the general public." See Newell, "Editor's Notes," *Journal of American Folklore* 2, no. 4 (1889): 1. While the "general public" may not have interpreted popular traditions through scientific models, the role of popular traditions on the stage, in literature, and in political discussions was pervasive.

57. Joel Chandler Harris's "collections" of animal tales were often cited as the impetus for more sustained attention to black folktales. Newell, almost certainly, was referring to Harris's wildly popular *Uncle Remus: His Songs and His Sayings* (1880) when he stated that "it is but within a few years that attention has been called to the

existence . . . of a great number of tales related to animals, which have been preserved in an interesting collection." See "On the Field and Work," 5.

58. George Frederickson, *The Black Image in the White Mind: The Debate on Afro-American Character and Destiny, 1817–1914* (Middleton, Connecticut: Wesleyan University Press, 1987), 207–12, 280–81.

59. Newell in a letter to Franz Boas, quoted in Rosemary Levy Zumwalt, "On the Founding of the American Folklore Society and the *Journal of American Folklore*," in *The American Folklore Society: 100 Years*, ed. William Clements (Washington: American Folklore Society, 1988), 8–10; Newell, "On the Field and Work," 5.

60. William Wiggins, "Afro-Americans As Folk: from Savage to Civilized," in *American Folklore Society: 100 Years*, 29; Newell, "On the Field and Work," 5.

61. Stewart Culin, "Reports Concerning Voodooism," *Journal of American Folklore* 2, no. 6 (1899): 232–33.

62. Culin explains that after the client "gave the doctor a sum of money equal to about eight dollars," the doctor returned the bottle filled with a clear tasteless fluid, that seemed to be pure water, and directed him to drink it; ". . . within four weeks afterwards [the client] was married to the woman of his choice." In his account, Culin implies that the client was only given water and that the efficacy of the ritual was owing to the client's willingness to participate and believe in the ritual. See Culin, "Reports Concerning Voodooism," 233.

63. Alcee Fortier, "Customs and Superstitions of Louisiana," *Journal of American Folklore* 1, no. 2 (1888): 136–38.

64. Irwin Russell, "A Christmas-Night in the Quarters," *Poems* (New York: Century, 1917), 3, 7–8.

65. This was the paradox that Plessy and his lawyers sought to expose. Homer Plessy, who was one-eighth black, had the physical traits of a white man. He and his lawyers argued that because he was visibly white, he was entitled to all the privileges of a white man.

66. *Roberts v. City of Boston*, 59 Mass. (5 Cush.) 198 (1850).

67. Logan, *The Betrayal of the Negro*, 175.

68. *Plessy v. Ferguson*, 163 US 537 (1896).

69. *Ratliff v. Beale*, 74 Miss. 247 So. 864 (1896).

70. David Theo Goldberg, "Racial Rule," in *Relocating Postcolonialism*, ed. David Theo Goldberg and Ato Quayson (Oxford, UK: Blackwell Press, 2002), 86 [82–102].

71. Goldberg, "Racial Rule," 87.

72. Charles Chesnutt, "The Courts and the Negroes," in *Charles W. Chesnutt: Stories, Novels and Essays*, ed. Werner Sollors (New York: Library of America, 2002), 900, 902 [895–905].

73. *Plessy v. Ferguson*.

Chapter 2

1. Richard and Clarissa Armstrong sailed aboard the *Averick* from New Bedford, Massachusetts, to the Hawaiian Islands, remaining briefly in Honolulu before being sent to the Marquesas Islands, then Maui and finally back to Oahu. See David Forbes, compiler, *Hawaiian National Bibliography, 1780–1900, vol. 4, 1881–1900* (Honolulu: University of Hawai'i Press, 2003), 222.

2. Punahou School, *The Oahu College at the Sandwich Island* (Boston: T. R. Marvin, 1856), 2.

3. William Richards, "Office Record," *State Archives Digital Collections*, State of Hawai'i http://archives1.dags.hawaii.gov/gsdl/collect/governme/index/assoc/HASH8366/47733f3b.dir/Richards,%20William.jpg, accessed 2011-01-29; Forbes, *Hawaiian National Bibliography*, vol. 4, 30–31.

4. The Hawaiian "provisional government," which was comprised mainly of U.S.-identified missionaries and businessmen and had as its president Sanford Dole, attempted to enforce a treaty annexing Hawai'i to the United States in 1893. Spurred by protests from Queen Lili'uokalani and the Kanaka Maoli, President Grover Cleveland rejected the annexation treaty. The provisional government then moved to maintain its power as the "Republic of Hawai'i" until it was able to secure annexation rights from the U.S. Congress under President McKinley in 1898. See Noenoe Silva, *Aloha Betrayed: Native Hawaiian Resistance to American Colonialism* (Durham: Duke University Press, 2004), 129–73, 160, 199. See also Helen Geracimos, *Shaping History: The Role of Newspapers in Hawaii* (Honolulu: University of Hawai'i Press, 1996), 93–104, 113–17.

5. See also Laura Lyons. "Dole, Hawai'i, and the Question of Land under Globalization," in *Cultural Critique and the Global Corporation*, ed. Purnima Bose, Laura Lyons, and Christopher Newfield (Bloomington: Indiana University Press, 2010), 64–101.

6. Eric Covey, "Dole," in *The Business of Food: Encyclopedia of the Food and Drink Industries*, ed. Gary J. Allen, Ken Albala (Westport, Connecticut: Greenwood, 2007), 140.

7. Samuel Armstrong, "Letter to the Cousins," December 22, 1860, Mission Houses Museum Library.

8. I follow Hawaiian Studies scholar Noenoe Silva in using the designation Kanaka Maoli as an identification for the indigenous peoples of Hawai'i and their descendants.

9. Referencing images from U.S.-based periodicals, Noenoe Silva shows how "American cartoonists borrowed stock images of Africans and African Americans" to "justify taking over the government from Kalakaua and Lili'uokalani. . . . By borrowing the ready-made 'black' stereotype the cartoonist was able to signify the queen's

racial difference immediately, a shorthand way to convey that she was essentially, naturally, unfit to rule." See Silva, *Aloha Betrayed*, 176–77. See also Geracimos, *Shaping History*, 103.

10. Richard Armstrong, journal entry, January 1, 1848, Mission Houses Museum Library.

11. Mary F. M. Armstrong, *America: Richard Armstrong. Hawaii* (Hampton, Virginia: Hampton Normal School Steam Press, 1887), 29–30.

12. Lee Baker, *Anthropology and the Racial Politics of Culture* (Durham: Duke University Press, 2010), 36–37.

13. For more on the influence of Armstrong's experiences in Hawai'i, see Mary Frances Armstrong and Helen Ludlow, *Hampton and Its Students* (Chicago: Afro-Am Press, 1969), 38–39; Samuel Armstrong, *Lessons from the Hawaiian Islands* (Hampton, Virginia: Normal School Printing Office, 1884); Robert Engs, *Educating the Disfranchised and Disinherited: Samuel Chapman Armstrong, 1839–1893* (Knoxville: University of Tennessee Press, 1999), 73–74; Francis Peabody, *Education for Life: The Story of Hampton Institute* (New York: Doubleday, Page, 1918), 88–89.

14. S. Armstrong, *Lessons from the Hawaiian Islands*, 213–14.

15. *Ibid.*, 216, 222.

16. Ngugi wa Thiong'o, *Decolonising the Mind: The Politics of Language in African Literature* (Portsmouth, New Hampshire: Heinemann, 1986), 3. Silva references Thiong'o in articulating the cultural imperialism enacted by nineteenth-century missionaries in Hawai'i. See *Aloha Betrayed*, 2, 125.

17. Silva, *Aloha Betrayed*, 144.

18. Silva explains that in the Hawaiian language, *pono* is related to concepts such as balance, completeness, material well-being, and the ideal behavior for ali'i or chiefs. When translated from Hawaiian into the English language writing system, pono was linked to the Christian concept of "righteousness" or morality. See Silva, *Aloha Betrayed*, 44; Silva, *Kanawai E Ho'opau I Na Hula Kuolo Hawai'i:* The Political Economy of Banning the Hula," *Hawaiian Journal of History* 34 (2000): 37.

19. Noel J. Kent, *Hawaii: Islands under the Influence* (Honolulu: University of Hawai'i Press, 1993), 28.

20. Quoted in Silva, "The Political Economy of Banning the Hula," 39.

21. See Amy Stillman, "Of People Who Love the Land: Vernacular History in the Poetry of Modern Hawaiian Hula," *Amerasia Journal* 28, no. 3 (2002): 85–108.

22. S. Armstrong, "Letter to the Cousins."

23. Whereas Richard Armstrong and Edward Beckwith supported advanced education for the missionaries and their children, who would in turn, maintain and expand the missionary project throughout the Pacific, Samuel Armstrong sought to turn the "native" or African American students into civilizing agents.

24. Engs, *Educating the Disenfranchised and Disinherited*, 58.

25. S. Armstrong, Letter to Archibald Hopkins, 1/15/1863, in Edith Armstrong Talbot, *Samuel Chapman Armstrong: A Biographical Study* (New York: Negro Universities Press, 1969), 86.

26. Peabody, *Education for Life*, 74.

27. *Ibid*., 78.

28. For a detailed history of Armstrong's work with the Freedmen's Bureau and the American Missionary Association, see Engs, *Educating the Disenfranchised and Disinherited*; James Anderson, "The Hampton Model of Normal School Industrial Education, 1868–1915" in *The Education of Blacks in the South, 1860–1935* (Chapel Hill: University of North Carolina Press, 1998), 33–78; Waters, *Strange Ways and Sweet Dreams: Afro-American Folklore from the Hampton Institute* (Boston: G. K. Hall, 1983), 13–17. Mary Farmer-Kaiser, *Freedwomen and the Freedmen's Bureau: Race, Gender, and Public Policy in the Age of Emancipation* (New York: Fordham University Press, 2010), 35–36.

29. *Ibid*., xiii.

30. Nathaniel Shaler, "The Negro Problem," *Atlantic Monthly* 54 (1884): 697–98; Shaler, "Race Prejudice," *Atlantic Monthly* 58 (1886): 510–13. For a detailed account of the exchange between Shaler and Samuel Armstrong, see Donald Waters, *Strange Ways and Sweet Dreams.*

31. James Anderson details Armstrong's model of industrial education in *The Education of Blacks in the South*, 33–78.

32. Frances Johnston, *The Hampton Album: 44 Photographs from an Album of the Hampton Institute*, ed. Lincoln Kirstein (New York: Museum of Modern Art/Doubleday, 1966). Photographs from this series also appeared on the cover of *Southern Workman.* "The Old Folks at Home," for example, was featured on the cover of *Southern Workman* 30, no.10 (October 1901).

33. Peabody, *Education for Life*, xiii.

34. Shawn Michelle Smith, *American Archives: Gender, Race and Class in Visual Culture* (Princeton: Princeton University Press, 1999), 171.

35. Quoted in Engs, *Educating the Disenfranchised and Disinherited*, 77.

36. *Ibid*., 76.

37. The Hampton Student Singers took as their motto "Singing and Building," because the funds raised during their performances went to the construction of new buildings on the Hampton campus. See Armstrong, Fenner, and Ludlow, *Hampton and Its Students*, 127.

38. *Ibid.*

39. Regina Bendix, *In Search of Authenticity*, 91.

40. Armstrong, Fenner, and Ludlow, *Hampton and Its Students*, 128–32.

41. Allen, Garrison, and Wares observed this tendency while collecting songs from

freedmen for *Slave Songs of the U.S.* The authors note, "[I]t is often indeed no easy matter to persuade them to sing their old songs, even as a curiosity, such is the sense of dignity that has come with freedom." See William Francis Allen, *Slave Songs of the United States* (New York: A. Simpson, 1867), x. See also Engs, *Educating the Disfranchised and Disinherited*, 77.

42. Waters links Armstrong's tactical approach to finding and exposing, or "spying out," black folklore to Armstrong's military background. See Waters, *Strange Ways*, 41.

43. S. Armstrong, "Principal's Report," in *Annual Report* (Hampton, Virginia: Normal School Printing Press, 1885), 28–29.

44. S. Armstrong, "Editorial Reply," *Southern Workman* 7, no. 5 (1878): 35.

45. Engs, *Educating the Disfranchised and Disinherited*, 78.

46. W. I. Lewis, "Letter," *Southern Workman* 7, no. 5 (1878): 35.

47. S. Armstrong, "Editorial Reply," 35.

48. "Conjure Doctors in the South," *Southern Workman* 7, no. 4 (1878): 30.

49. *Ibid.*

50. *Ibid.*, 31.

51. *Ibid.*, 30–31.

52. Philip Bruce, *Plantation Negro as Freedman: Observations on His Character, Conditions and Prospects in Virginia* (New York: G. P. Putnam's Sons, 1889), 115.

53. S. Armstrong, "Editorial Introduction to Student Papers on Conjuring," *Southern Workman* 7, no. 4 (1878): 26.

54. For more on nineteenth-century attitudes toward conjure, see Jeffrey Anderson, "The Invisible Conjurer: The Disappearance of Conjure from Conceptions of Black Society," in *Conjuring in African American Society* (Baton Rouge: Louisiana State University Press, 2003), 1–24.

55. "Conjure Doctors in the South," 30.

56. Anderson, "The Hampton Model," 90–91.

57. As cited in Sharps, "Happy Days and Sorrow Songs," 30.

58. In the developmental model of evolution, differences between races or cultures were not considered inherent, but instead were understood to be a product of environmental pressures and socio-historical conditions. This meant that a race or culture could develop along evolutionary lines, and their progress could be measured by comparing their growth to more "civilized" cultures. See Baker, *Anthropology and the Racial Politics of Culture*, 64.

59. Bacon, "Circular Letter," *Southern Workman* 22, no. 12 (1893): 179–81.

60. *Ibid.*

61. *Ibid.*

62. *Ibid.*, 179.

63. Armstrong capitalized on his connections with wealthy Northern families such as the Bacons and the Woolseys in his fundraising drives, and implied that Rebecca Bacon had endorsed his solicitations when, in actuality, he made such insinuations without her knowledge. See Waters, *Strange Ways and Sweet Dreams*, 5.

64. Claire Strom, "Alice Bacon," in *American National Biography, Volume One*, ed. John Garraty and Mark Carnes (New York: Oxford University Press, 1999), 840.

65. Robert Rosenstone, "'Learning from the 'Imitative' Japanese': Another Side of the American Experience in the Mikado's Empire," *American Historical Review* 85, no. 3 (1980): 576.

66. Bacon, *Japanese Girls and Women*, 258.

67. Bacon, *A Japanese Interior*, 228.

68. *Ibid.*, xiii.

69. *Ibid.*

70. Bacon, *Japanese Girls and Women*, vii–viii. As Johannes Fabin explains in his well-known critique of traditional ethnographic methods, the "objects" of ethnographic inquiry are often spoken about, but not spoken to, or, as Takami Kuwayama states, "They are excluded from the dialogic circle of ethnography." See Johannes Fabin, *Time and the Other: How Anthropology Makes Its Objects* (New York: Columbia University Press, 1983), 85; Takami Kuwayama, *Native Anthropology: The Japanese Challenge to Western Academic Hegemony* (Melbourne: Trans Pacific Press, 2004), 7. Self-reflexive ethnography has offered one method through which ethnographers, fieldworkers, folklorists, and anthropologists have attempted to address the politics of representation and questions of subjectivity/objectivity and positionality. Of this approach, Patrick Mullen asserts, "[T]he ethnographer must recognize his own subjective position as an influence on the fieldwork and subsequent cultural representations of the people being studied." He suggests that reciprocal ethnography constitutes an approach where "folklorists and other social scientists" work closely with the group being studied through the exchange of materials, the testing of interpretations, and ongoing dialogue in an effort to recognize and include multiple subjective positions. See Patrick Mullen, *The Man Who Adores Negro: Race and American Folklore* (Chicago: University of Illinois Press, 2008), 9, 11; for a critique of Mullen's ability to realize a truly reciprocal approach in his own fieldwork, see Elaine Lawless, "'Reciprocal' Ethnography: No One Said It Was Easy," *Journal of Folklore Research* 37, no. 2/3 (2000): 197–206.

71. Bacon, "Work and Method of the Hampton Folklore Society," *Journal of American Folklore* 11, no. 40 (1898): 17–21, 20.

72. Bacon, "Circular Letter," *Southern Workman* 22, no. 12 (1893): 180–81.

73. *Ibid.*

74. *Ibid.*

75. Bacon, "Work and Method of the Hampton Folklore Society," 18–19.

76. Lee Baker reads Bacon's work as an extension of Armstrong's missionary project to expose and eradicate black folklore en route to civilizing Hampton's African American students, while Jon Cruz situates Bacon within the frame of Newell's scientistic approach to categorizing and classifying black folk culture. Waters, on the other hand, locates Bacon in relation to both the Armstrong and Newell traditions, but ultimately aligns Bacon more closely with Newell and the American Folklore Society. While Waters most readily recognized Bacon's contribution to folklore studies—an emphasis on context when collecting oral folklore—he reads this contribution within rather than beyond the frame provided by the American Folklore Society. What I suggest here, however, is that one of Bacon's most significant contributions to folklore studies was an attention to the politics of folklore collection and a willingness to engage voices that went beyond the prominent white male practitioners of her day to include approaches articulated by African American scholars and intellectuals who re-focused attention on the racial politics of folklore studies and the cultural, creative, and political significance of documenting black folk traditions. See Baker, *Anthropology and the Racial Politics of Culture*, 48–49; Jon Cruz, *Culture on the Margins: The Black Spiritual and the Rise of American Cultural Interpretation* (Princeton: Princeton University Press, 1999), 171–75; Waters, *Strange Ways and Sweet Dreams*, 34–42.

77. Shaler, "Science and the African Problem," *Atlantic Monthly* 66 (1890): 36–45. For a detailed parsing of the construction and deployment of "cultural evolution" versus "biological determinism" in twentieth-century discourse and thought, see George Stocking Jr. "Turn-of-the-Century Concept of Race," *Modernism/Modernity* 1, no. 1 (1994): 4–16.

78. In a letter to Bacon, Shaler suggested that the group consider the following: "First: are there any survivors of the later importations of blacks from Africa? If so, where are they? Can their children of pure blood be identified? Second: What portion of colored people . . . are of mixed blood? Third: Are there any families among the Negroes characterized by straight hair . . . I suspect the existence of some Arab blood among our Negroes." See "Department of Folklore and Ethnology," *Southern Workman* 22, no. 12 (1893): 179–80. For more on Shaler's influence see Waters, *Strange Ways and Sweet Dreams*, 33–34.

79. "Department of Folklore and Ethnology," 179.

80. Bacon, "Circular Letter," 180–81.

81. Bacon, "Work and Method of the Hampton Folklore Society," 18.

82. William Wells Newell, "Folk-Lore," in *Johnson's Universal Cyclopedia* (New York: A. J. Johnson, 1893–97), 453; W. W. Newell, "The Study of Folk-Lore," *Transactions of the New York Academy of Sciences* 9 (1890): 134.

83. Zumwalt, *American Folklore Scholarship*, 6.

84. Bacon, "Work and Method of the Hampton Folklore Society," 20.

85. See for example Alan Dundes, "Texture, Text, and Context," *Southern Folklore Quarterly* 28 (1971): 251–65; Tim Lloyd, "On the Differences between Folklore Fieldwork and Oral History," in *Oral History in the Digital Age*, edited by Doug Boyd, Steven Cohen, Brad Rakerd, and Dean Rehberger (Washington, D.C.: Institute of Museum and Library Services, 2012, http://ohda.matrix.msu.edu/2012/06/on-the-differences-between-folklore-fieldwork-and-oral-history/ Web, 10 April 2013; Jeff Todd Titon, "Text," *Journal of American Folklore* 108, no. 430 (1995): 432–48.

Chapter 3

1. Vivian Patterson, ed., *Carrie Mae Weems: The Hampton Project* (Williamstown, Massachusetts: Aperture, 2000), 72.

2. Patterson, *Carrie Mae Weems: The Hampton Project*, n.p.

3. Although Weems's exhibition was scheduled to travel from Williams College to Hampton University, Hampton withdrew the invitation. Jeanne Zeidler, Hampton University Museum director, stated that Hampton had "profound reservations about the direction of the project" and about the "generalizations" being made about the students and education at Hampton. Weems, on the other hand, argued that Hampton was "the perfect site for beginning a critical dialogue that focuses on the problematic nature of assimilation, identity and the role of education." For more on these divergent perspectives see Jeanne Zeidler, "A View From Hampton University Museum," in *Carrie Mae Weems: The Hampton Project*, ed. Patterson, 77; Denise Ramzy and Katherine Fogg, "Interview: Carrie Mae Weems," in *Carrie Mae Weems: The Hampton Project*, ed. Patterson, 78.

4. For more on contributing and participating members of the Hampton Folklore Society, see *Twenty-Two Years' Work of the Hampton Normal and Agricultural Institute at Hampton, Virginia* (Hampton, Virginia: Normal School Press, 1893); Waters, *Strange Ways and Sweet Dreams*, 7–8; Ronald Sharps, "Happy Days and Sorrow Songs: Interpretations of Negro Folklore by Black Intellectuals, 1893–1928" (diss., George Washington University, 1991), 80–81; "Hampton Folklore Society file," Hampton University Archives (HUA).

5. "Mr. Vascar Barnette, Circulation Manager of *The Colored American*," *Colored American Magazine*, 1902-09-13, HUA.

6. Sharps, "Happy Days and Sorrow Songs," 83.

7. *Ibid.*, 102, italics added.

8. Waters, *Strange Ways and Sweet Dreams*, 13.

9. *Ibid.*, 84 n129.

10. W. E. B. Du Bois, Letter to Paul Hanus, 1916-07-19, HUA.

11. Portia Smiley, Letter to Hollis Frissell, 1912-12-02, HUA; Smiley letter to Miss Myrte, 1918-06-19, HUA; Smiley letter to Miss Myrte, 1922-02-21, HUA.

12. "A Contribution from South Carolina," *Southern Workman* 23, no. 3 (March 1894): 46; "Contributions from Correspondents," *Southern Workman* 23, no. 12 (December 1894): 209–10.

13. "Some Side Lights on History," *Southern Workman* 23, no. 4 (April 1894): 65 [65–66].

14. Waters, *Strange Ways and Sweet Dreams*, 55.

15. Sharps, "Happy Days and Sorrow Songs," 91.

16. For a more detailed discussion of the Hampton Folklore Society collection see Sharps, "Happy Days and Sorrow Songs," and Waters, *Strange Ways and Sweet Dreams.*

17. Alice Bacon, "American Folk-lore Society," *Southern Workman* 24, no. 2 (Feb 1895): 31 [30–32].

18. Robert Russa Moton, "Negro Folk-Songs," *Southern Workman* 24, no. 2 (1895): 31 [31–32].

19. *Ibid.*

20. *Ibid.*

21. *Ibid.*

22. *Ibid.*, 32.

23. Alice Bacon, "Work and Methods of the Hampton Folk-Lore Society," *Journal of American Folk-Lore* 11, no. 40 (1898): 21.

24. Robert Moton, *Finding A Way Out: An Autobiography* (New York: Doubleday, 1921), 59.

25. Even in his later writings and work, Moton continued to insist on the necessity of context in understanding black folklore and educated others on the significance of black folk culture. In "The Major," Walter Brown recalls, Moton "seemed at his best when leading in the singing of spirituals. . . . At the opening of each school year, and especially for the benefit of the new students, it was his custom to tell the origins of the spirituals—how they came into being and the conditions from which they sprang—and why the spirituals should be cherished." See Walter Brown, "The Major," in *Robert Russa Moton of Hampton and Tuskegee*, ed. William Hughes and Frederick D. Patterson (Chapel Hill: University of North Carolina Press, 1956), 75. For more on Moton's attention to contextualizing frameworks see also Waters, *Strange Ways and Sweet Dreams*, 48–49.

26. Rosemary Hathaway, "The Unbearable Weight of Authenticity: Zora Neale Hurston's *Their Eyes Were Watching God* and a Theory of 'Touristic Reading,'" *Journal of American Folklore* 117, no. 464 (2004): 169, 177 [168–90].

27. Lee Baker, *Anthropology and the Racial Politics of Culture* (Durham, North Carolina: Duke University Press, 2010), 59.

28. Daphne Lamothe, *Inventing the New Negro: Narrative, Culture and Ethnography* (Philadelphia: University of Pennsylvania Press, 2008), 30.

29. Quoted in Baker, *Anthropology*, 61.

30. Melvin Wade, "The Intellectual and Historical Origins of Folklore Scholarship By Black Americans: A Study of the Response to the Propaganda of Racial Superiority at Hampton (Virginia) Institute 1893–1939," unpublished manuscript, 1982-06-14, HUA.

31. Robert Moton, "Captain Moton's Story," *Southern Workman* 25, no. 9 (1986): 185–86.

32. Susan Meisenhelder, "Conflict and Resistance in Zora Neale Hurston's *Mules and Men*," *Journal of American Folklore* 109, no. 433 (1996): 271–72 [267–88].

33. Robert Russa Moton, *What the Negro Thinks* (New York: Doubleday, Doran, 1929), 1.

34. Alice Bacon, "Editorial," *Southern Workman* 28, no. 6 (1899): 201.

35. Henry Louis Gates Jr., "The Trope of a New Negro and the Reconstruction of the Image of the Black," *Representations* 24 (Autumn 1988): 132.

36. *Ibid.*, 136–37.

37. Wilson Moses traces the founding of the ANA back to this missionary and civilizing impulse, explaining: "The uplift of black people was seen as being dependent upon character building and the elevation of moral life . . . to be carried out through the work of an educated black elite. This was the genesis of the idea of the American Negro Academy . . ." (73). See Wilson Moses, *The Golden Age of Black Nationalism: 1850–1925* (Oxford: Oxford University Press, 1988), 73. It is important to note that while members of the ANA, throughout the 1890s, would have been in general agreement with the main tenets of the organization, there were distinctions among members' ideological and philosophical understandings of their "mission." As an extension of this race consciousness, for example, Crummell encouraged African Americans to participate in missionary work promoting Anglo-Christianity and "civilization" in Africa. See Carole Lynn Stewart, "Challenging Liberal Justice: The Talented Tenth Revisited," in *Re-Cognizing W. E. B. Du Bois in the Twenty-First Century*, ed. Mary Keller and Chester J. Fontenot Jr. (Macon, Georgia: Mercer University Press, 2007), 131–32. Stewart contends that while Du Bois may have concurred with Crummell's impulse to recover a positive meaning of black racial identity, he "fundamentally disagreed" with Crummell's plans for African colonization and with the colonization mindset generally. Instead, Stewart proposes that Du Bois offered his readers "another understanding of civilization as an arena for exchange rather than as a process of acquisition" (131–32). Also see Chris Long, "Rapporteur's Commentary," in *Re-Cognizing W. E. B. Du Bois*, ed. Keller and Fontenot, 231. Long further distinguishes Du Bois's attention to Africa from that of Crummell's missionary-driven ideology, noting that Du Bois's

attention stemmed from a desire to "make it clear that Africans had a cultural integrity prior to the advent of colonialism" (231).

38. For example, Crummell argued that through the "civilization of the Negro race . . . by scientific processes of literature, art, and philosophy . . . ," black people could then take their "place in the world of culture and enlightenment." See Alexander Crummell, "Civilization, the Primal Need of the Race (1898)," in *The American Negro Academy Occasional Papers, 1–22*, ed. American Negro Academy (New York: Arno Press, 1969), 3–4. Similarly, in "The Conservation of the Races," Du Bois urged black people to develop black literature, black art, and black culture that were "not a servile imitation of Anglo-Saxon culture, but a stalwart originality which shall unswervingly follow Negro ideals." See W. E. B. Du Bois, "The Conservation of the Races," in *The American Negro Academy Occasional Papers, 1–22*, ed. American Negro Academy (New York: Arno Press, 1969), 8, 10.

39. "More Letters Concerning the 'Folk-Lore Movement' at Hampton," *Southern Workman* 23, no. 1 (January 1894): 5.

40. Alexander Crummell, "Founder's Day Address," *Southern Workman* 25, no. 3 (1896): 48.

41. Michele Valerie Ronnick, "Introduction," in *The Autobiography of William Sanders Scarborough: An American Journey from Slavery to Scholarship*, by William Scarborough (Detroit: Wayne State University Press, 2005): 8.

42. William Scarborough, "Address by Prof. W. H. Scarborough," *Southern Workman* 25, no. 7 (1896): 144–45.

43. Scarborough, "The Negro in Fiction as Portrayer and Portrayed," *Southern Workman* 28, no. 9 (1899): 358–62.

44. Anna Julia Cooper, "Womanhood: A Vital Element in the Regeneration and Progress of the Race," in *The Voice of Anna Julia Cooper*, ed. Charles Lemert and Esme Bhan (Lanham, Maryland: Rowman and Littlefield, 1998), 61, 64. In "Anna Julia Cooper and the Black Orator," Todd Vogel poses a question that has skirted the perimeters of Cooper's studies over the past two decades: "Was Cooper an 'elitist' . . . Or did she use her fancy language to change the ways race works in the country?" In his essay, Vogel concludes that Cooper was a master rhetorician who "reforged the masters' tools . . . [to create] an alternative social theory for the nation." He further asserts that Cooper sought to change the conditions of African American men and women by changing public sentiment and perceptions. To do this, Vogel asserts, Cooper had to enter the dominant cultural discourse on its own terms and then, through rhetorical maneuvering, alter and invert the terms of the discourse. Contrary to Vogel's analysis, Kevin Gaines puts forth a less generous interpretation of Cooper's work. In "The Woman and Labor Questions," Gaines contends that Cooper's work is rooted in "Western ethnocentrism, staunch religious piety and late-Victorian bourgeois sen-

sibility." He argues that out of the multiplicity of Cooper's voices "emerged that of a Southern, nativist apologist for antilabor views." For further analysis of Cooper's rhetorical strategy see Todd Vogel, *Rewriting White: Race, Class and Cultural Capital in Nineteenth Century America* (New Brunswick: Rutgers University Press, 2004), 86; Hazel Carby, *Reconstructing Womanhood: The Emergence of the Afro-American Woman Novelist* (New York: Oxford University Press, 1987), 95–120; Shirley Logan, *We Are Coming: The Persuasive Discourse of Nineteen-Century Black Women* (Carbondale: Southern Illinois University Press, 1999), 113–26. For a critique of Cooper's "elitist" position, see Kevin Gaines, *Uplifting the Race: Black Leadership, Politics, and Culture in the Twentieth Century* (Chapel Hill: University of North Carolina Press, 1996), 128–51.

45. In this way Cooper demonstrates what bell hooks cogently identifies as a feminist commitment to "eradicating the ideology of domination that permeates Western culture on various levels . . . a commitment to reorganizing U.S. society." See bell hooks, *Ain't I a Woman: Black Women and Feminism* (Boston: South End Press, 1981), 194.

46. Evidence of Cooper's involvement with the Hampton Folklore Society is documented in "Hampton School Record," *Southern Workman* 22, no. 4 (March 1894): 54–55; "More Letters Concerning the Folk-lore Movement at Hampton," *Southern Workman* 23, no. 1 (January 1894): 5; "The Asheville Folk-lore Society," *Southern Workman* 23, no. 5 (May 1894): 84; "Folk-lore and Ethnology," *Southern Workman* 23, no. 7 (July 1894): 131–33; "Letter to Moton," 1909-03-26, HUA; "Letter to Moton," 1909-11-07, HUA; and Alice Bacon photograph with Cooper's comments inscribed on the back: "My good friend Miss Alice M. Bacon . . . Wrote a Review in S. W'km'n of *A Voice from the South* and secured favorable notice of it from Wm Dean Howells. Secured for me post of summer editor on the *Workman* for two summers which lead [*sic*] to employment in Hampton Institute for a number of yrs . . . ," Anna Julia Cooper Papers 1881–1958, Moorland-Spingarn Research Center.

47. For example, Vivian May contends, "As an educator and activist, Cooper held to her conviction that all forms of education, be they classical, professional, or vocational, full-time or part-time, should be sites of liberation." May convincingly argues that Cooper "sought to foster in her students and in her community what Paulo Freire would later describe as *concientización*—an overtly critical and political consciousness centered around the struggle for self-determination." See Vivian May, *Anna Julia Cooper, Visionary Black Feminist: A Critical Introduction* (New York: Routledge, 2007), 64.

48. Anna Julia Cooper, "Paper by Mrs. Cooper," *Southern Workman* 23, no. 7 (July 1894): 133.

49. As a cultural historian, Mia Bay contends that nineteenth-century African Americans contested white supremacy by "stripping white theories of black inferi-

ority down to the self- interested and dehumanizing stories that gave them life." In this way, Bay asserts, African Americans were able to show that "white Americans deemed blacks a lesser species only to rationalize their own exploitation and abuse of people of color." See Mia Bay, *The White Image in the Black Mind: African-American Ideas about White People, 1830–1925* (New York: Oxford University Press, 2000), 9.

50. Hazel Carby, *Reconstructing Womanhood: The Emergence of the Afro-American Woman Novelist* (New York: Oxford University Press, 1987), 101–2.

51. Patricia Hill Collins, *Black Feminist Thought: Knowledge, Consciousness, and the Politics of Empowerment* (Boston: Unwin Hyman, 1990), 221–38.

52. Cooper, "Paper by Mrs. Cooper," 133.

53. *Ibid.*

54. *Ibid.*

55. "Letters Concerning the 'Folk-Lore Movement,'" 5.

56. Vivian May, "Anna Julia Cooper's Philosophy of Resistance: Why African Americans Must 'Reverse the Picture of the Lordly Man Slaying the Lion . . . [and] Turn Painter,'" *Philosophia Africana* 12, no. 1 (2009): 43–44 [41–65].

57. For a discussion of "socialized ambivalence" as it relates to the African American literary tradition see Bell, *The Contemporary Novel*, 68, 81.

58. My use of "sites" of memory here is a deliberate allusion to the impressive collection *History and Memory in African American Culture*, in which Robert O'Meally and Genevieve Fabre borrow Pierre Nora's concept of "*lieux de memorie*," or sites of memory, to characterize how African Americans have maintained and articulated memories as a form of alternative history. In the first essay in the collection, Melvin Dixon asserts that these "sites have been used by African American writers . . . to enlarge the frame of cultural reference for the depiction of black experiences by anchoring that experience in memory—a memory that ultimately rewrites history." See Melvin Dixon, "The Black Writer's Use of Memory," in *History and Memory in African American Culture*, ed. Genevieve Fabre and Robert G. O'Meally (New York: Oxford University Press, 1994), 20; Fabre and O'Meally, "Introduction," in *History and Memory in African-American Culture.*

59. Helen Lock, "'Building Up from Fragments': The Oral Memory Process in Some Recent African-American Written Narratives," in *Essentials of the Theory of Fiction*, ed. Michael Hoffman and Patrick Murphy (Durham: Duke University Press, 2005), 297, 299.

60. "Folklore and Ethnology," *Southern Workman* 23, no. 8 (August 1894): 149 [149–150].

61. *Ibid.*, 150.

62. "Folklore and Ethnology," *Southern Workman* 23, no. 10 (October 1894): 179–80.

63. Daniel Webster Davis, "Echoes from a Plantation Party," *Southern Workman*

28, no. 2 (February 1899), 54. For a detailed discussion of the cultural significance and diasporic variations of ring shouts, ring ceremonies, and ring dances, see Sterling Stuckey, *Slave Culture: Nationalist Theory and the Foundations of Black America* (New York: Oxford University Press, 1987), 3-97. For a discussion of Webster's work collecting ring plays, see Waters, *Strange Ways and Sweet Dreams*, 49–50.

64. "News from Washington Workers," *Southern Workman* 23, no. 4 (April 1894): 66.

65. Gene Bluestein, *The Voice of the Folk* (Amherst: University of Massachusetts Press, 1972), 4.

66. "Paper by Mrs. Anna Julia Cooper," 133.

67. bell hooks, "Postmodern Blackness," *Postmodern Culture: An Electronic Journal of Interdisciplinary Criticism* 1, no. 1 (1990): par. 5.

68. "Paper by Mrs. Anna Julia Cooper," 133.

69. Mary Helen Washington, "Introduction," *A Voice from the South: Anna Julia Cooper* (New York: Oxford University Press, 1998), xliii.

70. Anna Julia Cooper, "The Negro as Presented in American Literature," in *The Voice of Anna Julia Cooper*, ed. Charles Lemert and Esme Bhan, 138.

71. *Ibid.*, 141.

72. *Ibid.*, 149.

73. Cooper, "The Ethics of the Negro Question," in *The Voice of Anna Julia Cooper*, ed. Lemert and Bhan, 209.

74. Cooper, "The Negro as Presented in American Literature," in *The Voice of Anna Julia Cooper*, ed. Lemert and Bhan, 140.

75. *Ibid.*, 135, 159.

76. May, "Philosophy," 46, 44.

77. For more on Cooper's ethics of democratic exchange see Janice Fernheimer, "Arguing from Difference: Cooper, Emerson, Guizot, and a More Harmonious America," in *Black Women's Intellectual Traditions: Speaking Their Minds*, ed. Carol Conaway and Kristen Waters (Burlington: University of Vermont Press, 2007), 295–96.

78. See Karen Baker-Fletcher, *A Singing Something: Womanist Reflections on Anna Julia Cooper* (New York: Crossroad Press, 1994).

79. Cooper, "The Negro as Presented in American Literature," in *The Voice of Anna Julia Cooper*, ed. Lemert and Bhan, 159.

80. Cooper, "Ethics of the Negro Question," in *The Voice of Anna Julia Cooper*, ed. Lemert and Bhan, 206.

81. Elizabeth Alexander, "We Must Be About Our Father's Business: Anna Julia Cooper and the Incorporation of the Nineteenth Century African-American Woman Intellectual," *Signs* 20, no. 2 (1995): 345 [336–56].

82. *Ibid.*, 350.

83. Cooper, "Woman versus the Indian," in *The Voice of Anna Julia Cooper*, ed. Lemert and Bhan, 94–94.

84. *Ibid.*, 95 (italics in original).

85. Toni Cade Bambara, *The Salt Eaters* (1980; rpt. New York: Vintage, 1992), 258.

86. Helen Lock, "'Building Up from Fragments,'" 299.

87. Charles Chesnutt, *Conjure Tales and Stories of the Color Line*, ed. William Andrews (New York: Penguin, 1992), 65.

Chapter 4

1. Scarborough, "The Negro in Fiction as Portrayer and Portrayed," *Southern Workman* 28 (September 1899): 359 [358–61].

2. Gene Andrew Jarrett, "The Dialect of New Negro Literature," in *A Companion to African American Literature*, ed. Jarrett (Oxford: Blackwell, 2010), 171 [169–84].

3. Jarrett labels this form of literary realism "minstrel realism" to capture the ways in which nineteenth-century protocols of racial authenticity drawn from the minstrel and plantation traditions created racially determined and differentiated criteria for what constituted realism. See Jarrett, "'Entirely Black Verse from Him Would Succeed,'" in *Deans and Truants: Race and Realism in African American Literature*, ed. Gene Andrew Jarrett (Philadelphia: University of Pennsylvania Press, 2007), 29–51. Houston Baker uses the phrase "tight spaces" to denote a post-Reconstruction United States context, although he notes that this condition extends well before and after the post-Reconstruction period, in which blackness was controlled, contained, framed, and/or exiled via the institutionalization of human life. See Baker, *Turning South Again: Re-Thinking Modernism/Re-Reading Booker T.* (Durham: Duke University Press, 2001), 15, 26.

4. In an 1895 letter to Alice Ruth Moore (Dunbar-Nelson), Dunbar queried Alice about her thoughts on "preserving . . . those quaint old tales . . . of our fathers," which he noted had been made famous by "Joel Chandler Harris, Thomas Nelson Page, Ruth McEnery Stuart and others," wondering whether there was a place for this folklore in African American literature or whether it was better to "ignore the past" and the potential fame representing these tales might generate. See "Paul Laurence Dunbar to Alice Ruth Moore (Dunbar-Nelson), April 17, 1895," in *Letters from Black America*, ed. Pamela Newkirk (New York: Farrar, Straus and Giroux, 2009), 270.

5. William Dean Howells's 27 June 1896 review of *Majors and Minors* and his subsequent "Introduction" for *Lyrics of Lowly Life* was emblematic, if not prescriptive, of mainstream literary assessments of Dunbar's work. In the now infamous review of *Majors and Minors*, Howells asserts of Dunbar's Majors, or Standard English verse, that there was nothing exceptional about them other than that they were written by a

black man. Regarding his dialect poems, however, Howells claims that it is then "we feel ourselves in the presence of a man with a direct and fresh authority to do the kind of thing he is doing." See William Dean Howells, "Life and Letters," *Harpers Weekly* (27 June 1896): 630. Grace Isabel Colbron provides a review along similar lines, tellingly asserting:

> It is therefore no belittling of the true literary value of Paul Dunbar's earlier works, his exquisite poems, and the sketches in *Folks from Dixie*, to say that they touched us so deeply because they gave us what we asked for—the glow of a warm heart thrown on [an] . . . almost unknown corner of our country's many-sided life. When this promising poet, from whom we expected work of increasing power along the same lines, forsakes his own people and gives us a picture of the life of the white inhabitants of an Ohio town, he challenges us to judge him without the plea of his especial fitness for the work.

See Grace Isabel Colbron, "Across the Color Line," *Bookman* 8 (December 1898): 339 [338–41].

6. As Kevin Young notes, "From his first book and mythologized death on, Dunbar's names would be recalled with reverence. . . . The Dunbar name went on to grace many African American institutions, from societies to high schools, across the country. . . . 'Dunbar' almost came to be synonymous with black." See Kevin Young, *The Grey Album: On the Blackness of Blackness* (Minneapolis: Greywolf Press, 2012), 91.

7. Alice Dunbar-Nelson, for instance, argued that contrary to Howells's evaluations, Dunbar expressed himself most fully in his Standard English verse. See Alice Dunbar-Nelson, "The Poet and His Song," *A.M.E. Review* 12 (October 1914): 124 [121–35].

8. Jay Martin and Gossie Hudson, "Introduction," in *The Paul Laurence Dunbar Reader* (New York: Dodd, Mead, 1975), 17.

9. For a detailed description of Dunbar's and Douglass's involvement in the World's Columbian Exposition, see Shelley Fisher Fishkin and David Bradley, "General Introduction," in *The Sport of the Gods and Other Essential Writings*, ed. Shelley Fisher Fishkin and David Bradley (New York: Modern Library, 2005), xix–xxiv.

10. See Daryl Dance, *From My People: 400 Years of African American Folklore* (New York: W. W. Norton, 2002), xxxvi; Joanne Braxton, "Acknowledgments," in *The Collected Poetry of Paul Laurence Dunbar*, by Paul Laurence Dunbar (Charlottesville: University of Virginia Press, 1993), vii; Henry Louis Gates Jr., "Foreword," in *In His Own Voice: The Dramatic and Other Uncollected Works of Paul Laurence Dunbar*, ed. Herbert Woodward Martin and Ronald Primeau (Athens: Ohio University Press, 2002), xi.

11. Paul Laurence Dunbar, Letter to Dr. Henry Tobey, 13 July 1895, in *The Paul Laurence Dunbar Reader*, 430–31; Dunbar, "The Poet," in *Collected Poetry*, 191.

12. As Gates notes, this aspect of Dunbar's legacy—and the tradition of African Americans memorizing and reciting poetry by black writers more generally—deserves a study of its own, and indeed Lena Ampadu has added numerous additional examples of this practice through her own collection of personal interviews, and she asserts not only the aesthetic value but also the functional value of this tradition. See Gates, "Foreword," in *In His Own Voice*, xi; and Lena Ampadu, "The Poetry of Paul Laurence Dunbar and the Influence of African Aesthetics: Dunbar's Poems and the Tradition of Masking," in *We Wear the Masks: Paul Laurence Dunbar and the Politics of Representative Reality*, ed. Willie Harrell Jr. (Kent, Ohio: Kent State University Press, 2012), 3–16.

13. Paul Laurence Dunbar, "Negro Music," *Chicago Record*, 1899, reprinted in *In his Own Voice*, 183 [183–85].

14. In *Culture on the Margins*, Jon Cruz argues that Frederick Douglass invited readers to hear slave songs not as alien music but as "testimonies" of the slaves' inner lives. See John Cruz, *Culture on the Margins: The Black Spiritual and the Rise of American Cultural Interpretation* (Princeton: Princeton University Press, 1999), 3.

15. Dunbar, "Negro Music," 183.

16. *Ibid.*, 184.

17. Howells, "Introduction" [to *Lyrics of Lowly Life*], in *The Life and Works of Paul Laurence Dunbar*, ed. Lida Wiggins (Naperville, Illinois: J. L. Nichols, 1907), 15.

18. Howells, "Introduction," 14–15.

19. *Ibid.*, 16.

20. *Ibid.*

21. L.B.A., "Review of *Poems of Cabin and Field*," *Southern Workman* 28, no. 12 (December 1899): 506–7; Susan Showers, "Review of *The Fanatics*," *Southern Workman* 30, no. 6 (June 1901): 364–65; "Review of *Sport of the Gods*," *Southern Workman* 30, no. 10 (October 1901): 557; Helen Ludlow, "Review of *Candle-Lightin' Time*," *Southern Workman* 30, no. 12 (December 1901): 696–97; "Review of *When Malindy Sings*," *Southern Workman* 32, no. 12 (December 1903): 630–3l; "Review of *Li'l Gal* and *Heart of Happy Hollow*," *Southern Workman* 33, no. 12 (December 1904): 692–93; "Review of *Howdy, Honey, Howdy*," *Southern Workman* 34, no. 11 (November 1905): 628; "Review of *Joggin' Erlong*," *Southern Workman* 36, no. 1 (January 1907): 52.

22. "Review of *When Malindy Sings*," 630.

23. Ludlow, "Review of *Candle-Lightin' Time*," 696.

24. Young, *The Grey Album*, 99.

25. Gates, *Figures in Black*, 171–72. Gavin Jones similarly suggests that this form of masking might be operative in Dunbar's fiction, asking, "Do the 'plantation tradition'

aspects of Dunbar's stories act as an emotional smokescreen, disarming readers, leaving them vulnerable to the sudden dagger of his moral revolt?" (187). Jones, however, does not make the same distinction Young posits, between black dialect as a product of white literary conventions and black vernacular as a form of everyday African American expression. See Gavin Jones, *Strange Talk: the Politics of Dialect Literature in Gilded Age America* (Berkeley: University of California Press, 1999), 186–94.

26. Dunbar, "Fishin'," *Southern Workman* 30, no. 1 (January 1901): 761–62; Dunbar, "Speakin' at de Co'te House," *Southern Workman* 30, no. 9 (September 1901): 485; Dunbar, "Wadin' in de Creek," *Southern Workman* 32, no. 7 (July 1903): 319–20; Dunbar, "The Forest Greeting," *Southern Workman* 32, no. 12 (December 1903): 616; Dunbar, "The Tuskegee Song," *Southern Workman* 35, no. 5 (May 1906): 291.

27. See "Negro in Literature," in *In His Own Voice*, 205–6.

28. See Ray Sapirstein, "Picturing Dunbar's Lyrics," *African American Review* 41, no. 2 (Summer 2007): 331 [327–39]. For more on the close and influential relationship Dunbar maintained with his mother, see Joanne M. Braxton, "Dunbar, the Originator," *African American Review* 41, no. 2 (Summer 2007): 205–14.

29. *Southern Workman* 30, no. 10 (October 1901): 560.

30. Sapirstein, "Picturing Dunbar's Lyrics," 327.

31. *Ibid.*, 333.

32. Gene Jarrett and Thomas Lewis Morgan, "Introduction," in *The Complete Short Stories of Paul Laurence Dunbar*, ed. Gene Jarrett and Thomas Lewis Morgan (Athens: Ohio University Press, 2005), xvii.

33. Dunbar, *Complete Stories*, 351.

34. Dunbar, "A Defender of the Faith," in *The Complete Short Stories of Paul Laurence Dunbar*, ed. Jarrett and Morgan, 352.

35. Jarrett and Morgan, "Introduction," xx.

36. "Review of *The Strength of Gideon and Other Stories*," in *New York Commercial Advertiser*, 1 June 1900.

37. For an expanded discussion of the counter-text created in Kemble's illustrations, see Adam Sonstegard, "Kemble's Figures and Dunbar's Folks: Picturing the Work of Graphic Illustrations in Dunbar's Short Fiction," in *We Wear the Masks*, ed. Harrell, 116–37.

38. See Stuart Hall, "The Spectacle of the 'Other,'" in *Representation: Cultural Representations and Signifying Practices* (1997, rpt. London: Sage, 2003), 249, 270, 274 [223–90].

39. Betty Kuyk, *African Voices in African American Heritage* (Bloomington: Indiana University Press, 2003), 139.

40. Gates, *Figures in Black*, 167–68.

41. Bernard Bell, *Afro-American Novel and Its Tradition* (Amherst: University of Massachusetts Press, 1987), 18.

42. Craig Werner, "Early Twentieth Century," in *The Concise Oxford Companion to African American Literature,* ed. William Andrews, Frances Foster, and Trudier Harris (New York: Oxford University Press, 2001), 466 [466–69].

43. Dunbar, *Collected Poems,* 14, 317.

44. *Ibid.,* 2–3.

45. Mikhail Bakhtin, *The Dialogic Imagination: Four Essays,* ed. Michael Holquist; trans. Caryl Emerson and Michael Holquist (Austin: University of Texas Press, 1981), 68, 83.

46. Dunbar, *The Sport of the Gods,* 56–57.

47. *Ibid.,* 57.

48. Dunbar, although friends with Booker T. Washington and commissioned by Washington to write the alma mater for Tuskegee, never embraced Washington's stance on industrial education or his accommodationist approach to addressing African American civil rights in the South. Based on her study of Dunbar's private correspondences, Joanne Braxton found Dunbar to be "a 'race man' much more closely aligned with the W. E. B. Du Bois line of thinking than with the more accommodationist views of Booker T. Washington," asserting Dunbar's essays on "suffrage, civil rights and higher education for Blacks might be seen to *anticipate* those of Du Bois." See Braxton, "Introduction," in *The Collected Poems of Paul Laurence Dunbar,* ed. Braxton, xx.

49. George Frederickson, *The Black Image in the White Mind: The Debate on Afro-American Character and Destiny, 1817–1917* (New York: Harper and Row, 1971), 210–11.

50. Dunbar, *The Sport of the Gods,* 41 (italics added).

51. *Ibid.,* 44.

52. *Ibid.,* 45.

53. *Ibid.,* 49.

54. *Ibid.,* 50.

55. *Ibid.,* 51.

56. Lawrence Rodgers, "Paul Laurence Dunbar's *The Sport of the Gods*: The Doubly Conscious World of Plantation Fiction, Migration, and Ascent," *American Literary Realism* 24, no. 3 (Spring 1992): 42–57.

57. Madhu Dubey, "Narration and Migration: Jazz and Vernacular Theories of Black Women's Fiction," *American Literary History* 10, no. 2 (Summer 1998): 298 [291–316].

58. Quoted in Philip Foner and Ronald L. Lewis, ed., *Black Workers: A Documen-*

tary History from Colonial Times to the Present (Philadelphia: Temple University Press, 1989), 6–8.

59. James Weldon Johnson, *Black Manhattan* (1930, rpt. New York: Arno Press, 1968), 128.

60. *Ibid.*, 78.

61. James Weldon Johnson, *Negro Americans, What Now?* (New York: AMS Press, 1971), 91–92.

62. Dunbar, *The Sport of the Gods*, 78.

63. Anand Prahlad, "Africana Folklore: History and Challenges," *Journal of American Folklore* 118, no. 469 (2005): 265 [245–70]. Here I borrow the phrase "discourse of folkness" from John Roberts, "African American Diversity and the Study of Folklore," *Western Folklore, Special Issue* 52 nos. 2, 3, 4 (April, July, October 1993): 158–59 [157–72]. Arjun Appadurai further explains this paradox in relation to the concepts of "the Native," which operates in ways similar to "the folk." As Kirin Narayan explains of Appadurai's assertion: "[T]he term [Native] is linked to place. 'Natives' are incarcerated in bounded geographical spaces, immobilized and untouched yet paradoxically available to the mobile outsider." See Narayan, "How Native is 'Native' Anthropology?" *American Anthropologist* 95, no. 3 (September 1993): 676 [671–86].

64. See William Andrews, "Introduction," in *The Sport of the Gods* (New York: Signet Classics, 2011), n.p.

65. Dunbar, *The Sport of the Gods*, 216–17.

66. Howells, "Life and Letters," 630.

67. Dunbar, Letter to William Dean Howells, 1896-07-13, in *The Paul Laurence Dunbar Reader*, ed. Martin and Hudson, 435.

68. Quoted in Benjamin Brawley, *Paul Laurence Dunbar: Poet of His People* (Chapel Hill: University of North Carolina Press, 1936), 60.

69. Alice Dunbar Nelson, "The Poet and His Song," 124.

70. Houston Baker, "The 'Limitless' Freedom of Myth: Paul Laurence Dunbar's *The Sport of the Gods* and the Criticism of Afro-American Literature," in *The American Self: Myth, Ideology, and Popular Culture*, ed. Sam Girgus (Albuquerque: University of New Mexico Press, 1981), 135 [124–43].

71. Dunbar, *The Sport of the Gods*, 122–23.

72. *Ibid.*, 203.

73. *Ibid.*, 243.

74. *Ibid.*, 238.

75. Dickson Bruce, *Black American Writing from the Nadir: The Evolution of a Literary Tradition, 1877–1915* (Baton Rouge: Louisiana State University Press, 1989), 97.

76. Rodgers, "Paul Laurence Dunbar's *The Sport of the Gods*," 48, italics added.

Chapter 5

1. Chesnutt's editor, Walter Hines Page, suggested that Chesnutt compose more conjure tales like "The Goophered Grapevine," to be published as a collection of short stories. Within seven weeks Chesnutt returned to Page with six more conjure tales, four of which, "The Conjurer's Revenge," "Sis' Becky's Pickaninny," "The Gray Wolf's Ha'nt," and "Hot-Foot Hannibal" would join the earlier compositions "The Goophered Grapevine" (1887), "Po' Sandy" (1889), and "Mars Jeems' Nightmare" (1889) to become *The Conjure Woman*. Two of the stories, "Tobe's Tribulations" and "A Victim of Heredity," were not accepted by the publisher, and instead Chesnutt published them in *Southern Workman* and *Self Culture Magazine*, respectively. Richard Brodhead has argued that Page's role in selecting and rejecting stories amounted to "a virtual censorship" in which the "darkest," most subversive stories were rejected by Page under the auspice of maintaining literary coherence and aesthetic quality. See Richard Brodhead, "Introduction," in *The Conjure Woman and Other Conjure Tales* by Charles W. Chesnutt (Durham: Duke University Press, 1993), 18 [1–21]. For more on the publication history and editorial practices related to *The Conjure Woman*, see Brodhead, "Introduction," in *The Conjure Woman* by Chesnutt, 15–18; Helen Chesnutt, *Charles Waddell Chesnutt: Pioneer of the Color Line* (Chapel Hill: University of North Carolina, 1952); Charles Chesnutt, *"To Be an Author": Letters of Charles W. Chesnutt, 1889–1905*, ed. Joseph R. McElrath Jr. and Robert C. Leitz (Princeton NJ: Princeton University Press, 1997), 105–6.

2. Bruce Jackson, "Introduction," in *The Negro and His Folklore in Nineteenth-Century Periodicals* (Austin: University of Texas Press, 1967), xxiii.

3. H. Chesnutt, *Charles Waddell Chesnutt*, 20.

4. William Andrews, for instance, argues that Chesnutt utilized irony to alter the plantation frame employed by Page, Harris, and others. See William Andrews, "The Significance of Charles W. Chesnutt's 'Conjure Stories,'" in *Charles W. Chesnutt: Selected Writings*, ed. SallyAnn Ferguson (Boston: Houghton Mifflin, 2001), 337 [370–87]. Joseph McElrath similarly situates Chesnutt in relation to the white literary establishment, interrogating how Chesnutt negotiated his relationships with William Dean Howells. See Joseph McElrath, "W. D. Howells and Race: Charles Chesnutt's Disappointment of the Dean," *Nineteenth-Century Literature* 51 (March 1997): 474–99. Other scholars such as M. Giulia Fabi and Gene Jarrett focus on Chesnutt's role in exposing and subverting the fictions of race associated with the various literary traditions. Fabi, for instance, argues convincingly that Chesnutt and other nineteenth-century African American writers engaged in a "radical revision of prevalent literary modes" and used "metanarrative clues [to] call attention to those revisionary practices." See M. Giulia Fabi, "Reconstructing the Race: The Novel After Slavery," in

The Cambridge Companion to the African American Novel, ed. Maryemma Graham (Cambridge, UK: Cambridge University Press, 2004), 34 [34–49]. For more on this strategy of subversive engagement, see also Gene Jarrett, "The Dialect of New Negro Literature," in *A Companion to African American Literature*, ed. Gene Jarrett (Oxford: Blackwell University Press, 2010), 169–84.

5. According to Bruce Jackson, "With the last decade of the [19th] century we move into modern times. The Negro discovers the value of his folklore himself and, as the 'Folk-lore and Ethnology' series [produced by the Hampton Folklore Society] in *Southern Workman* indicates, begins to take seriously his own cultural heritage." See Jackson, *The Negro and His Folklore*, xxiii.

6. Chesnutt, "Lonesome Ben," *Southern Workman* 29, no. 3 (March 1900): 137–45; Chesnutt, "Tobe's Tribulations," *Southern Workman* 29, no. 11 (November 1900): 656–64; Chesnutt, "The Free Colored People of North Carolina," *Southern Workman* 31, no. 3 (March 1902): 136–41; "Review of *The Conjure Woman*," *Southern Workman* 28, no. 5 (May 1899): 194–95; "Review of *The Marrow of Tradition*," *Southern Workman* 30, no. 12 (December 1901): 655–96.

7. H. Chesnutt, *Charles Waddell Chesnutt*, 111, 155.

8. For a detailed account of Chesnutt's early years as a teacher and then stenographer, see H. Chesnutt, *Charles Waddell Chesnutt*, 1–42.

9. Robert Moton, *Finding a Way Out* (New York: Doubleday, Page, 1920), 61–62.

10. H. Chesnutt, *Pioneer*, 14–15.

11. Richard Brodhead, for example, argues that "uneducated rural blacks seem (as they always do) profoundly other to this writer," further asserting that the outlook Chesnutt internalizes through his schooling "organizes his sense of difference" from the masses of uneducated black people. Cash takes this assertion further, explaining that it is something of a mystery that Chesnutt "chose the folklore laden theme of conjure stories to drive his initial attempts at publication, especially considering his apparent aversion to folk beliefs and the people who sustained its practices." Cash can only explain this as Chesnutt's concession to "the formula of using folklore to attain literary success," a formula, which Cash contends, Chesnutt would eventually abandon. See Richard Brodhead, "Introduction," in *The Journals of Charles W. Chesnutt*, ed. Richard Brodhead (Durham: Duke University Press, 1993), 14; Wiley Cash, "Those Folks Downstairs Believe in Ghosts": The Eradication of Folklore in the Novels of Charles W. Chesnutt," in *Charles Chesnutt Reappraised: Essays on the First Major African American Fiction Writer*, ed. David Garrett Izzo and Maria Orban (Jefferson, North Carolina: McFarland, 2009), 74, 70 [69–80].

12. Chesnutt's investment in making visible customs and traditions as they exist across color lines is documented in his many indictments of the folkways and "stateways" that governed race relations. As several of Chesnutt's non-fiction essays, such

as “What is a White Man?,” “The Disfranchisement of the Negro,” and “The Courts and the Negro” attest, Chesnutt possessed a deep awareness of how the rhetoric of folklore and the distortion of black folk customs were being co-opted to support segregationists’ agendas. See Chesnutt, “What is a White Man?” in *Charles Chesnutt: Stories, Novels and Essays*, ed. Werner Sollors (New York: Library of America, 2002), 837–44; Chesnutt, “The Disfranchisement of the Negro,” in *Charles Chesnutt*, ed. Sollors, 874–94; Chesnutt, “The Courts and the Negro,” in *Charles Chesnutt*, ed. Sollors, 895–905.

13. For more on the protocols of authenticity see Jarrett, “Entirely Black Verse From Him Would Succeed,”, 29–51.

14. Robert Hemenway, “The Functions of Folklore in Charles Chesnutt’s *The Conjure Women*,” *Journal of the Folklore Institute* 13, no. 3 (1976): 287 [283–309].

15. Alan Dundes, “The Study of Folklore in Literature and Culture: Identification and Interpretation,” *Journal of American Folklore* 78, no. 308 (April–June 1965): 136–42.

16. Karen Beardslee, *Literary Legacies, Folklore Foundations: Selfhood and Cultural Tradition in Nineteenth* (Knoxville: University of Tennessee Press, 2001), xiv, xx.

17. See Eric J. Sundquist, “The Origin of the Cakewalk,” in *To Wake the Nations: Race in the Making of American Literature* (Cambridge: Belknap Press of Harvard University Press, 1993), 276–93. Gloria Oden also discusses the significance of African cultural retentions and black folk culture in Chesnutt’s fiction. See Gloria Oden, “Chesnutt’s Conjure as African Survival,” *MELUS* 5, no. 1 (Spring 1978): 38–48. For studies that focus on Chesnutt’s use of folklore as providing an alternative history of slavery and African American experiences, see William Andrews, “Introduction,” in *Conjure Tales and Stories of the Color Line* (New York: Penguin, 1992), vii–xvi; Richard Baldwin, “The Art of the Conjure Woman,” in *Selected Writings*, 346–357; Robert Stepto, “‘The Simple but Intensely Human Inner Life of Slavery’: Story Telling and the Revision of History in Charles W. Chesnutt’s ‘Uncle Julius Tales,’” in *History and Tradition in Afro-American Culture*, ed Gunter Lenz (Frankfurt: Campus Verlag, 1984), 29–55.

18. Bronislaw Malinowski, quoted in Alan Dundes, “Meta Folklore and Oral Literary Criticism,” in *Readings in American Folklore*, ed. Jan Brunvand (New York: W. W. Norton, 1979), 406 [404–15].

19. *Ibid.*, 405.

20. Dan Ben-Amos, “Folklore in Context,” in *Readings in American Folklore*, ed. Brunvand, 436 [428–43].

21. *Ibid.*, 436–37.

22. Mikhail Bakhtin, “Discourse and the Novel,” in *The Norton Anthology of Theory and Criticism*, ed. Vincent Leitch (New York: W. W. Norton), 1205 [1190–1220].

23. See Regina Bendix, *In Search of Authenticity: The Formation of Folklore Studies* (Madison: University of Wisconsin Press, 1997), 198–99.

24. Chesnutt, "Superstitions and Folk-lore of the South," in *Charles W. Chesnutt: Stories, Novels and Essays*, 864 [864–71].

25. *Ibid.*, 854, 865.

26. *Ibid.*, 869, 870.

27. *Ibid.*, 870–71.

28. Sundquist, *To Wake the Nations*, 297.

29. John Edgar Wideman, "Charles Chesnutt and the WPA Narratives: The Oral and Literate Roots of Afro-American Literature," in *The Slave's Narrative*, ed. Charles Davis and Henry Louis Gates Jr. (Oxford, UK: Oxford University Press, 1985), 60 [59–77].

30. Sandra Molyneaux, "Expanding the Collective Memory: Charles Chesnutt's *The Conjure Woman Tales*," in *Memory, Narrative and Identity*, ed. Amritjit Singh, Joseph Skerrett, and Robert E. Hogan (Boston: Northeastern University Press, 1994), 166 [164–78].

31. Yvonne Chireau, *Black Magic: Religion and the African American Conjuring Tradition* (Berkeley: University of California Press, 2003), 13, 20.

32. For more on the various powers held by conjure doctors and their place within the black community, see Chireau 15–20; Albert Raboteau, *Slave Religion: The "Invisible Institution" in the Antebellum South* (New York: Oxford University Press, 1978), 283; Stephanie Mitchem, *African American Folk Healing* (New York: New York University Press, 2007), 21.

33. Raboteau, *Slave Religion*, 281.

34. *Ibid.*, 284.

35. *Ibid.*

36. Harry M. Hyatt, *Hoodoo, Conjuration, Witchcraft, Rootwork: Beliefs Accepted by Many Negroes and White Persons, These Being Orally Recorded among Blacks and Whites*, 5 vols. (Washington: American University Bookstores, 1970), epigraph to vol. 1.

37. See, for example, "Conjure Doctors in the South," *Southern Workman* 7, no. 4 (April 1878): 30–31; "About the Conjuring Doctors," *Southern Workman* 7, no. 5 (May 1878): 38–39; "Conjuring and Conjure-Doctors," *Southern Workman* 24, no. 7 (July 1895): 117–18; "Some Conjure Doctors We Have Heard Of," *Southern Workman* 26, no. 2 (February 1897): 37–38.

38. Mary Owen, *Among the Voodoos* (1881), qtd. in Newbell Niles Puckett, *Folk Beliefs of the Southern Negro* (Chapel Hill: University of North Carolina Press, 1926), 189.

39. "Chills Cured," *Southern Workman* 28, no. 8 (August 1899): 314–15.

40. Frank de Caro and Rosan Augusta Jordan, *Re-Situating Folklore: Folk Contexts*

and Twentieth-Century Literature and Art (Knoxville: University of Tennessee Press, 2004), 6.

41. Zora Neale Hurston, *Their Eyes Were Watching God* (1937, rpt. New York: Harper and Row, 1990), 7.

42. In *Re-Situating Folklore*, Frank de Caro and Rosan Jordan explain how folklore involves and models a dynamic narrative strategy: "[B]ecause there is a 'teller'/performer and an actively participating 'audience,' folkloric communication involves an element of performance and a degree of direct feedback influencing the performance in process . . . it continually evolves in response to its performance context [and] those 'items' performed commonly undergo change in the course of being transmitted." See de Caro and Jordan, *Re-Situating Folklore*, 2.

43. Chesnutt, "Post-Bellum, Pre-Harlem," in *Charles Chesnutt*, ed. Sollors, 907; "Signs and Superstitions," *Southern Workman* 24, no. 5 (May 1895): 78.

44. Sundquist, *To Wake the Nations*, 359.

45. Charles Chesnutt, *Conjure Tales and Stories of the Color Line*, ed. William Andrews (New York: Penguin, 1992), 13.

46. *Ibid.*, 23–24.

47. Anna Julia Cooper, "The Negro as Presented in American Literature," in *The Voice of Anna Julia Cooper*, 135.

48. Hemenway, "Functions of Folklore," 287.

49. Chesnutt, *Conjure Tales*, 6.

50. In the first story, it was disclosed that Aunt Peggy is not only a conjure doctor, but as Julius explains, "dey say she went out ridin' de niggers at night, fer she wuz a witch 'sides bein' a conjuh 'oman" (Chesnutt, *Conjure Tales*, 26). In the Hampton collection, hags are especially terrifying figures since they invade a person during sleep, when he or she is least able to defend himself or herself. Once the besieged individual falls asleep, the witch, or "hag," takes over the person's being, "riding" him or her through the night, causing extreme mental and physical duress. Upon awaking, the affected individual is typically worn down and susceptible to whatever actions the hag seeks to induce.

51. Sundquist, *To Wake the Nations*, 371.

52. Chesnutt, *Conjure Tales*, 38.

53. Molyneaux, "Expanding the Collective Memory," 165.

54. Beardslee, *Literary Legacies*, 77; Arlene Elder, "Charles Waddell Chesnutt: Art or Assimilation?" in *The "Hindered Hand": Cultural Implications of Early African-American Fiction* (Westport, Connecticut: Greenwood Press, 1978), 159; William Andrews, *The Literary Career of Charles Chesnutt* (Baton Rouge: Louisiana State University Press, 1980), 60.

55. Chesnutt, *Conjure Tales*, 49.

56. *Ibid.*, 54.

57. *Ibid.*, 61.

58. *Ibid.*

59. Indeed, Melvin Dixon, reading their relationship within the frame of the seduction narrative, contends that they have become quite more than friends, asserting that the rabbit's foot functions as a phallic symbol enacting a sexual exchange between Julius and Annie. See Melvin Dixon, "The Teller as Folk Trickster in Chesnutt's *The Conjure Woman*," *College Language Association Journal* 18 (December 1974): 186–97.

60. Molyneaux, "Expanding the Collective Memory,"174; Peter Caccavari, "A Trick of Mediation: Charles Chesnutt's Conflicted Literary Relationship with Albion Tourgee," in *Literary Influence and African-American Writers*, ed. Tracy Mishkin (New York: Garland, 1996), 147–48.

61. Cooper, "Ethics of the Negro Question," 209.

62. Ryan Simmons, *Chesnutt and Realism: A Study of the Novels* (Tuscaloosa: University of Alabama Press, 2006), 5.

63. Matthew Wilson, "Who Has the Right to Say? Charles W. Chesnutt, Whiteness and the Public Sphere," *College Literature* 26, no. 2 (Spring 1999): 29 [18–35].

64. Jeanne Fox-Friedman, "Howard Pyle and the Chivalric Order in America: King Arthur for Children," *Arthuriana* 6, no. 1 (1996): 81, 87 [77–95].

65. Charles Chesnutt, *The Colonel's Dream* (1905, rpt. New York: Negro Universities Press, 1970), 26.

66. *Ibid.*, 38.

67. T. J. Jackson Lears, *No Place of Grace: Antimodernism and the Transformation of American Culture* (Chicago: University of Chicago Press, 1994), xvi, 57.

68. Chesnutt, *The Colonel's Dream*, 49.

69. Roger Abrahams, "Sincerities: William Wells Newell and the Discovery of Folklore in Late Nineteenth Century America," in *Folklore in American Life*, ed. Jane Becker and Barbara Franco (Lexington, Massachusetts: Museum of Our National Heritage, 1998), 62 [61–75].

70. Chesnutt, *The Colonel's Dream*, 146, 147.

71. *Ibid.*, 149–50.

72. Cooper, "Womanhood," in *The Voice of Anna Julia Cooper*, eds. Lemert and Bhan, 55.

73. See Dean McWilliams, *Charles W. Chesnutt and the Fictions of Race* (Athens: University of Georgia Press, 2004), 168–69.

74. Chesnutt, *The Colonel's Dream*, 271.

75. For a detailed discussion of the significance of the "extraction of Peter's body,"

and how that event comes to symbolize for French the "utter intransigence toward black equality," see McWilliams, *Charles W. Chesnutt and the Fictions of Race*, 176–77.

76. Charles Mills, *The Racial Contract* (Ithaca, New York: Cornell University Press, 1999), 18.

Conclusion

1. Franz Boas, "Letter to Hurston," 3 May 1927, Franz Boas Papers, Folk Life Center, Library of Congress.

2. Zora Neale Hurston, "'Halimuhfack" recording with explanation." Recorded by Herbert Halpert, 18 June 1939, Hurston Sound Recordings, Folk Life Center, Library of Congress.

3. Zora Neale Hurston, *Mules and Men* (1935, reprint New York: HarperPerennial, 2008), 1.

4. Ralph Ellison, "Twentieth Century Fiction," in *Shadow and Act* (1953; reprint New York: Vintage, 1995), 27 [24–44].

5. *Ibid.*, 28.

6. Ralph Ellison, "Flying Home," in *Flying Home and Other Stories*, ed. John Callahan (New York: Random House, 1996), 17.

7. Colson Whitehead, *John Henry Days* (New York: Anchor, 2002), 4.

BIBLIOGRAPHY

Abrahams, Roger D. "Rough Sincerities: Williams Wells Newell and the Discovery of Folklore in Late Nineteenth Century America." In *Folklore in American Life*, ed. Jane Becker and Barbara Franco, 61–75. Lexington, MA: Museum of Our National Heritage, 1998.

"About the Conjuring Doctors." *Southern Workman* 7, no. 5 (May 1878): 38–39.

Alexander, Elizabeth. "We Must Be About Our Father's Business: Anna Julia Cooper and the Incorporation of the Nineteenth Century African-American Woman Intellectual." *Signs* 20, no. 2 (1995): 336–56.

Alice Bacon photograph. Anna Julia Cooper Papers 1881–1958, Moorland-Spingarn Research Center.

Allen, William Francis, Charles Pickard Ware, and Lucy McKim Garrison. *Slave Songs of the United States*. New York: A. Simpson, 1867.

Ampadu, Lena. "The Poetry of Paul Laurence Dunbar and the Influence of African Aesthetics: Dunbar's Poems and the Tradition of Masking." In *We Wear the Masks: Paul Laurence Dunbar and the Politics of Representative Reality*, ed. Willie Harrell Jr., 3–16. Kent, OH: Kent State University Press, 2012.

Anderson, James. "The Hampton Model." In *New Perspectives on Black Educational History*, ed. P. Vincent Franklin and James Anderson. Boston: G. K. Hall, 1978.

Anderson, Jeffrey. *Conjure in African American Society*. Baton Rouge: Louisiana State University Press, 2003.

Andrews, William. "Introduction." In *Conjure Tales and Stories of the Color Line*, vii–xvi. New York: Penguin, 1992.

———. "Introduction." In *The Sport of the Gods*, n.p. New York: Signet Classics, 2011.

———. *The Literary Career of Charles Chesnutt*. Baton Rouge: Louisiana State University Press, 1980.

———. "The Significance of Charles W. Chesnutt's 'Conjure Stories.'" In *Charles W. Chesnutt: Selected Writings*, ed. SallyAnn Ferguson, 370–87. Boston: Houghton Mifflin Company, 2001.

Armstrong, Mary F. M. *America: Richard Armstrong. Hawaii*. Hampton, VA: Hampton Normal School Steam Press, 1887.

Armstrong, Mary, and Helen Ludlow. *Hampton and Its Students*. Chicago: Afro-Am Press, 1969.

Armstrong, Richard. Journal entry. 1 January 1848. Mission Houses Museum Library.

Armstrong, Samuel. "Editorial Introduction to Student Papers on Conjuring." *Southern Workman* 7, no. 4 (1878): 26.

———. "Editorial Reply." *Southern Workman* 7, no. 5 (1878): 35.

———. "Letter to Archibald Hopkins." 15 Jan 1863. In *Samuel Chapman Armstrong: A Biographical Study*, by Edith Armstrong Talbot, 86. New York: Negro Universities Press, 1969.

———. "Letter to the Cousins." 22 Dec 1860. Mission Houses Museum Library.

———. "Lesson from the Hawaiian Islands." Hampton, VA: Normal School Printing Office, 1884.

———. "Principal's Report." In *Annual Report*. Hampton, VA: Normal School Printing Press, 1885.

"The Asheville Folk-lore Society." *Southern Workman* 23, no. 5 (May 1894): 84.

Bacon, Alice. "American Folk-lore Society." *Southern Workman* 24, no. 2 (Feb 1895): 30–32.

———. "Circular Letter." *Southern Workman* 22, no. 12 (1893): 180–81.

———. "Editorial." *Southern Workman* 28, no. 6 (1899): 201.

———. *Japanese Girls and Women*. Boston, New York: Houghton Mifflin, 1891.

———. *A Japanese Interior*. Boston: Houghton Mifflin, 1893.

———."Some Side Lights on History." *Southern Workman* 23, no. 4 (April 1894): 65–66.

———. "Work and Method of the Hampton Folklore Society." *Journal of American Folklore* 9, no. 40 (1898): 17–21.

Baker, Houston. *Blues, Ideology and Afro-American Literature: A Vernacular Theory*. Chicago: University of Chicago Press, 1984.

———. "The 'Limitless' Freedom of Myth: Paul Laurence Dunbar's *The Sport of the Gods* and the Criticism of Afro-American Literature." In *The American Self: Myth, Ideology, and Popular Culture*, ed. Sam Girgus, 124–43. Albuquerque: University of New Mexico Press, 1981.

———. *Turning South Again: Re-Thinking Modernism/Re-Reading Booker T.* Durham, NC: Duke University Press, 2001.

Baker, Lee. *Anthropology and the Racial Politics of Culture*. Durham, NC: Duke University Press, 2010.

Baker-Fletcher, Karen. *A Singing Something: Womanist Reflections on Anna Julia Cooper.* New York: Crossroad Press, 1994.

Bakhtin, Mikhail. *The Dialogic Imagination: Four Essays*, ed. Michael Holquist, translated by Caryl Emerson and Michael Holquist. Austin: University of Texas Press, 1981.

———. "Discourse and the Novel." In *The Norton Anthology of Theory and Criticism*, ed. Vincent Leitch, 1190–1220. New York: W. W. Norton, 2010.

Baldwin, Richard. "The Art of The Conjure Woman." In *Charles W. Chesnutt: Selected Writings*, ed. SallyAnn Ferguson, 346–57. Boston: Houghton Mifflin, 2001.

Bambara, Toni Cade. *The Salt Eaters*. 1980. Reprint, New York: Vintage, 1992.

Bassett, F. S. "The International Folk-Lore Congress of the World's Columbian Exposition, Chicago, July, 1893/Address by Lieutenant F. S. Bassett." Accessed 17 March 2011. http://en.wikisource.org/w/index.php?title=The_International_Folk-Lore_Congress_of_the_World%27s_Columbian_Exposition,_Chicago,_July,_1893/Address_by_Lieutenant_F._S._Bassett&oldid=2511450.

Bay, Mia. *The White Image in the Black Mind: African-American Ideas about White People, 1830–1925*. New York: Oxford University Press, 2000.

Beardslee, Karen. *Literary Legacies, Folklore Foundations: Selfhood and Cultural Tradition in Nineteenth- and Twentieth-Century American Literature*. Knoxville: University of Tennessee Press, 2001.

Bederman, Gail. *Manliness and Civilization: A Cultural History of Gender and Race in the United States, 1880–1917*. Chicago: University of Chicago Press, 1995.

Bell, Bernard. *The Afro-American Novel and Its Tradition*. Amherst: University of Massachusetts Press, 1987.

———. *The Contemporary African American Novel: Its Folk Roots and Modern Literary Branches*. Amherst: University of Massachusetts Press, 2004.

Ben-Amos, Dan. "Folklore in Context." In *Readings in American Folklore*, ed. Jan Brunvand, 428–43. New York: W. W. Norton, 1979.

———. "Toward a Definition of Folklore in Context." *Journal of American Folklore* 84, no. 331 (January 1971): 3–15.

Bendix, Regina. *In Search of Authenticity: The Formation of Folklore Studies*. Madison: University of Wisconsin Press, 1997.

Bluestein, Gene. *The Voice of the Folk: Folklore and American Literary Theory*. Amherst: University of Massachusetts Press, 1972.

Boas, Franz. "Letter to Hurston." 3 May 1927. Franz Boas Papers. Folk Life Center, Library of Congress.

Brawley, Benjamin. *Paul Laurence Dunbar: Poet of His People*. Chapel Hill: University of North Carolina Press, 1936.

Braxton, Joanne, ed. *The Collected Poetry of Paul Laurence Dunbar*, by Paul Laurence Dunbar. Charlottesville: University of Virginia Press, 1993.

———. "Dunbar, The Originator." *African American Review* 41, no. 2 (Summer 2007): 205–14.

Brodhead, Richard. Introduction. *The Conjure Woman and Other Conjure Tales*, by Charles W. Chesnutt, 1–21. Durham, NC: Duke University Press, 1993.

———. Introduction. *The Journals of Charles W. Chesnutt*, by Charles W. Chesnutt, ed. Richard Brodhead. Durham: Duke University Press, 1993.

Bronner, Simon. *American Folklore Studies: An Intellectual History*. Lawrence: University Press of Kansas, 1986.

———. *Folk Nation: Folklore in the Creation of American Tradition*. Wilmington, DE: Scholarly Resources, 2002.

Brown, Walter. "The Major." In *Robert Russa Moton of Hampton and Tuskegee*, ed. William Hardin Hughes and Frederick D. Patterson. Chapel Hill: University of North Carolina Press, 1956.

Bruce, Dickson. *Black American Writing from the Nadir: The Evolution of a Literary Tradition, 1877–1915*. Baton Rouge: Louisiana State University Press 1989.

Bruce, Philip. *Plantation Negro as Freedman: Observations on His Character, Conditions and Prospects in Virginia*. New York: G. P. Putnam's Sons, 1889.

Caccavari, Peter. "A Trick of Mediation: Charles Chesnutt's Conflicted Literary Relationship with Albion Tourgee," in *Literary Influence and African-American Writers*, ed. Tracy Mishkin, 129–53. New York: Garland, 1996.

Carby, Hazel. *Reconstructing Womanhood: The Emergence of the Afro-American Woman Novelist*. New York: Oxford University Press, 1987.

Carroll, Anne. *Word, Image and the New Negro: Representation and Identity in the Harlem Renaissance*. Bloomington: Indiana University Press, 2005.

Cash, Wiley. "'Those Folks Downstairs Believe in Ghosts': The Eradication of Folklore in the Novels of Charles W. Chesnutt." In *Charles Chesnutt Reappraised: Essays on the First Major African American Fiction Writer*, ed. David Garrett Izzo and Maria Orban, 69–80. Jefferson, NC: McFarland, 2009.

Chesnutt, Charles. *Charles Chesnutt: Stories, Novels and Essays*, ed. Werner Sollors. New York: Library of America, 2002.

———. *The Colonel's Dream*. 1905. Reprint, New York: Negro Universities Press, 1970.

———. *The Conjure Woman*. 1899. Reprint in *Conjure Tales and Stories of the Color Line*, ed. William Andrews. New York: Penguin *Books*, 1992.

———. *Conjure Tales and Stories of the Color Line*, ed. William Andrews. New York: Penguin, 1992.

———. "The Free Colored People of North Carolina." *Southern Workman* 31, no. 3 (March 1902): 136–41.

———. "Lonesome Ben." *Southern Workman* 29, no. 3 (March 1900): 137–45.

———. "Tobe's Tribulations." *Southern Workman* 29, no. 11 (November 1900): 656–64.

———. *"To Be an Author": Letters of Charles W. Chesnutt, 1889–1905*, ed. Joseph R. McElrath Jr. and Robert C. Leitz. Princeton: Princeton University Press, 1997.

Chesnutt, Helen. *Charles Waddell Chesnutt: A Pioneer of the Color Line*. Chapel Hill: University of North Carolina Press, 1952.

"Chills Cured." *Southern Workman* 28, no. 8 (August 1899): 314–15.

Chireau, Yvonne. *Black Magic: Religion and the African American Conjuring Tradition.* Berkeley: University of California Press, 2003.

Christian, Barbara. "The Race for Theory." *Cultural Critique* 6 (Spring 1987): 51–63.

Colbron, Grace Isabel. "Across the Color Line." *Bookman* 8 (December 1898): 338–41.

Collins, Patricia Hill. *Black Feminist Thought: Knowledge, Consciousness, and the Politics of Empowerment.* Boston: Unwin Hyman, 1990.

"Conjure Doctors in the South." *Southern Workman* 7, no. 4 (1878): 2.

"Conjuring and Conjure-Doctors." *Southern Workman* 24, no. 7 (July 1895): 117–18.

"A Contribution from South Carolina." *Southern Workman* 23, no. 3 (1894): 46–47.

"Contributions from Correspondents." *Southern Workman* 23, no. 12 (1894): 209–10.

Cooper, Anna Julia. *The Voice of Anna Julia Cooper*, ed. Charles Lemert and Esme Bhan. Lanham, MD: Rowman and Littlefield, 1998.

———. "Paper by Mrs. Anna J. Cooper." *Southern Workman* 23, no. 7 (1894): 133.

Covey, Eric. "Dole." In *The Business of Food: Encyclopedia of the Food and Drink Industry.* Edited by Gary Allen and Ken Albala. Westport, Connecticut: Greenwood, 2007.

Crane, T. F. "Recent Folk-Lore Publications" *Nation* 12 (June 1890): 475–76.

Crummell, Alexander. "Civilization, the Primal Need of the Race (1898)." In *The American Negro Academy Occasional Papers, 1–22*, ed. American Negro Academy. New York: Arno Press, 1969.

———. "Founder's Day Address." *Southern Workman* 25, no. 3 (1896): 48.

Cruz, John. *Culture on the Margins: The Black Spiritual and the Rise of American Cultural Interpretation.* Princeton, NJ: Princeton University Press, 1999.

Culin, Stewart. "Reports Concerning Voodooism." *Journal of American Folklore* 2, no. 6 (1899): 232–33.

Dance, Daryl. *From My People: 400 Years of African American Folklore.* New York: W. W. Norton, 2002.

Davis, Daniel Webster. "Echoes from a Plantation Party." *Southern Workman* 28, no. 2 (February 1899): 54–59.

Davis, Gerald L. "Thomas Washington Talley: Early Twentieth-Century African American Folklore Theorist." *New York Folklore* 18, nos.1–4 (2000): 91–102.

de Caro, Frank, and Rosan Augusta Jordan. *Re-Situating Folklore: Folk Contexts and Twentieth-Century Literature and Art.* Knoxville: University of Tennessee Press, 2004.

"Department of Folklore and Ethnology." *Southern Workman* 22, no. 12 (1893): 179–80.

Dixon, Melvin. "The Black Writer's Use of Memory." In *History and Memory in African American Culture*, ed. Geneviève Fabre and Robert G. O'Meally, 18–27. New York: Oxford University Press, 1994.

———. "The Teller as Folk Trickster in Chesnutt's *The Conjure Woman*." *College Language Association Journal* 18 (December 1974): 186–97.

Du Bois, W. E. B. "The Conservation of the Races." In *The American Negro Academy Occasional Papers, 1–22*, ed. American Negro Academy. New York: Arno Press, 1969.

———. "Letter to Paul Hanus." 19 July 1916. Hampton University Archives.

Dubey, Madhu. "Narration and Migration: *Jazz* and Vernacular Theories of Black Women's Fiction." *American Literary History* 10, no. 2 (Summer 1998): 291–316.

Dunbar, Paul Laurence. *The Collected Poetry of Paul Laurence Dunbar*. Edited by Joanne Braxton. Charlottesville: University of Virginia Press, 1993.

———. *The Complete Stories of Paul Laurence Dunbar*, ed. Gene Andrew Jarrett and Thomas Lewis Morgan. Athens: Ohio University Press, 2005.

———. "Fishin." *Southern Workman* 30, no. 1 (January 1901): 761–2.

———. "The Forest Greeting." *Southern Workman* 32, no. 12 (December 1903): 616.

———. *In His Own Voice: The Dramatic and Other Uncollected Works of Paul Laurence Dunbar*, ed. Herbert Woodward Martin and Ronald Primeau. Athens: Ohio University Press, 2002.

———. *The Paul Laurence Dunbar Reader*, ed. Jay Martin and Gossie Husdon. New York: Dodd, Mead, 1975.

———. "Speakin' at de Co'te House." *Southern Workman* 30, no. 9 (September 1901): 485.

———. *The Sport of the Gods*. New York: Arno Press, 1969.

———. "The Tuskegee Song." *Southern Workman* 35, no. 5 (May 1906): 291.

———. "Wadin' in de Creek." *Southern Workman* 32, no. 7 (July 1903): 319–20.

Dundes, Alan. "The Study of Folklore in Literature and Culture: Identification and Interpretation." *Journal of American Folklore* 78, no. 308 (April–June 1965): 136–42.

———. "Meta Folklore and Oral Literary Criticism." In *Readings in American Folklore*, ed. Jan Brunvand, 404–15. New York: W. W. Norton, 1979.

———, ed. *Mother Wit from the Laughing Barrel: Readings in the Interpretation of Afro-American Folklore*. Englewood Cliffs, NJ: Prentice-Hall, 1973.

———. "Texture, Text, and Context." *Southern Folklore Quarterly* 28 (1971): 251–65.

Dwyer-Shick, S. A.. "The American Folklore Society and Folklore Research in America, 1888–1940." Diss., University of Pennsylvania, 1979.

Elder, Arlene. *The "Hindered Hand": Cultural Implications of Early African-American Fiction*. Westport, CT: Greenwood Press, 1978.

Ellison, Ralph. *Shadow and Act*. 1953. Reprint, New York: Random House, 1964.

———. *Flying Home and Other Stories*, ed. John Callahan. New York: Random House, 1996.

Engs, Robert Francis. *Educating the Disfranchised and Disinherited: Samuel Chapman Armstrong, 1839–1893*. Knoxville: University of Tennessee Press, 1999.

Ernest, John. *Chaotic Justice: Rethinking African American Literary History.* Chapel Hill: University of North Carolina Press, 2009.

Evans, Brad. *Before Cultures: The Ethnographic Imagination in American Literature, 1865–1920.* Chicago: University of Chicago, 2005.

Fabi, M. Giulia. "Reconstructing the Race: The Novel After Slavery." In *The Cambridge Companion to the African American Novel,* ed. Maryemma Graham, 34–49. Cambridge, UK: Cambridge University Press, 2004.

Fabin, Johannes. *Time and the Other: How Anthropology Makes Its Objects.* New York: Columbia University Press, 1983.

Fabre, Geneviève, and Robert G. O'Meally. Introduction. *History and Memory in African-American Culture,* ed. Geneviève Fabre and Robert G. O'Meally. New York: Oxford University Press, 1994.

Farmer-Kaiser, Mary. *Freedwomen and the Freedmen's Bureau: Race, Gender, and Public Policy in the Age of Emancipation.* New York: Fordham University Press, 2010.

Favor, J. Martin. *Authentic Blackness: The Folk in the New Negro Renaissance.* Durham, NC: Duke University Press, 1999.

Fernheimer, Janice. "Arguing from Difference: Cooper, Emerson, Guizot, and a More Harmonious America." In *Black Women's Intellectual Traditions: Speaking Their Minds,* ed. Carol Conaway and Kristen Waters, 295–96. Burlington, VT: University of Vermont Press, 2007.

Fishkin, Shelley Fisher, and David Bradley, ed. "General Introduction." In *The Sport of the Gods and Other Essential Writings,* xix–xxiv. New York: Modern Library, 2005.

"Folk-lore and Ethnology." *Southern Workman* 23, no. 7 (July 1894): 131–33.

"Folklore and Ethnology." *Southern Workman* 23, no. 8 (August 1894): 149–50.

Foner, Philip, and Ronald L. Lewis, ed. *Black Workers: A Documentary History from Colonial Times to the Present.* Philadelphia: Temple University Press, 1989.

Forbes, David, compiler. *Hawaiian National Bibliography, 1780–1900, volume 4, 1881–1900.* Honolulu: University of Hawai'i Press, 2003.

Fortier, Alcee. "Customs and Superstitions of Louisiana." *Journal of American Folklore* 1, no. 2 (1888): 136–38.

Fox-Friedman, Jeanne. "Howard Pyle and the Chivalric Order in America: King Arthur for Children." *Arthuriana* 6, no. 1 (1996): 77–95.

Frederickson, George. *The Black Image in the White Mind: The Debate on Afro-American Character and Destiny, 1817–1914.* 1971. Reprint, Middletown, CT: Wesleyan University Press, 1987.

Freund, Hugo. "Cultural Evolution, Survivals, and Immersion: The Implications for Nineteenth-Century Folklore Studies." In *The American Folklore Society: 100*

Years, ed. William Clements, 12–15. Washington: American Folklore Society, 1988.

Gaines, Kevin. *Uplifting the Race: Black Leadership, Politics, and Culture in the Twentieth Century.* Chapel Hill: University of North Carolina Press, 1996.

Gates, Henry Louis Jr. *Figures in Black: Words, Signs, and the Racial Self.* New York: Oxford University Press, 1987.

———. Foreword to *In His Own Voice: The Dramatic and Other Uncollected Works of Paul Laurence Dunbar*, ed. Herbert Woodward Martin and Ronald Primeau. Athens: Ohio University Press, 2002.

———. *The Signifying Monkey: A Theory of Afro-American Literary Criticism.* New York: Oxford University Press, 1988.

———. "The Trope of a New Negro and the Reconstruction of the Image of the Black." *Representations* 24 (Autumn 1988): 129–55.

Geracimos, Helen. *Shaping History: The Role of Newspapers in Hawaii.* Honolulu: University of Hawai'i Press, 1996.

Goldberg, David Theo. "Racial Rule." In *Relocating Postcolonialism*, ed. David Theo Goldberg and Ato Quayson, 82–102. Oxford, UK: Blackwell Press, 2002.

Hall, Stuart. "The Spectacle of the 'Other.'" In *Representation: Cultural Representations and Signifying Practices*, 223–90. 1997. Reprint, London: Sage, 2003.

"Hampton Folklore Society file." Hampton University Archives.

"Hampton School Record." *Southern Workman* 22, no. 4 (March 1894): 54–55.

Harris, Joel Chandler. *Uncle Remus: His Songs and His Sayings.* Boston: Houghton, Mifflin, 1893.

Hathaway, Rosemary. "The Unbearable Weight of Authenticity: Zora Neale Hurston's *Their Eyes Were Watching God* and a Theory of 'Touristic Reading.'" *Journal of American Folklore* 117, no. 464 (2004): 168–90.

Hemenway, Robert. "The Functions of Folklore in Charles Chesnutt's *The Conjure Woman.*" *Journal of the Folklore Institute* 13 (1976): 283–309.

hooks, bell. *Ain't I a Woman: Black Women and Feminism.* Boston: South End Press, 1981.

———. "Postmodern Blackness." *Postmodern Culture: An Electronic Journal of Interdisciplinary Criticism* 1, no. 1 (1990).

Howells, William Dean. "Introduction" to *Lyrics of Lowly Life*. In *The Life and Works of Paul Laurence Dunbar*, by Lida Wiggins, 15. Naperville, IL: J. L. Nichols, 1907.

———. "Life and Letters." *Harpers Weekly* (27 June 1896): 630.

Hurston, Zora Neale. "'Halimuhfack' recording with explanation." Recorded by Herbert Halpert, 18 June 1939. Hurston Sound Recordings, Folk Life Center, Library of Congress.

———. *Mules and Men.* 1935. Reprint, New York: Harper Perennial, 2008.

———. *Their Eyes Were Watching God.* 1937. Reprint, New York: Harper and Row, 1990.

Hyatt, Harry M. *Hoodoo, Conjuration, Witchcraft, Rootwork: Beliefs Accepted by Many Negroes and Whites Persons These Being Orally Recorded among Black and Whites*, 5 volumes. Washington: American University Bookstores, 1970.

Jackson, Bruce. *The Negro and His Folklore in Nineteenth Century Periodicals.* Austin: University of Texas Press, 1967.

Jarrett, Gene Andrew. "The Dialect of New Negro Literature." In *A Companion to African American Literature*, ed. Gene Andrew Jarrett, 169–84. Oxford, UK: Blackwell, 2010.

———. "Entirely Black Verse From Him Would Succeed." In *Deans and Truants: Race and Realism in African American Literature*, 29–51. Philadelphia: University of Pennsylvania Press, 2007.

Jarrett, Gene Andrew, and Thomas Lewis Morgan. "Introduction. In *The Complete Stories of Paul Laurence Dunbar*, by Paul Laurence Dunbar, xv–xliv. Athens: Ohio University Press, 2005.

Johnson, James Weldon. *Black Manhattan.* 1930. Reprint, New York: Arno Press, 1968.

———. *Negro Americans, What Now?* New York: AMS Press, 1971.

Johnston, Frances. *The Hampton Album: 44 Photographs from an Album of the Hampton Institute.* New York: Museum of Modern Art/Doubleday, 1966.

Jones, Gavin. *Strange Talk: The Politics of Dialect Literature in Gilded Age America.* Berkeley: University of California Press, 1999.

Kachun, Mitchell. "Society for the Collection of Negro Folklore." In *Organizing Black America: An Encyclopedia of African American Associations*, ed. Nina Mjagkij, 536. New York: Garland, 2004.

Kelley, Robin. "Notes on Deconstructing the Folk." *American Historical Review* 97, no. 5 (December 1992): 1400–1408.

Kent, Noel J. *Hawaii: Islands under the Influence.* Honolulu: University of Hawai'i Press, 1993.

Kuwayama, Takami. *Native Anthropology: The Japanese Challenge to Western Academic Hegemony.* Melbourne: Trans Pacific Press, 2004.

Kuyk, Betty. *African Voices in African American Heritage.* Bloomington: Indiana University Press, 2003.

Lamothe, Daphne. *Inventing the New Negro: Narrative, Culture, and Ethnography.* Philadelphia: University of Pennsylvania Press, 2008.

Lawless, Elaine. "'Reciprocal' Ethnography: No One Said It Was Easy." *Journal of Folklore Research* 37, no. 2/3 (May–December 2000): 197–205.

L.B.A. "Review of *Poems of Cabin and Field*." *Southern Workman* 28, no. 12 (December 1899): 506–7.

Lears, T. J. Jackson. *No Place of Grace: Antimodernism and the Transformation of American Culture*. Chicago: University of Chicago Press, 1994.

"Letter to Moton." 26 March 1909. Hampton University Archives.

"Letter to Moton." 7 November 1909. Hampton University Archives.

Levine, W. Lawrence. *Black Culture and Black Consciousness*. New York: Oxford University Press, 1978.

Lewis, W. I. "Letter." *Southern Workman* 7, no. 5 (1878): 1.

Lhamon, W. T. Jr. *Jump Jim Crow*. Cambridge, MA: Harvard University Press, 2003.

———. *Raising Cain: Blackface Performance from Jim Crow to Hip Hop*. Cambridge, MA: Harvard University Press, 1998.

Lloyd, Tim. "On the Differences between Folklore Fieldwork and Oral History." In *Oral History in the Digital Age*. Ed. Doug Boyd, Steve Cohen, Brad Rakerd, and Dean Rehberger. Washington D.C.: Institute of Museum and Library Services, 2012. Accessed 10 April 2013. http://ohda.matrix.msu.edu/2012/06/on-the-differences-between-folklore-fieldword-and-oral-history/.

Lock, Helen. "'Building Up from Fragments': The Oral Memory Process in Some Recent African-American Written Narratives." In *Essentials of the Theory of Fiction*, ed. Michael Hoffman and Patrick Murphy. Durham, NC: Duke University Press, 2005.

Logan, Rayford Whittingham. *The Betrayal of the Negro, from Rutherford B. Hayes to Woodrow Wilson*. New York: Da Capo, 1997.

Logan, Shirley. *We Are Coming: The Persuasive Discourse of Nineteen-Century Black Women*. Carbondale: Southern Illinois University Press, 1999.

Lomax, Bess Hawes, and Bessie Jones. *Step It Down; Games, Plays, Songs and Stories from the Afro-American Heritage*. New York: Harper and Row, 1972.

Long, Chris. "Rapporteur's Commentary." In *Re-Cognizing W. E. B. Du Bois*, ed. Mary Keller and Chester J. Fontenot, 231. Macon, GA: Mercer University Press, 2007.

Lott, Eric. "Love and Theft: The Racial Unconscious of Blackface Minstrelsy." *Representations* 39 (Summer 1992): 23–50.

Ludlow, Helen. "Review of *Candle-Lightin' Time*." *Southern Workman* 30, no. 12 (December 1901): 696–97.

Lyons, Laura. "Dole, Hawai'i, and the Question of Land under Globalization." In *Cultural Critique and the Global Corporation*, ed. Purnima Bose, Laura Lyons, and Christopher Newfield, 64–101. Bloomington: Indiana University Press, 2010.

Martin, Jay, and Gossie Hudson, eds. "Introduction." In *The Paul Laurence Dunbar Reader*. New York: Dodd, Mead, 1975.

May, Vivian. *Anna Julia Cooper, Visionary Black Feminist: A Critical Introduction.* New York: Routledge, 2007.

———. "Anna Julia Cooper's Philosophy of Resistance: Why African Americans Must 'Reverse the Picture of the Lordly Man Slaying the Lion . . . [and] Turn Painter.'" *Philosophia Africana* 12, no. 1 (2009): 41–65.

McBride, Dwight. *Why I Hate Abercrombie & Fitch: Essays on Race and Sexuality.* New York: New York University Press, 2005.

McCaskill, Barbara, and Caroline Gebhard, eds. *Post-Bellum, Pre-Harlem, African American Literature and Culture 1877–1919.* New York: New York University Press, 2006.

McElrath, Joseph. "W. D. Howells and Race: Charles Chesnutt's Disappointment of the Dean." *Nineteenth-Century Literature* 51 (March 1997): 474–99.

McNeil, William. "A History of American Folklore Scholarship before 1908." Diss., Indiana University, 1980.

McWilliams, Dean. *Charles W. Chesnutt and the Fictions of Race.* Athens: University of Georgia Press, 2004.

Meisenhelder, Susan. "Conflict and Resistance in Zora Neale Hurston's *Mules and Men.*" *Journal of American Folklore* 109, no. 433 (1996): 267–88.

"Members of the American Folk-lore Society." *Journal of American Folklore* 1, no. 1 (April–June 1888): 94–96.

Mills, Charles. *The Racial Contract.* Ithaca, NY: Cornell University Press, 1999.

Mitchem, Stephanie. *African American Folk Healing.* New York: New York University Press, 2007.

Molyneaux, Sandra. "Expanding the Collective Memory: Charles Chesnutt's *The Conjure Woman Tales.*" In *Memory, Narrative, and Identity,* ed. Amritjit Singh, Joseph Skerrett, and Robert E. Hogan. Boston: Northeastern University Press, 1994.

"More Letters Concerning the 'Folk-Lore Movement' at Hampton." *Southern Workman* 23, no. 1 (1894): 5.

Moses, Wilson. *The Golden Age of Black Nationalism: 1850–1925.* Oxford: Oxford University Press, 1988.

Moton, Robert. "Captain Moton's Story." *Southern Workman* 25, no. 9 (1896): 185–86.

Moton, Robert Russa. *Finding a Way Out: An Autobiography.* Garden City, NY: Doubleday Page, 1921.

———. "Negro Folk-Songs." *Southern Workman* 24, no. 2 (1895): 30–32.

———. *What the Negro Thinks.* New York: Doubleday, Doran, 1929.

"Mr. Vascar Barnette, Circulation Manager of *The Colored American.*" *Colored American Magazine.* 13 September 1902. Hampton University Archives.

Mullen, Patrick. *The Man Who Adores Negro: Race and American Folklore.* Chicago: University of Illinois Press, 2008.

Nadell, Martha. *Enter the New Negroes: Images of Race in American Culture*. Cambridge, MA: Harvard University Press, 2004.

Narayan, Kirin. "How Native is 'Native' Anthropology?" *American Anthropologist* 95, no. 3 (September 1993): 671–86.

Nelson, Alice Dunbar. "The Poet and His Song." *A.M.E. Review* 12 (October 1914): 121–35.

Newell, William Wells. "Additional Collection Essential to Correct Theory in Folk-Lore and Mythology." *Journal of American Folklore* 3, no. 8 (January–March 1890): 23–32.

———. "Folk-lore." In *Johnson's Universal Cyclopedia*, vol. 3, 453. New York: A. J. Johnson, 1893–97.

———. "Editor's Notes." *Journal of American Folklore* 2, no. 4 (1889): 1.

———. "First Annual Meeting of the American Folk-lore Society." *Journal of American Folklore* 3, no. 8 (January–March 1890): 1–16.

———. "The Importance and Utility of the Collection of Negro Folk-lore." *Southern Workman* 23, no. 7 (July 1894): 131–32.

———. "Introduction." *Journal of American Folklore* 2, no. 4 (January–March 1889): 1–2.

———. "Myths of Voodoo Worship and Child Sacrifice in Hayti." *Journal of American Folklore* 1, no. 1 (April–June 1888): 16–30.

———. "The Necessity of Collecting the Traditions of the Native Races." *Journal of American Folklore* 1, no. 2 (July–September 1888): 162–63.

———. "On the Field and Work of a Journal of American Folk-Lore." *Journal of American Folklore* 1, no. 1 (April–June 1888): 3–7.

———. "Theories of Diffusion of Folk-Tales." *Journal of American Folklore* 8, no. 28 (January–March 1895): 7–18.

———. "Third Annual Meeting of the American Folk-lore Society." *Journal of American Folklore* 5, no. 16 (January-March 1892): 1–8.

Pamela Newkirk, ed. *Letters from Black America*. New York: Farrar, Straus and Giroux, 2009.

"News from Washington Workers." *Southern Workman* 23, no. 4 (April 1894): 66.

Ngugi wa Thiong'o. *Decolonising the Mind: The Politics of Language in African Literature*. Portsmouth, NH: Heinemann, 1986.

Nicholls, David. *Conjuring the Folk: Forms of Modernity in African America*. Ann Arbor: University of Michigan Press, 2000.

Oden, Gloria. "Chesnutt's Conjure as African Survival." *MELUS* 5, no. 1 (Spring 1978): 38–48.

"The Old Cabinet: Simplicity." *Scribner's Monthly* 16 (May–October 1878): 434–35.

Patterson, Vivian, ed. *Carrie Mae Weems: The Hampton Project*. Williamstown, MA: Aperture, 2000.

Peabody, Francis. *Education for Life: The Story of Hampton Institute*. New York: Doubleday, Page, 1918.

Peterson, Carla. "Commemorative Ceremonies and Invented Traditions: History, Memory, and Modernity in the 'New Negro' Novel of the Nadir." In *Post-Bellum, Pre-Harlem, African American Literature and Culture, 1877–1919*, ed. Caroline Gebhard and Barbara McCaskill, 34–56. New York: New York University Press, 2006.

Plessy v. Ferguson. 163 U.S. 537 (1896).

Prahlad, Sw. Anand. "Africana Folklore: History and Challenges." *Journal of American Folklore* 118, no. 469 (205): 245–70.

Puckett, Newbell Niles. *Folk Beliefs of the Southern Negro*. Chapel Hill: University of North Carolina Press, 1926.

Punahou School. *The Oahu College at the Sandwich Island*. Boston: T. R. Marvin, 1856.

Raboteau, Albert. *Slave Religion: The "Invisible Institution" in the Antebellum South*. New York: Oxford University Press, 1978.

Ramzy, Denise, and Katherine Fogg. "Interview: Carrie Mae Weems." In *Carrie Mae Weems: The Hampton Project*, ed. Vivian Patterson, 78. Williamstown, MA: Aperture, 2000.

Ratliff v. Beale. 74 Mississippi 247 (1890).

"Review of *The Conjure Woman*." *Southern Workman* 28, no. 5 (May 1899): 194–95.

"Review of *Howdy, Honey, Howdy*." *Southern Workman* 34, no. 11 (November 1905): 628.

"Review of *Joggin' Erlong*." *Southern Workman* 36, no. 1 (January 1907): 52.

"Review of *Li'l Gal* and *Heart of Happy Hollow*." *Southern Workman* 33, no. 12 (December 1904): 692–93.

"Review of *The Marrow of Tradition*." *Southern Workman* 30, no. 12 (December 1901): 655–96.

"Review of *The Strength of Gideon and Other Stories*." In *Paul Laurence Dunbar: A Bibliography*, by Eugene Metcalf Jr., 137. Metuchen, NJ: Scarecrow Press, 1973.

"Review of *When Malindy Sings*." *Southern Workman* 32, no. 1 (January 1903): 630.

"Review of *When Malindy Sings*." *Southern Workman* 32, no. 12 (December 1903): 630–3l.

"Review of '*Sport of the Gods*.'" *Southern Workman* 30, no. 10 (October 1901): 557.

Richards, William. "Office Record." State Archives Digital Collections, State of Hawai'i. Accessed 29 January 2011. http://archives1.dags.hawaii.gov/gsdl/collect/governme/index/assoc/HASH8366/47733f3b.dir/Richards,%20William.jpg.

Roberts v. City of Boston. 59 Mass. (5 Cush.) 198 (1850).

Roberts, John. "African American Diversity and the Study of Folklore." *Western Folklore* Special Issue 52 no. 2, 3, 4 (April, July, October 1993): 157–72.

———. "Grand Theory, Nationalism, and American Folklore." *Journal of Folklore Research* 45, no. 1 (2008): 45–54.

Rodgers, Lawrence. "Paul Laurence Dunbar's *The Sport of the Gods*: The Doubly Conscious World of Plantation Fiction, Migration, and Ascent." *American Literary Realism* 24, no. 3 (Spring 1992): 42–57.

Ronnick, Michele Valerie. "Introduction." In *The Autobiography of William Sanders Scarborough: An American Journey from Slavery to Scholarship*, by William Scarborough. Detroit: Wayne State University Press, 2005. 1–22.

Rose, Julie. "The World's Columbian Exposition." Accessed January 2004. http://xroads.virginia.edu/~MA96/WCE/title.html.

Rosenstone, Robert. "'Learning from the "Imitative" Japanese': Another Side of the American Experience in the Mikado's Empire." *American Historical Review* 85, no. 3 (1980): 572–95.

Russell, Irwin. "A Christmas-Night in the Quarters." *Poems*. New York: Century, 1888.

Sapirstein, Ray. "Out from behind the Mask: The Illustrated Poetry of Paul Laurence Dunbar and Photography at Hampton Institute." Diss., University of Texas, Austin, 2005.

———. "Picturing Dunbar's Lyrics." *African American Review* 41, no. 2 (Summer 2007): 327–39.

Scarborough, William. "Address by Prof. W. H. Scarborough." *Southern Workman* 25, no. 7 (1896): 144–45.

———. "The Negro in Fiction as Portrayer and Portrayed." *Southern Workman* 28, no. 9 (1899): 358–62.

Schulman, Bruce. "Interactive Guide to the World's Columbian Exposition." Accessed January 2004. http://users.vnet.net/schulman/Columbian/columbian.html.

Seward, Adrienne Lanier. "The Legacy of Early Afro-American Folklore Scholarship." In *Handbook of American Folklore*, ed. Richard Dorson, 48–56. Bloomington: Indiana University Press, 1983.

Shaler, Nathaniel. "The Negro Problem." *Atlantic Monthly* 54 (1884): 696–709.

———. "Race Prejudice." *Atlantic Monthly* 58 (1886): 510–18.

———. "Science and the African Problem." *Atlantic Monthly* 66 (1890): 36–45.

Sharps, Ronald. "Happy Days and Sorrow Songs: Interpretations of Negro Folklore by Black Intellectuals, 1893–1928." Diss., George Washington University, 1991.

Shockley, Evie. *Renegade Poetics: Black Aesthetics and Formal Innovation in African American Poetry*. Iowa City: University of Iowa Press, 2011.

Showers, Susan. "Review of *The Fanatics*." *Southern Workman* 30, no. 6 (June 1901): 364–65.

Shuman, Amy, and Charles Briggs. "Introduction." *Western Folklore* Special Issue 52 no. 2, 3, 4 (April, July, October 1993): 109–34.

"Signs and Superstitions." *Southern Workman* 24, no. 5 (May 1895): 78.

Silva, Noenoe. *Aloha Betrayed: Native Hawaiian Resistance to American Colonialism*. Durham, NC: Duke University Press, 2004.

———. *"He Kanawai E Hoʻopau I Na Hula Kuolo Hawaiʻi:* The Political Economy of Banning the Hula." *Hawaiian Journal of History*, vol. 34 (2000): 29–48.

Simmons, Ryan. *Chesnutt and Realism: A Study of the Novels*. Tuscaloosa: University of Alabama Press, 2006.

Smedley, Audrey. *Race in North America: Origin and Evolution of a Worldview*. Boulder, CO: Westview Press, 1999.

Smiley, Portia. "Letter to Hollis Frissell." 2 December 1912. Hampton University Archives.

———. "Letter to Miss Myrte." 21 February 1922. Hampton University Archives.

———. "Letter to Miss Myrte." 19 June 1918. Hampton University Archives.

Smith, Shawn Michelle. *American Archives: Gender, Race and Class in Visual Culture*. Princeton, NJ: Princeton University Press, 1999.

"Some Conjure Doctors We Have Heard Of." *Southern Workman* 26, no. 2 (February 1897): 37–38.

"Some Side Lights on History." *Southern Workman* 23, no. 4 (April 1894): 65–66.

Sonstegard, Adam. "Kemble's Figures and Dunbar's Folks: Picturing the Work of Graphic Illustrations in Dunbar's Short Fiction." In *We Wear the Masks: Paul Laurence Dunbar and the Politics of Representative Reality*, ed. Willie Harrell Jr., 116–37. Kent, OH: Kent State University Press, 2012.

Sotiropoulos, Karen. *Staging Race: Black Performers in Turn of the Century America*. Cambridge, MA: Harvard University Press, 2006.

Stancil, Cassandra. "An Early Model for the Study of African-American Folklore: Carter G. Woodson and the *Journal of Negro History*." *New York Folklore* 18, nos. 1–4 (2000): 103–17.

Stepto, Robert. "'The Simple but Intensely Human Inner Life of Slavery': Story Telling and the Revision of History in Charles W. Chesnutt's 'Uncle Julius Tales.'" In *History and Tradition in Afro-American Culture*, ed. Gunter Lenz, 29–55. Frankfurt: Campus Verlag, 1984.

Stewart, Carole Lynn. "Challenging Liberal Justice: The Talented Tenth Revisited." In *Re-Cognizing W. E. B. Du Bois in the Twenty-First Century*, ed. Mary Keller and Chester J. Fontenot Jr., 131–32. Macon, GA: Mercer University Press, 2007.

Stillman, Amy. "Of People Who Love the Land: Vernacular History in the Poetry of Modern Hawaiian Hula." *Amerasia Journal* 28, no. 3 (2002): 85–108.

Stocking, George W., Jr. *Race, Culture, and Evolution: Essays in the History of Anthropology*. 1968. Reprint, Chicago: University of Chicago Press, 1982.

———. "Turn-of-the-Century Concept of Race." *Modernism/Modernity* 1, no. 1 (1994): 4–16.

Strom, Claire. "Alice Bacon." In *American National Biography, Vol. 1*, ed. John Garraty and Mark Carnes, 840. New York: Oxford University Press, 1999.

Sumner, William Graham. *Folkways*. 1906. New York: Blaisdell, 1966.

Sundquist, Eric J. *To Wake the Nations: Race in the Making of American Literature*. Cambridge, MA: Belknap Press of Harvard University Press, 1993.

"Through the Looking Glass." *Chicago Tribune* (1 November 1893): 9.

Titon, Jeff Todd. "Text." *Journal of American Folklore* 108, no. 430 (1995): 432–448.

Tolls, Robert. *Blacking Up: The Minstrel Show in Nineteenth Century America*. New York: Oxford University Press, 1974.

Twenty-Two Years' Work of the Hampton Normal and Agricultural Institute at Hampton, Virginia. Hampton, VA: Normal School Press, 1893.

Vance, Lee J. "The Study of Folk-Lore." *Forum* 22 (1896–97): 249.

Vogel, Todd. *Rewriting White: Race, Class, and Cultural Capital in Nineteenth Century America*. New Brunswick, NJ: Rutgers University Press, 2004.

Wade, Melvin. "The Intellectual and Historical Origins of Folklore Scholarship by Black Americans: A Study of the Response to the Propaganda of Racial Superiority at Hampton (Virginia) Institute 1893–1939." Unpublished manuscript, Hampton University Archives, 1982.

Washington, Mary Helen. Introduction. *A Voice from the South: Anna Julia Cooper*. New York: Oxford University Press, 1998.

Waters, Donald. *Strange Ways and Sweet Dreams: Afro-American Folklore from the Hampton Institute*. Boston: G. K. Hall, 1983.

Watkins, Mel. *On the Real Side: Laughing, Lying and Signifying*. New York: Simon and Schuster, 1995.

Wells, Ida B., and Frederick Douglass. "No 'Nigger Day,' No 'Nigger Pamphlet!'" *Indianapolis Freeman* (25 March 1893): 4.

Werner, Craig. "Early Twentieth Century." In *The Concise Oxford Companion to African American Literature*, ed. William Andrews, Frances Foster, and Trudier Harris, 466–69. New York: Oxford University Press, 2001.

Whitehead, Colson. *John Henry Days*. New York: Anchor, 2002.

Wideman, John Edgar. "Charles Chesnutt and the WPA Narratives: The Oral and Literate Roots of Afro-American Literature." In *The Slave's Narrative*, ed. Charles Davis and Henry Louis Gates Jr., 59–77. Oxford, UK: Oxford University Press, 1985.

Wiggins, William. "Afro-Americans As Folk: From Savage to Civilized." In *American Folklore Society: 100 Years*, ed. William Clements, 29. Washington: American Folklore Society, 1988.

Wilson, Matthew. "Who Has the Right to Say? Charles W. Chesnutt, Whiteness and the Public Sphere." *College Literature* 26, no. 2 (Spring 1999): 18–35.

Wright, A. R. "Presidential Address: The Folklore of Past and Present." *Folklore* 38, no. 1 (March 1927): 13–39.

Young, Kevin. *The Grey Album: On the Blackness of Blackness*. Minneapolis, MN: Greywolf Press, 2012.

Zeidler, Jeanne. "A View from Hampton University Museum." In *Carrie Mae Weems: The Hampton Project*, ed. Vivian Patterson, 76–77. Williamstown, MA: Aperture, 2000.

Zumwalt, Rosemary Levy. *American Folklore Scholarship: A Dialogue of Dissent*. Bloomington: Indiana University Press, 1988.

———. "On the Founding of the American Folklore Society and the *Journal of American Folklore*." In *The American Folklore Society: 100 Years*, ed. William Clements, 8–10. Washington: American Folklore Society, 1988.

INDEX

Page numbers in **bold** indicate illustrations.

DEC 04 2013

CPSIA information can be obtained at www.ICGtesting.com
Printed in the USA
BVOW02*0929260913

332029BV00002B/13/P